Trying to Get Over

Trying to Get Over

AFRICAN AMERICAN DIRECTORS AFTER BLAXPLOITATION, 1977–1986

Keith Corson

University of Texas Press *Austin*

Printed in the United States of America
First edition, 2016

Requests for permission to reproduce material from this work should be sent to:
Permissions
University of Texas Press
P.O. Box 7819
Austin, TX 78713-7819
http://utpress.utexas.edu/index.php/rp-form

♾ The paper used in this book meets the minimum requirements of ANSI/NISO Z39.48-1992 (R1997) (Permanence of Paper).

LIBRARY OF CONGRESS CATALOGING-IN-PUBLICATION DATA
Corson, Keith, author.
Trying to get over : African American directors after blaxploitation, 1977–1986 / Keith Corson. — First edition.
pages cm
Includes bibliographical references and index.
ISBN 978-1-4773-0907-0 (cloth : alk. paper)
ISBN 978-1-4773-0908-7 (pbk. : alk. paper)
ISBN 978-1-4773-0909-4 (library e-book)
ISBN 978-1-4773-0910-0 (non-library e-book)
1. African Americans in motion pictures. 2. African Americans in the motion picture industry. 3. African American motion picture producers and directors. 4. Motion pictures—United States—History—21st century. 5. Blaxploitation films—United States—History and criticism. I. Title.
PN1995.9.N4C623 2016
791.43′652996073—dc23

2015023681

doi:10.7560/309070

In Memory of

MANNING MARABLE

ROBERT SKLAR

JAMAA FANAKA

MARK BEHR

Contents

Acknowledgments

THIS BOOK WOULD NOT HAVE BEEN POSSIBLE WITHout the guidance and encouragement of a handful of mentors I've been lucky enough to have over the years. Ed Guerrero's influence was established beforehand from what he put down on the page in *Framing Blackness*, but getting the chance to work with him one-on-one at New York University was an absolute privilege. I couldn't have asked for a better consigliere, as his support for this project was unwavering, and his humor and zest for life always put everything in the proper perspective. S. Craig Watkins, the Hardest Working Man in Academia, was incredibly gracious with his time and patiently helped me find my way through countless drafts, concepts, and false starts. Melinda Barlow gave me the initial push to start this project and provided me with the confidence to pursue a doctorate. She is the perfect model for matching scholarship with pedagogy and made the University of Colorado at Boulder a transformative experience. Jeff Crouse's passion for art and justice made me realize that film studies has the same creative potential as filmmaking itself. The conversations we shared on our Thursday pizza-and-a-foreign-film outings made me a more thoughtful and introspective person.

There has been a spoil of riches in terms of the people I've had the opportunity to work with over the years. All of them have influenced this project. At NYU, Richard Allen, Manthia Diawara, Dan Streible, Anna McCarthy, Jung Bong Choi, Robert Sklar, and Sheril Antonio all helped shape this book. Paula Massood at Brooklyn College deserves special mention for being so generous with her time and offering invaluable advice. My cohorts in the PhD program at NYU deserve thanks as well, not only for providing feedback on this project but also for serving as a makeshift support group. I owe an enormous debt of gratitude to Nate

Brennan, Benjamin Min Han, Michelle Kelley, Benjamin Olin, Intan Paramaditha, and Anastasia Saverino. Robyn Citizen and Noah Tsika also provided insight and encouragement. At the University of Texas, Jennifer Fuller, Thomas Schatz, Joni Jones, and Meta DuEwa Jones helped make Austin a life-changing experience. At the University of Colorado, Ernesto Acevedo-Muñoz, Bruce Kawin, Carl Weiman, and James Brody gave me a foundation that I still pull from in and out of the classroom. Thanks also to George Junne at the University of Northern Colorado for making the trek down to Boulder to share his perspective on an early iteration of this project.

Many thanks to all of the people who have given me the opportunity to share my ideas and research in the classroom. To Marshall Boswell, Rebecca Finlayson, Rashna Richards, and everyone in the English Department at Rhodes College, thank you for being so incredibly supportive and welcoming. Thanks to Ellen Daugherty and Remy Miller at Memphis College of Art for giving me the freedom to explore new topics and develop my own approach to teaching film. Thanks to Allison Graham at the University of Memphis as well. Most of all, a thank you is in order to all of the students I've had the pleasure to teach at Rhodes, MCA, UM, and NYU for allowing me to work through this material and for keeping me honest.

Big thanks are in order to Jim Burr and everyone at the University of Texas Press for making the writing of this book such a great experience. To my peer readers, cloaked in mystery but forceful in your contributions, thank you so much for making this book better and for believing in the project. Katherine Streckfus is an amazing copy editor and deserves special praise. She offered helpful suggestions throughout and worked diligently to make up for my lackluster public school education.

The interviews for this book not only helped to provide crucial information that added depth in context, but also, and more importantly, made this project personal. Thanks to Michael Schultz for setting aside an entire day to talk with me in Santa Monica and for not getting scared off by my obsessive need to unpack every detail of *Disorderlies*. Thanks to Fred Williamson for taking the time to talk. The Hammer is easily the coolest dude on the planet. Thanks to William Branch, Richard Wesley, Gary Stromberg, and David Dashev for talking to me about their collaborations and providing texture to the book. A deep, heartfelt thank you goes out to Tsia Moses, Carol Moses-Robinson, and Wilma Butler for trusting me to tell part of Gil's story. Unquestionably, Gil was a genius, and his spirit lives on through his family. Jamaa Fanaka, my friend for life, was the most invested person in this project. It's my hope that I've done him justice in the following pages.

Thanks to Ian Strachan and everyone at the College of the Bahamas for organizing the Sidney Poitier International Conference and Film Festival in February 2010. Thanks to Mary Huelsbeck at the Black Film Center and Archive at Indiana University for allowing me access to a number of interviews, clippings, and press kits, not to mention arranging a personal screening of the elusive *Passing Through*. Thanks to the staff in the rare books and manuscripts division at New York Public Library's Schomburg Center for Research in Black Culture for all of the help and guidance. An extra-special note of thanks is due to Fred Adams and everyone at HistoryMakers for allowing me to visit their Chicago offices to access oral histories, and later, inviting me to be a test user of their online archive.

NYU's Inter-University Doctoral Consortium afforded me the opportunity to spend a semester at Columbia University working with Manning Marable, who became a great adviser and took an interest in my scholarship. It was a singular pleasure getting to work with Dr. Marable. His fingerprints can be found throughout this book as a key source of inspiration.

My wife, Jamie, obviously, deserves the most thanks of all for being there with me every step of the way and for humoring me during the never-ending game of "Six Degrees of Michael Schultz" that researching this book inspired. Mom, thanks for raising children who read and for giving me carte blanche to rent whatever I wanted at the video store. Dad, thanks for modeling hard work and for making the movie theater a second home. My sister Brenda, thanks for taking care of me, making me laugh, and for always being the smarter person I'm struggling to keep up with. Thanks to all of the Clays, Corsons, Darts, Gaspards, and Von Roenns. Thanks to Sean, Adam, Damian, Nic, Rachael, Dave, Krish, Nicola, Emma, Marc, Mike, Ryan, Lily, Jen, and Christy for being great friends. And finally, to my best friend in the world, Ginger. You were by my side, literally, for the writing of most of this book and taught me more about life than anyone else I've ever known. The wisdom of a dog is something to behold. You were the wisest of them all.

Introduction

THE META-COMMENTARY OF CURTIS MAYFIELD'S soundtrack for *Super Fly* (1972, Gordon Parks Jr.) is one of the most remarked-upon elements of the blaxploitation-era classic, adding depth to the narrative by providing much-needed context and reflection. Mayfield's lyrics and plaintive vocals humanize the film's cocaine-dealing protagonist Youngblood Priest (Ron O'Neal) and clearly convey a political dimension that is not made explicit in the film, helping to define the story as a meditation on the structural inequalities and moral relativism of capitalism. Within the limited space of a pop/soul song structure, major themes and observations are crystallized into short lyrics. Nowhere is this aim more clearly expressed than in the title song, where Mayfield frames the struggle of Priest, and of African Americans as a whole, as a matter of "trying to get over." The idea of getting over—the struggle to gain entry into a society that has historically excluded and exploited blacks economically, politically, and culturally—is not the creation of Mayfield; nor is it specific to 1972. Whether it takes the form of financial accumulation and legitimization (as it does for *Super Fly*'s protagonist), the attempt to earn a living wage and join the middle class, or the desire for legal and political enfranchisement, the black experience in America has been defined by the ongoing struggle to gain access to the same rights and privileges enjoyed by whites. More to the point, the history of race and class in America has been defined by the disenfranchised trying to get over.

Getting over would be a recurring theme during the blaxploitation cycle, with Mayfield's use of the term at the beginning of the cycle bookended by a film like *The Monkey Hu$tle* (1976, Arthur Marks), which was released during blaxploitation's final year and has characters repeatedly uttering some derivation of the term "get over." Outside of film texts, the blaxploitation era was largely about getting over for the black actors, writers, and directors who finally found an entry point into an industry that had been resistant to black involvement since its inception. From 1972 to 1976, the American film industry made an unprecedented number of films targeting black spectators, with the percentage of US theatrical releases that had an identifiable black focus actually exceeding the demographic representation of African Americans as a whole.[1]

The barriers for black directors in Hollywood began to disappear a few years before the boom in black-focused production, with Gordon Parks, directing the adaptation of his autobiographical novel *The Learning Tree* (1969) for Warner Bros., becoming the first African American to direct a studio feature. Of course, Parks was not the first African American to direct a feature film. The earliest race film productions of Oscar Micheaux predated *The Learning Tree* by half a century.[2] However, the separate cinema of filmmakers like Micheaux and Spencer Williams existed on the margins of the mainstream film industry. These works were produced in places like Chicago and Dallas, far removed from Hollywood, the major studios, and mainstream distribution.

Gordon Parks and his peers represent the first group of black directors to get over in Hollywood and make films within the framework of the dominant motion picture industry. A number of first-time black directors emerged over the following years, bolstered by the blaxploitation cycle. Parks was joined by the likes of Melvin Van Peebles, Ossie Davis, Bill Gunn, Ivan Dixon, Oscar Williams, William Crain, and his son Gordon Parks Jr., who all directed multiple features in the 1970s. Beginning with *The Learning Tree*, close to sixty features were credited to black directors before the end of the blaxploitation cycle.

Blaxploitation's sudden demise at the end of 1976 reversed the momentum for black filmmakers, part of a decade-long retrenchment in Hollywood's production of black-focused features. There is a decided void separating the blaxploitation era and the black film explosion that came a few years after the arrival of Spike Lee and his independent breakthrough *She's Gotta Have It* (1986). Features with African American themes—to say nothing of features actually made by black directors—were few and far between in the intervening years, creating a steep decline in black representation and opportunities. Blaxploitation's stars receded into the margins of Hollywood, while the handful of black directors who were able to make inroads during the early 1970s were no longer directing after 1976. From 1977 to 1986, the number of black-oriented features dipped dramatically and opportunities for black directors became scarce. Ironically, one of the few black-focused films made during this era was titled *Getting*

Over (1981, Bernie Rollins); it was produced by and starred John Daniels, but made by a white director.[3] *Getting Over* was financed and ultimately self-released by Daniels after both major and minor studios passed on distributing the low-budget comedy. It slipped into obscurity even though he used the same mode of production that had been successful for his blaxploitation-era features *The Candy Tangerine Man* (1975, Matt Cimber) and *Black Shampoo* (1976, Greydon Clark).[4] *Getting Over* is an optimistic tale of breaking into the music business through hard work and good luck, but getting over in the film industry after the fall of blaxploitation was easier said than done for Daniels.

This book focuses on the work of the handful of black directors (eight, to be exact) who ventured to make commercial films for theatrical release during this time, trying to get over in Hollywood after the fall of blaxploitation. Hollywood's move away from making black-focused features, and the diminished opportunities for independent production, severely limited opportunities for black directors, but the eight filmmakers in this study found ways to make films despite changes in financing, distribution, and exhibition. Completing twenty-four features between 1977 and 1986, these filmmakers were not part of a collective. Their films vary in style, tone, and perspective, to say nothing of their disparate approaches to navigating the film industry. However, the output of black directors in these years not only exhibits a connective thread from the blaxploitation cycle to Spike Lee and beyond, but also provides a window through which to examine the political and cultural landscape of the 1970s and 1980s.

Even so, why focus this study on directors? Regardless of the collaborative nature of the medium or the machinations of the film industry, there is a unique connotation of power associated with the director. The same holds true for the producer in television and the writer in theater. Denzel Washington taking a turn as Walter Lee Younger on Broadway does not strip Lorraine Hansberry of her status as the central creative force in *A Raisin in the Sun*, even if in this case the star actor overshadows the playwright somewhat. The symbolic power in the title of "director" alone makes the position a perfect entry point for analyzing the political economy of the film industry. African Americans gaining access to the director's chair is important in and of itself, to say nothing of their filmic texts and levels of creative input.

It is also worth pointing out that, since this is a study of directors, I will be in conversation with ideas relating to authorship and the contested legacy of the *auteur* theory. Early debates about the validity of the *auteur* as a workable concept within a collaborative medium like cinema generally pushed toward polarities, either arguing for the director as the primary voice of a text or bypassing the concept altogether in favor of the filmic system as a disembodied "author." When siding with the possibility of individual authorship, most theorists tread cautiously, using a case-by-case basis to evaluate the contributions of directors, and granting a privileged few with *auteur* status.

What I would like to suggest, particularly for this study, is that the authorship of film directors can be placed on a scale rather than viewed as a binary (i.e., the static notion that Orson Welles is an *auteur*, but Michael Curtiz is not). The director always plays a role in authoring the text, but the extent of that contribution is dependent on a host of factors. The *Auteur* theory often assumes an idealized world in which directors can assert control over a film by the sheer force of their brilliance and creativity. Rarely is proper attention given to external factors that influence just how much of a director's voice is heard in the final cut of a film. When considering the economically and culturally compromised position of African American directors in Hollywood, it is important that we not use a simplistic model for assessing their contributions. This study assumes that aspects of the director's voice exist in each text, but uses production histories and industry analysis to place their contributions on the scale of authorship.

Marginalized by Hollywood and neglected by scholars, the central figures of this book are the black directors who aspired to find a popular audience in the decade following blaxploitation's demise, creating a space for expression despite the fact that the structure and sensibilities of the commercial film industry discouraged black involvement. I will argue for the importance of filmmakers such as Michael Schultz, Fred Williamson, and Jamaa Fanaka, placing their work within a broader historical trajectory of African American cinema and locating three very different approaches to making commercial films. In addition to figures primarily identified as filmmakers, the lesser-known directorial careers of Sidney Poitier, Richard Pryor, and Prince provide a space to examine black celebrity and the negotiation of power and creative control within Hollywood. The brief cinematic careers of Gilbert Moses and Stan Lathan, on the other hand, underscore the limited opportunities in Hollywood for even the most talented black artists. Together, these eight directors help illustrate the shifting dialogue concerning race, power, and access during a time that has gone largely unexplored.

Scholarly discussions of African Americans in cinema during this period have generally emphasized issues of representation, focusing on the star personas of Eddie Murphy and Richard Pryor, problematic Hollywood texts like *The Color Purple* (1985, Steven Spielberg), or popular tropes such as the black buddy in films like *Lethal Weapon* (1987, Richard

Donner). This is not meant to criticize the work of scholars such as Mark Reid, Jacqueline Bobo, or Ed Guerrero, who have made invaluable contributions to the field. Instead, the lack of scholarship regarding the work of black directors during this era speaks to a broader trend in which topics relating to African Americans have received scant attention, leaving scholars like Reid, Bobo, and Guerrero in the unenviable position of trying to relate the complexities of black experiences in cinema either through broad histories and theories or via anecdotal case studies. In this book I attempt to paint in some of the brushstrokes missing from existing scholarship to provide a more complete understanding of the era through a dialogue between black artists and the motion picture industry.

Christopher Sieving's excellent book *Soul Searching: Black-Themed Cinema from the March on Washington to the Rise of Blaxploitation* provides a model for expanding the discussion of African American cinema, in his case by taking on the otherwise underexamined decade before blaxploitation.[5] *Trying to Get Over*, in many ways, attempts to function as a bookend on the other side of the blaxploitation cycle, detailing the following decade, but filtered through the work of black directors and the changing structure of the US film industry. As such, the eight filmmakers at the center of this study were chosen because they made commercially distributed films. Obviously, other African American directors were also active during this time, working on projects ranging from short subjects to experimental, avant-garde, documentary, public broadcasting, and festival circuit films. While I appreciate and admire the work of filmmakers such as St. Clair Bourne, Michelle Parkerson, and William Greaves, their films fall outside the scope of this project. Although some of the LA Rebellion filmmakers are discussed in chapter 5, I do not foreground their work for the same reason, as their lack of commercial intent and their orientation eschewed Hollywood and mainstream audiences.

The fact that the work of the eight directors in the following chapters has largely been ignored, dismissed, or marginalized by scholars and critics is enough to warrant a serious reevaluation. How is it that the work of serious-minded black artists making resistant cinema has been so undervalued by film scholars and cultural historians? Part of the answer relates to lingering reservations about popular entertainment, and in particular about genre filmmaking practices. If these films are recalled at all, it is largely by film cultists who look at them through either an ironic or a nostalgic lens. What I would like to do is to reclaim these films from critics and cultists, reevaluating their importance by considering the broader context in which they were produced.

Taking these films seriously may defy traditional logic, as many of the works in my corpus have been deemed unimportant because they were poorly received critically and labeled low art (i.e., as genre, commercial films), or because they had low box-office numbers and therefore were not seen as indicative of broader social trends and audience tastes. I would like to move past some of the value judgments that have played a role in the scholarly neglect of these films and instead provide a historical framework through which they can be engaged. At the same time, I unapologetically make my own valuations, whether it is championing the work of Michael Schultz or refuting the critical trashing of *Under the Cherry Moon* (1986, Prince), which I see as one of the more nuanced and interesting American films of the 1980s. The films made by African American directors between 1977 and 1986 are important documents in charting the changing landscape of black politics and culture in the Carter and Reagan years, particularly since they share a perspective that was largely absent from the national discourse.

CHAPTER ONE

Blaxploitation Reconsidered

AFRICAN AMERICAN DIRECTORS AND THE POLITICAL ECONOMY OF HOLLYWOOD

BILL GUNN'S 1981 NOVEL *RHINESTONE SHARECROPping* provides a rare glimpse into the life of a black screen artist at the end of the blaxploitation cycle. Loosely autobiographical—the names have been changed to protect the innocent—the novel recounts the end of Gunn's tumultuous decade working as a director and writer in Hollywood, giving voice to African Americans marginalized within mainstream cinema.

Hollywood first reached out to Gunn based on his reputation in New York theater, hiring him to write the adapted screenplay for *The Landlord* (1970, Hal Ashby).[1] The producers were looking for a black writer to help retain an air of authenticity for the film's black characters; they wanted to avoid the same white liberal idealism of other Hollywood meditations on race, while Gunn envisioned expressing his ideas to a broader audience. His opportunities seemed limitless when he arrived in Hollywood. But his experiences in the movie business proved frustrating, leaving him feeling like a perpetual outsider because of his race and sexual orientation, not to mention his intellect. Unhappy with the final cut of *The Landlord*, Gunn felt that the finished film shifted his intended tone of the story and diminished his contributions.

The same year that *The Landlord* was released, Gunn was offered a chance to write and direct for Warner Bros. The company gave him a small budget and the creative freedom to make a feature of his choosing. The final product, *Stop* (1970), was not what the studio had had in mind from their young black director.[2] Instead of a film that could easily be marketed to tap into black box-office dollars, *Stop* explores issues of sexuality through an affluent white couple on vacation in Puerto Rico. Both husband and wife engage in extramarital liaisons, including same-sex coupling; through them the film touches on the search for self-fulfillment at the heart of the sexual revolution. Warner Bros. refused to promote the film and quietly opened it on a single screen at a Texas drive-in, then pointed to the predictably poor audience response during its one week in release as evidence that *Stop* was not commercially viable.[3] The film has been out of circulation ever since, never appearing on television or home video.[4] Gunn's second picture, *Ganja & Hess* (1973), which he made outside of the major studios, was equally problematic. His long battle over the final cut of the film with the production company Kelly/Jordan Enterprises resulted in his postmodernist classic being reshaped by the studio into an indecipherable attempt at genre convention.

Gunn's final commercial film project, working as a screenwriter on the Muhammad Ali biopic *The Greatest* (1977, Tom Gries and Monte Hellman), proved to be the most disheartening, with Gunn forced to deal with a litany of racial insensitivities from the white producers along with Ali's own concerns over the supposedly feminizing qualities of his character in the screenplay.[5] After being fired off of *The Greatest*, Gunn was convinced that the Ali biopic could very well be the last black-focused film made in Hollywood. Looking around to notice the dramatic exclusion of black screen artists, Gunn used the fictional veil of his novel *Rhinestone Sharecropping* to sum up the mood of the film industry in the immediate aftermath of the blaxploitation cycle:

> Cleola and me had just heard on the phone that B.C. Pictures and five other major studios announced mainly through the columns that they were not planning to produce any more Black Pictures. There are a few in production, they will be finished. "It was discovered that as many 'Blacks' went to see Jaws as went to see Sounder?" And taking the racial element out of the industry could possibly prove healthier in the long run. The industry will of course continue its effort to integrate what has unfortunately been referred to as the white film until an acceptable racial balance has been achieved to the satisfaction of the community at large.[6]

Writing *Rhinestone Sharecropping* became a way for Gunn to process the whole sordid affair of working on *The Greatest*. Publishing the novel through his friend and sometime collaborator Ishmael Reed's small press, Gunn spoke truth to power without indulging in a Hollywood tell-all, expressing key themes by filtering his experience through a fictionalized narrative. The novel provides a succinct analysis of the film industry and the circular logic of white producers and executives. The title itself is a clear articulation of Gunn's feelings about black labor and commercial filmmaking, as the glamour associated with Hollywood's dream factory masks the subjugated position of its creative talent. Among the insights of *Rhinestone Sharecropping*, Gunn proved most prescient by recognizing that opportunities for black artists in Hollywood would be dramatically changed starting in 1977.

HOLLYWOOD IN FLUX

Understanding the logic of the film industry during the blaxploitation cycle—and moving past some of the common misconceptions associated with the era—is critical when thinking about the decade that followed. While a shifting political and cultural climate informed the films of the blaxploitation era, the roots of the production cycle can be found in the struggling studio system in the late 1960s. The growing dominance of television, a host of big-budget flops, and the increasing percentage of foreign-made films on American screens all served as cause for panic in Hollywood. Studios began to rethink their methods of operation, and the US government instituted tax credits for independent financiers in an attempt to spur lagging domestic production. Thanks to the dismantling of the Production Code and the success of films like *Bonnie and Clyde* (1967, Arthur Penn), *The Graduate* (1967, Mike Nichols), and *Easy Rider* (1969, Dennis Hopper), Hollywood began reaching out toward a politicized youth counterculture with products that operated outside of the safe thematic boundaries of the Golden Age.

No longer the sole domain of the old guard of moguls, the changing structure of the major studios in the late 1960s made Hollywood more inclined to seek new responses to its financial pressures by catering their films to different sectors of the population, as the traditional target audience had fled to suburbia to spend their evenings at home watching television. With an ever-shrinking base of active filmgoers—a trend that had begun in the early 1950s—Hollywood had to maximize the profits from those still coming out to the theater, and African Americans remained one of the most loyal demographics at the box office.

In terms of black images in film, the opening up of film content was coupled with an unprecedented moment of political activism on the part of African Americans. Black Power had displaced the passive civil rights movement in capturing the zeitgeist of black political thought, bringing along a new investment in the arts. The Black Arts movement dictated a shift in literature, poetry, theater, and painting, while musically the aesthetic corollaries of black nationalism were articulated in free jazz, funk, and soul.[7] Cinema, on the other hand, had yet to incorporate an aesthetic aligned with black counterculture. While *Bonnie and Clyde* and *The Graduate* were connecting with young and disaffected white Americans, the venerable Sidney Poitier was reaching his peak of stardom in *Guess Who's Coming to Dinner* (1967, Stanley Kramer), *To Sir, with Love* (1967, James Clavell), and *In the Heat of the Night* (1967, Norman Jewison). Poitier's refined and unthreatening archetype may have been a hit with mainstream audiences, but his films were beginning to wear thin with black America.[8] For young African American audiences, the desexualized and passive Poitier character was as out of step with the times as the big-budget flop *Hello, Dolly!* (1969, Gene Kelly) was with the Woodstock generation.

Looking for an alternative to Poitier and an entry point for a young black audience, Hollywood began to cultivate football star Jim Brown as a bankable commodity, giving the green light to a handful of films with black protagonists. A number of the films released in 1969 and 1970 function along the lines of message movies from the previous two decades, with a foregrounding of black/white racial tensions and a clear political moral. *The Great White Hope* (1970, Martin Ritt), *The Angel Levine* (1970, Ján Kadár), and . . . *tick . . . tick . . . tick . . .* (1970, Ralph Nelson) are all good examples of Hollywood meditations on race that attempted to appeal to an audience aware of the Black Power movement, but still invested in the integrationist sentiments of the civil rights movement. At the same time, Hollywood also opened its doors for the first time to black directors, beginning with Gordon Parks filming the adaptation of his novel *The Learning Tree* in 1969.

The Learning Tree had been optioned six years earlier by independent producer Edward Funsten Jr., with Parks having it written into the contract that in the event of any eventual screen adaptation he would be guaranteed the option of directing.[9] The project was pitched to a number of studios in 1964, with United Artists, Columbia, and Universal all expressing interest. But Hollywood was hesitant to back a film with a first-time director that had no stars attached and was "predominantly Negro."[10] The possibility of shooting *The Learning Tree* as a modest film on 16 mm black-and-white stock in the mode of contemporary black-focused efforts *The Cool World* (1964, Shirley Clarke), *Nothing But a Man* (1964, Michael Roemer), and *One Potato, Two Potato* (1964, Larry Peerce) was briefly entertained, but Parks's insistence on rich, opulent visuals ruled out a bare-bones production.[11]

Having been a respected photographer for *Vogue* and *Life*, as well as an author, Parks was not artistically or financially dependent on making it in Hollywood, so he was able to dictate his own terms without fearing that his professional survival depended on studio validation. He waited another four years before finally beginning work on *The Learning Tree*, founding his own production company (Winger) to make the film for Warner Bros. *The Learning Tree* was far from a runaway success, earning $3 million at the box office after spending just under $2 million on production, but the film removed the barrier for black directors in Hollywood.[12]

The next year, three more black directors would join the Hollywood ranks, with Bill Gunn making *Stop* for Warner Bros., Columbia hiring Melvin Van Peebles to direct *Watermelon Man* (1970), and United Artists distributing Ossie Davis's *Cotton Comes to Harlem* (1970). Thematically, *Cotton Comes to Harlem* set the template for both the black action picture and the black cast comedy in the blaxploitation era. More importantly, *Cotton*'s success at the box office gave Hollywood hope that black-focused features had the possibility of being profitable. While the majority of black-themed releases in 1969 and 1970 were mildly received by audiences, *Cotton* was a hit, earning $5.2 million in rentals.[13] The following year, however, production of black-focused films dipped again, with only three films released by major studios, two of which starred Sidney Poitier. *The Organization* (1971, Don Medford) found Poitier appearing for the third time as his iconic detective character Virgil Tibbs, and the spiritual drama *Brother John* (1971, James Goldstone) reiterated the "Saint Sidney" archetype even as it moved away from the problem picture formula. The only other black-focused film released by a major studio that year was MGM's *Shaft* (1971, Gordon Parks).[14]

Coming a mere two months after the release of Melvin Van Peebles's wildly successful independent film *Sweet Sweetback's Baadasssss Song* (1971, released by exploitation distributor Cinemation), *Shaft* established a model for studios looking to garner black box-office dollars.[15] Both *Sweetback* and *Shaft* surpassed $10 million at the box office, figures made even more remarkable by their small budgets.[16] In addition, *Shaft* not only launched a film franchise (two sequels and a short-lived TV series on CBS), but also provided a hit soundtrack album, courtesy of Isaac Hayes, as well as a host of branded tie-ins, ranging from sunglasses to hair picks.

The dual success of *Sweetback* and *Shaft* in the summer and fall of 1971 prompted a sea change in Hollywood as a full slate of black-focused features was rushed into production. *Shaft* set a precedent for studio success and served as a character template for a host of films, but *Sweetback*'s independent production and distribution proved an epiphany for producers and distributors outside of major Hollywood studios. Studios and independent producers looked toward black-focused features following the success of these films, and the low-budget independent production of *Sweetback* became the dominant model in the blaxploitation years.

BLAXPLOITATION

The sudden surge of black-focused films in 1972 was conspicuous and became the subject of a great deal of debate and consternation, mostly revolving around the hotly contested term "blaxploitation." Today, the term is often used without regard to a fixed definition to situate films historically, politically, and thematically. The term itself operates as if notions of what blaxploitation is (and is not) were clear. Similar to *film noir* in its usage, "blaxploitation" is grounded temporally and thematically, if not strictly defined. Unfortunately, like *film noir*, "blaxploitation" has become synonymous with ideas of genre, often with all of the films that fall under its umbrella being assessed through a handful of supposedly representative texts. More than suggesting plot elements, "blaxploitation" in common usage connotes a fixed racial component (black protagonists, black target audience) and suggests limitations in artistic ambition, budget, and exhibition. Running counter to popular usage of the term, "blaxploitation" is best understood and defined through periodization rather than theme, functioning as a production cycle and not a genre.

The films that fall under the umbrella of blaxploitation are expansive in terms of genre and tone, including horror, westerns, comedies, romantic dramas, period pieces, and martial-arts films in addition to the urban-action vehicles most closely associated with the era. The term was originally conceived without regard to genre. Rooting the concept in aspects of spectatorship, *Variety* coined the term in 1972 following an explosion in releases targeting black audiences. Contrary to a persistent myth, it was not an invention of the National Association for the Advancement of Colored People (NAACP) or protest groups like the Coalition Against Blaxploitation; nor was it intended to be derogatory toward the films themselves, the performers who starred in them, or the spectators paying to see these movies in theaters. *Variety*'s use of the term "exploitation" was meant to comment on marketing strategies and distribution techniques used by major and minor studios and producers; the usage had been common in the magazine since the 1930s. In this context "exploitation" simply meant maximizing the take at the box office and recognizing current profit trends.

It is important to note that *Variety*'s use of the word "exploitation" was not interchangeable with accepted notions of "exploitation film," although

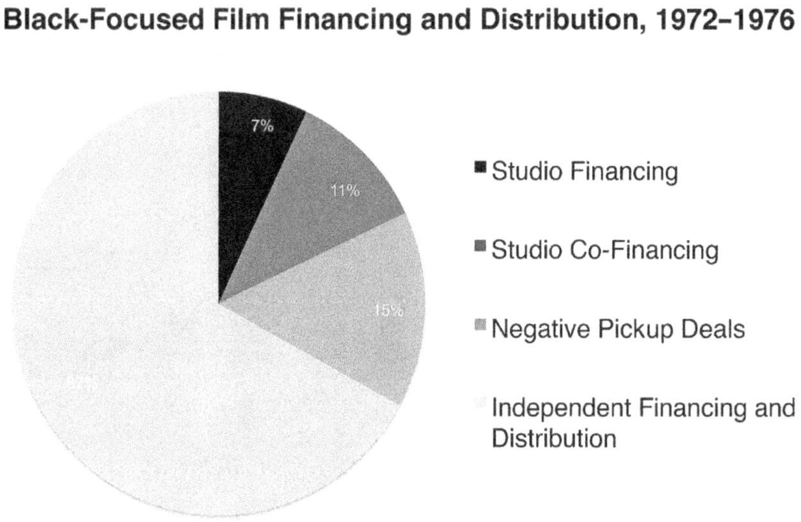

Figure 1

a number of blaxploitation films fit that rubric as well. It was only later, in 1972, that the term became synonymous with growing concerns among black intellectuals and civic leaders, with the Coalition Against Blaxploitation solidifying the idea that black-focused genre films were overwhelmingly "negative," leaving a stigma for many of the screen artists who worked during the era. This repurposing of meaning brought with it a value judgment that has obscured the original intent of the term "blaxploitation." Instead of signifying a production trend, "blaxploitation" has become an umbrella term with specific implications about genre, (mis)representation, and Hollywood's crass strategies of marketing to black youth. Lost in this debate over representation is a clear understanding of the film industry and the numerous ways in which African Americans participated in the filmmaking process.

Shaft and *Sweetback* encouraged studios and independent producers to find ways of replicating their success. The fact that both films were made by black directors helped open doors for others in the years to come. Parks returned to his previous year's success with the sequel *Shaft's Big Score* (1972), and five first-time black directors made studio-released features in the same year, including his son Gordon Parks Jr. and Mark Warren, Sidney Poitier, Hugh A. Robertson, and Ivan Dixon.[17] These directors tell only part of the story, as most black-focused features were made without the involvement of the major studios. As Figure 1 shows, less than one-third of blaxploitation-era releases were distributed by major studios,

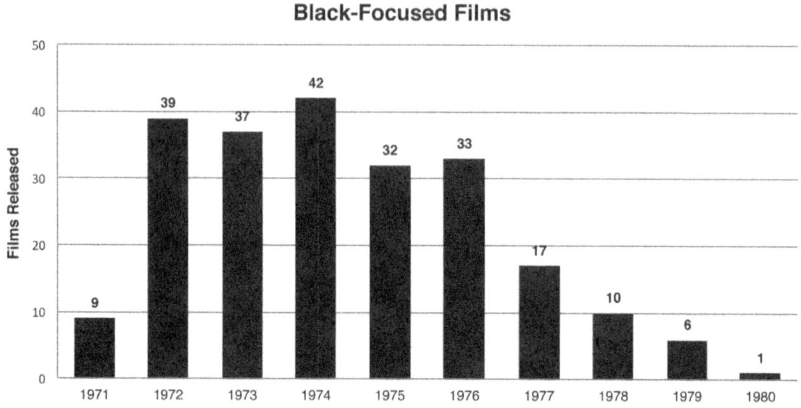

Figure 2

and the majority of those were either studio co-productions or negative pickup deals with independent financing. The majority of black-focused films between 1972 and 1976 were made by minor studios or independent producers and distributed without the help of the majors. Independent producers hoped to strike it rich by making the next *Sweetback*, or at least to turn a modest profit by piggybacking on a new trend. Independent productions fostered new opportunities for black directors as well. Ossie Davis utilized independent financing to make his modestly budgeted *Black Girl* (1972), while William Crain, Oscar Williams, Yaphet Kotto, Christopher St. John, and Michael Schultz all made their directorial debuts outside of the major studios in 1972.[18]

As Figure 2 shows, over the span of five years, from 1972 to 1976, more than thirty black-focused features were released annually. This surge coincided with an influx of black filmmakers. Young directors like Stan Lathan and Gilbert Moses brought their talents from other mediums (television and theater, respectively, in their case), while actors Raymond St. Jacques and Ron O'Neal took advantage of new opportunities to step behind the camera.[19] Even Motown founder Berry Gordy looked to take part in the new wave of black directors, crediting himself on *Mahogany* (1975), although it is widely believed that Tony Richardson was in fact the director. As studio investment in black-focused features began to wane after a disappointing box office year in 1974, independent productions remained steady and gave an entry point for black directors on low-budget genre features, including Sal Watts, Arthur Roberson, Horace Jackson, D'Urville Martin, Cliff Roquemore, Woodie King Jr., Fred Williamson, and Jamaa Fanaka.[20]

Of course, black-focused features were not the exclusive domain of black directors, particularly for exploitation studios like American International Pictures, which only used two black directors on its twenty-four black-focused films.[21] Even with studios beginning to scale back on black-focused productions as early as 1975, it is important to keep in mind that the opportunities for African Americans to make films still existed with independent features. But all that would change at the end of 1976.

While most scholars mark the beginning of blaxploitation either with the success of *Cotton Comes to Harlem* in 1970 or the arrival of *Shaft* and *Sweetback* in 1971, the end date for the cycle is less clear.[22] Dates range from 1974 and 1975 to 1979, with a few seeing blaxploitation as a generic construct that continued into the 1980s and 1990s. The output of major studios is commonly used to gauge blaxploitation's ending point, which has led scholars such as Ed Guerrero, Jesse Algeron Rhines, and Mark A. Reid to pinpoint 1974 as the final year of the cycle.[23] This assessment limits blaxploitation's output to the releases of a handful of companies, suggesting a stranglehold on the industry to match a later model of control from media conglomerates. However, the film industry in the 1970s was far more open and fluid than this model suggests, with minor studios and independents having access to theater screens and wielding modest power thanks to regulated markets and the dysfunction of their more established competitors. While the major studio model of *Shaft* was replicated by successful studio releases like *Super Fly* and *Cleopatra Jones*, the majority of black-oriented releases failed at the box office in 1973 and 1974, causing a shift away from blaxploitation features on the part of major studios by 1975. However, looking at the broader trend in black-focused productions allows a clearer understanding of the time frame and prompts a number of questions.

As Figure 2 indicates, black-focused productions remained relatively steady throughout 1976, with independents continuing their investment at a level beyond the output of major studios. The sudden decrease between 1976 and 1977—and the near erasure of black-focused features from the American film industry by the end of the decade—raises an interesting set of questions. Starting with the most obvious, what happened in 1976 to begin the decline? The common explanations for the demise of blaxploitation are as follows. First, the success of *Jaws* (1975, Steven Spielberg) changed the landscape of the industry, shifting the focus from a large stable of releases earning modest profits to a smaller selection of big-budget features that studios hoped would earn monumental returns at the box office. *Jaws*, released by Universal Pictures, coupled with Twentieth Century Fox's *Star Wars* (1977, George Lucas) to codify the blockbuster approach in Hollywood. Second, exhibition strategies were undergoing major transformations throughout the 1970s. The rise of the cineplex, largely coming in the form of two- or four-screen theaters being built in shopping malls, shifted exhibition venues to the suburbs, leaving distributors with little reason to continue making black-oriented features for single-screen urban venues and drive-ins.

The third and most often argued cause for the decline is that blaxploitation, like countless other niche subgenres, had simply run its course.[24] Whether the decline was rooted in a political awakening from the protests of the Coalition Against Blaxploitation, or in audience fatigue from the formulaic retreads of *Shaft* and *Sweetback*, black-focused films were no longer drawing the same number of spectators, and therefore were abandoned. While these explanations point out important factors in the shifting filmgoing practices, they fail to provide a compelling reason for the very sudden decrease in black-focused features after 1976. Blockbuster production, suburban exhibition, and changing tastes might account for a gradual change, but it does not account for the drastic shift in business philosophy evidenced in the empirical data of the era. The most logical explanation for the decline can be found in the details of film financing and the understanding that the majority of black-focused features were made and distributed outside of the major studios.

TAXPLOITATION

In an effort to combat runaway production, new tax rules introduced in the late 1960s had offered tax credits for movies shot in the United States. The 1969 Revenue Act was a boon to independent producers and low-budget filmmakers, allowing for a 100 percent tax write-off for individual film investment in modestly budgeted features made in America.[25] Thanks in part to the Paramount decree and the rebuilding of competing national cinemas following World War II, domestic production had dropped steadily throughout the 1950s and 1960s. Differentiation from television and improved technology helped to move productions off of studio lots. This new emphasis on location shooting sparked a growing number of American-financed features to use foreign locales. Some movies went overseas for the built-in production value of exotic locales, while others took advantage of lowered costs, as was the case with spaghetti westerns. American theaters also began carrying more imported films than ever before, ranging from art-house fare to low-budget sexploitation. The 1969 Revenue Act enticed studios to shoot their films stateside, but more importantly, it sparked independent investment in film production.

The scope of the blaxploitation cycle was a direct result of the Revenue Act, with tax shelters and no-risk investment becoming the impetus for independent financing of a large number of black-focused films in the 1970s. Melvin Van Peebles mortgaged his livelihood on *Sweetback*'s success, but independent financiers and small business investors looking for a tax write-off won regardless of box-office performance. Oftentimes, independent financiers expressed little or no interest in the quality of the films they backed. Regardless of the box-office return, they received a tax credit that would at least offset their investment, and at times exceed it with additional credits, as an investment of $150,000 could lead to a tax write-off of $450,000.[26] In practice, whether a film became a success or failed to gross dollar one at the box office, the investment paid off. The best-case scenario was that the film would become a runaway success at the box office, like *Sweetback*, and the investor would enjoy the profits. The worst-case scenario was that their taxes were paid to a filmmaker rather than to the federal government.

The federal Tax Reform Act of 1976 abolished these tax shelters, and, not coincidentally, within a few months independent production of black-focused features came to a grinding halt.[27] Without no-risk investment, minor distributors became more cautious and refused to invest in films targeting a black audience. In 1977 there were only eleven independently financed black-focused releases; in 1978 there were eight. Even these low numbers fail to be fully indicative of the decline, as a large portion of the black-focused films released in 1977 and 1978 were actually produced before the end of tax shelters, as they did not find distributors until a full one or two years after they were completed. Others films from 1977 and 1978 were international co-productions shot in the Philippines, Italy, or Hong Kong. By 1980, the bottom had dropped out; that year, no independently financed black-focused features found theatrical release.

The end of the blaxploitation cycle in 1976 not only marked a sharp decline in black-oriented features but also in effect closed the window of opportunity for black directors. With access to independent financing becoming increasingly difficult by 1977, the only other option for a black director would be to work for one of the major Hollywood studios. While the majors distributed twenty-seven features by African American directors between 1969 and 1976, the increasingly conservative studios all but required that a director have a track record. Not only would directors need to have numerous credits to their name, but they would have to show evidence that the films they made were often, if not always, financially successful. In essence, the field of black directors shrank to a handful of filmmakers who had been able to make the most of the climate of inclusion that accompanied the blaxploitation cycle.

THE END OF THE LINE

The end of no-risk independent financing and the conservative shift at the major studios would shut out young first-time black directors from the possibility of making a commercial film. Unfortunately, the closing of the doors to new black screen artists coincided with the departure of the most successful black directors from the blaxploitation years. Melvin Van Peebles had yet to match the success of *Sweetback* by the time the blaxploitation cycle had run its course, concentrating instead on writing and directing for the stage.[28] When he returned to filmmaking in 1977, he chose to work with a major studio, writing and directing a biopic about the first black stock-car-racing champion, Wendell Scott. Struggling to retain creative control over the project, Van Peebles had an intense falling out with the film's producers; he was fired by Warner Bros. midway through shooting *Greased Lightning* (a film eventually completed by Michael Schultz and released in 1977). Essentially blacklisted by Hollywood, Van Peebles became a day trader on Wall Street, and he appeared in a series of bizarre nightly news editorials on New York's WNBC in the 1980s. Remaining a film-industry outsider, he watched as his son Mario began to make a name for himself as an actor in the 1980s. Mario eventually followed in his father's footsteps as a director in the 1990s.

Ossie Davis's success with *Cotton Comes to Harlem*, and later with the Vietnam-veteran revenge fantasy *Gordon's War* (1973), was balanced by his financial failures. His attempts to cultivate a pan-African cinema with revolutionary rhetoric and black financing were ultimately disastrous. After finishing *Cotton*, Davis traveled to Africa to film an adaptation of Wole Soyinka's play *Kongi's Harvest* (1970), using US financing and a Swedish crew to make what he claimed to be the first feature film made in Nigeria.[29] Davis hoped the film would spark involvement in film production in Africa, furthering the momentum of Senegal's Ousmane Sembène while also placing black Americans in direct dialogue with African art and culture. However, the film had a small budget and poor production values and was rarely seen, taking three years to find a limited release in the United States. Davis's next project in Africa was even more ambitious: filming the original screenplay for *Countdown at Kusini* (1976) in Lagos with an expanded budget of $1.2 million provided by the black sorority Delta Sigma Theta.[30]

The Deltas looked at *Countdown at Kusini* as a chance to take a proactive stance against the supposedly negative stereotypes in blaxploitation films. The idea was to make a film that was black controlled on every level aside from the distribution, which was handled by Columbia. The end result, however, was disappointing. The tale of revolution in a fictitious African nation was panned by critics and lost money at the box office, causing embarrassment for the Deltas. The film was never made available to the public following its initial theatrical release.[31] The Deltas moved away from financing black films, and Davis was unable to find a workable model for a pan-African commercial cinema. He stopped directing after the release of *Countdown at Kusini*.

Meanwhile, Gordon Parks, the first black director to make a studio film and the most successful prior to 1976, was growing increasingly frustrated with Hollywood. Following *The Learning Tree*, he intended to make another film based on his own material, writing the original screenplay *Eagle in the Air*.[32] The story of a young black woman hitchhiking across Nevada was attached to MGM, but was never filmed. Instead, Parks signed on to direct *Shaft*, which led to his returning for the sequel *Shaft's Big Score* the following year.[33] His success on the first two *Shaft* films placed Parks at the center of the debates over negative representation, forcing him into the unenviable position of having to defend his work among fellow black intellectuals. Parks shuddered at the term "blaxploitation," and until his death in 2006 he remained upset anytime his films were discussed within the thematic framework of the production cycle.

After the first two *Shaft* films, Parks tried to move forward with another original screenplay, *An Endless Silence*.[34] The story focuses on a Korean War veteran suffering from posttraumatic stress disorder who is on the run from the law after kidnapping his deaf son. The drama has didactic elements about the treatment of soldiers that are an outgrowth of the antiwar movement, with Parks creating a narrative of black experiences that differs from anything else being released in theaters in the early 1970s. Again, the studios passed on Parks's original screenplay. Instead, he directed *The Super Cops* (1974) at MGM, moving away from black-focused features with a true-life story of New York City policemen patterned after the successful *Serpico* (1973, Sidney Lumet). Parks would make his final studio film for Paramount with the biopic of a blues legend in *Leadbelly* (1976), which was a passion project for the director. With a budget exceeding $2 million and three years invested in developing the project,

Parks was heartbroken when Paramount failed to put much effort into promoting the film.[35] Gordon Parks swore off Hollywood after *that*, turning to other creative outlets and never looking back.

His son Gordon Parks Jr., who had worked alongside his father on *The Learning Tree* before finding success on his own accord with *Super Fly*, would exit the ranks of black directors under much more tragic circumstances. Following *Super Fly*, he directed *Thomasine and Bushrod* (1974) at Columbia before making the sizably budgeted action film *Three the Hard Way* (1974) through the ambitious minor studio Allied Artists. He then returned to Columbia to make *Aaron Loves Angela* (1975) before stepping away from filmmaking to develop his own projects. In the mode of Ossie Davis before him, Gordon Parks Jr. hoped to establish a feasible model for filmmaking in Africa, founding the new production company African International Productions in 1979. With a third of the principal photography completed on *Revenge*, which was the first effort for the new company, Parks and three crew members died in a plane crash in Nairobi.[36]

Gordon Parks Jr. had passed away, his uncompromising father refused to work in Hollywood, Melvin Van Peebles was blacklisted, and no one would hire Ossie Davis because of his recent failures. Who did that leave? Struggling to find work after the fall of blaxploitation, other black directors who had made features during the era looked outside of Hollywood feature filmmaking for opportunities. Ivan Dixon, Mark Warren, and William Crain directed for television throughout the 1970s and 1980s, never making another theatrically distributed feature in America. Warren directed the Canadian teen sex comedy *The Kinky Coaches and the Pom Pom Pussycats* (1981, also known as *Heartbreak High*), while Crain directed the independently produced family western *The Kid from Not-So-Big* (1978), which was never released theatrically.

Oscar Williams, Cliff Roquemore, and D'Urville Martin remained on the margins of the film industry for a few years following 1976 before disappearing altogether. Martin would act in a handful of small films before his death in 1984. Roquemore directed the Rudy Ray Moore vehicle *Petey Wheatstraw* (1977), wrote the screenplay for Moore's *Disco Godfather* (1979, J. Robert Wagoner), and received his final screen credit as an associate producer on *Body and Soul* (1981, George Bowers). Oscar Williams, who had made *The Final Comedown* (1972), *Five on the Black Hand Side* (1973), and the Jim Kelly action film *Hot Potato* (1976), as well as writing the screenplays for *Black Belt Jones* (1974, Robert Clouse) and *Truck Turner* (1974, Jonathan Kaplan), unsuccessfully pursued work in Hollywood over the next decade. His only completed film following blaxploitation was *Whack Attack* (1978), a message movie about the dangers of the drug PCP written by Los Angeles psychiatrist Roland Jefferson. The search for a theatrical distributor for the film was abandoned in favor of trying to sell it as a TV movie-of-the-week, and it eventually aired on ABC in 1980.[37]

AFTERMATH

The end of tax shelters may have stifled independent financiers' interest in black-focused cinema, but Hollywood had done enough market research by 1977 to realize that African Americans made up a significant percentage of their filmgoing audience. In fact, numerous studies have shown that African Americans, approximately 12 to 13 percent of the general population, are disproportionately represented in film and television audiences. By the 1990s the NAACP had estimated that black audiences made up 25 percent of the domestic box office, a number that may have been even higher in the years before the rise of suburban multiplexes.[38] In transitioning away from the blaxploitation cycle and moving toward a blockbuster production model, studios were more than aware that black audiences were an important part of their consumer base. What Hollywood set out to do was merge approaches, making films for the broadest possible audiences while simultaneously appealing to the specific interests of the black filmgoing market. Hollywood's most disastrous attempt to reach black audiences via the blockbuster model came with Universal's big-budget musical *The Wiz* (1978, Sidney Lumet), a box-office disappointment that gave studios pause when considering tackling black-cast films in the blockbuster era.[39] While blaxploitation features were largely viable because of their modest returns on even more modest investments, *The Wiz*'s bloated budget necessitated massive returns both at the box office and through ancillary tie-ins that never materialized.

Rather than attempt to sell a mainstream and multiethnic audience on big-budget, black-cast features, Hollywood instead looked to find ways of incorporating black characters into otherwise white films. Universal president Thom Mount captured the mood of the industry when he told *Black Enterprise* magazine in 1982, "Black films are not capable of making money. . . . There's only one actor who's bankable—Richard Pryor—and one actress—Diana Ross, and we have Pryor under contract."[40] As Bill Gunn had predicted in *Rhinestone Sharecropping*, integration became the model for Hollywood films, taking a number of different forms outside of the Richard Pryor and Eddie Murphy approach of a black star in an otherwise white world. The addition of Billy Dee Williams to *The Empire Strikes Back* (1980, Irvin Kershner) gave the *Star Wars* franchise a more visible black presence, as did the casting of Paul Winfield in *Star Trek II: The Wrath of Khan* (1982, Nicholas Meyer). African Americans joined the ensemble in mainstream comedies like *Police Academy* (1984, Hugh Wilson), *Revenge of the Nerds* (1984, Jeff Kanew), and *Fast Times at Ridgemont High* (1982, Amy Heckerling), while complementary actors, such as Gregory Hines and Lou Gossett Jr., were often cast in more serious roles opposite whites.

Two dominant modes of black representation in the 1980s were urban criminality and the black buddy. Films like *Death Wish II* (1982, Michael Winner) and *Sudden Impact* (1983, Clint Eastwood) play on suburban fears and reiterate the Reagan presidency's scapegoating of people living in poverty, while dutiful black friends help their white counterparts achieve their goals in *Nighthawks* (1981, Bruce Malmuth) and *Running Scared* (1986, Peter Hyams). *Rocky III* (1982, Sylvester Stallone) manages to do both at the same time, with Rocky Balboa's dutiful friend Apollo Creed (Carl Weathers) helping him triumph against the urban menace Clubber Lang (Mr. T).

African Americans remained present in Hollywood, but they were kept in the margins, part of a strategy of tokenism that the film industry used to deflect charges of racism. Despite nominal representation, Hollywood in the 1980s was unquestionably a racist institution. Trying to locate personal racial animus on the part of studio executives to support this claim is beside the point, as the structure of the industry and its production strategies disenfranchised blacks and other minorities. Black audiences were underserved thanks to Hollywood's curious logic, whereby studios concluded that black-focused films could not be profitable despite only limited efforts to prove otherwise. More importantly, examples of black spectators coming out to see blockbuster films in the 1970s were presented as proof that black box-office dollars would remain constant regardless of the racial makeup of the films Hollywood chose to release.[41] Multiethnic casting became a way to assuage the needs of African American filmgoers without upsetting mainstream cinema's primary focus on white characters and audiences.

In terms of labor, the exclusion of African Americans from the filmmaking process was clearly evident. In 1982, only 3.7 percent of the members of the Directors Guild of America belonged to minority groups—including blacks, Hispanics, and Asians—with little evidence that anything was going to change.[42] A simple comparison of credited directors is even more striking, showing the dramatic difference between the blaxploitation cycle and the years to follow for black filmmakers. Twenty-eight different black directors made theatrically released films that were produced in the five-year span between 1972 and 1976. Over the next ten years, from 1977 to 1986, only nine black directors would see their names on the silver screen. Against all odds, Michael Schultz and Sidney Poitier found success at major studios, while Fred Williamson and Jamaa Fanaka adapted to the changing landscape of independent financing to create their own opportunities. These directors worked to counter the precipitous fall that came with the end of the blaxploitation cycle, finding ways to make films in a climate that discouraged their involvement.

CHAPTER TWO

Our Man in Hollywood

CREATIVITY AND COMPROMISE IN THE FILMS OF MICHAEL SCHULTZ

When Walter Gordon went to a Los Angeles movie theater in the summer of 1975 to see *Cooley High*, he was at once deeply moved and confused. To him, the film captured the essence of what it was like to grow up in the inner city, negotiating friendship and ambition with the constant presence of poverty and violence. Gordon had seen scores of blaxploitation films in the preceding years, but *Cooley High* was an epiphany for him. It moved beyond a fantasy of black heroism to truly capture the emotional reality of life in the ghetto. But Gordon paused when he looked at the credits of the film and saw that *Cooley High* had been directed by Michael Schultz. "I thought that Schultz was Jewish," he later recalled, "and I couldn't figure out how this white guy made a movie that was so authentically black."[1] After a bit of digging and asking around, Gordon discovered that his confusion was with the name itself. Michael Schultz was, in fact, African American. An aspiring director studying filmmaking at the University of California at Los Angeles at the time, Gordon wanted to make sure that no one ever would make the same mistake when seeing one of his films in the future. So, Walter Gordon became Jamaa Fanaka, adopting a Swahili name that he felt was "unmistakably black."[2]

Fanaka's personal anecdote is revealing, pointing to the relative anonymity of Michael Schultz. With a long career that includes some of the most iconic cinematic representations of blackness, Schultz is nevertheless rarely invoked in popular or scholarly discussions of African American filmmaking traditions. Before the arrival of Spike Lee, no black director made more films in Hollywood than Schultz, yet the two are rarely mentioned in the same breath. Lee's visibility—be it as an actor, commercial pitchman, sports fan, or interview subject—stands in sharp contrast to

Schultz, whose aversion to self-promotion has played a role in obscuring his importance as a filmmaker.

Aside from their varying degrees of name recognition, the careers of Schultz and Lee are strikingly similar. Both gained access to Hollywood studio productions, opened doors for minority employment on film crews, and expressed a nuanced aesthetic rooted in black cultural traditions while also incorporating established film language. Schultz remained a viable member of Hollywood's ranks through his ability to navigate an industry that largely excluded black artists from participating in mainstream productions in any capacity. The fact that Schultz's work lacked the outward markers of seriousness that accompany art-house offerings has likely played a role in his career not receiving critical attention or due acclaim. He worked primarily for major studios and made films that catered to popular taste. Yet his films provide a necessary counter-narrative to the exclusionary US film industry, providing a black political perspective within the structural framework of Hollywood productions. *Car Wash* (1976), *The Last Dragon* (1985), *Which Way Is Up?* (1977), and *Cooley High* (1975) provide thoughtful commentaries on race and class, intertwining drama and comedy to create deeply textured films. *Krush Groove* (1985) and *Sgt. Pepper's Lonely Hearts Club Band* (1978), in different ways, feature key moments of transition in popular music and document performances of some of the most important musicians of the twentieth century. Schultz's work with film stars is also particularly notable. *Carbon Copy* (1981) introduces a young Denzel Washington to film audiences, while the four films Schultz made with Richard Pryor provide the most compelling and nuanced screen performances of the comedian's career.

Schultz's career now spans five decades, starting with his work for the stage and including fifteen feature films and his prolific "side career" directing for television. He is a humble and reserved man, self-deprecating and quick to shower praise on the actors, writers, producers, and various collaborators who have accompanied him on his myriad projects. On set he has a quiet demeanor and spends time outside of principal photography doing the less than glamorous labor of rehearsing actors, rewriting scripts, and working with editors on final cuts, rather than engaging in self-promotion. While his name appears on the films he directs, his work is rarely seen as a form of authorial expression. Spanning genre, his films would seem to fall in line with auteurist readings of studio-era directors like Howard Hawks and Michael Curtiz, using close analysis of an entire filmography to unpack recurring themes and formal patterns even when a "directorial style" is not immediately clear.

What complicates this approach for Schultz is that his work fluctuates wildly in terms of both production modes and personal investment. He has made films on shoestring budgets and has also enjoyed the largesse of blockbuster-sized financing. He has cultivated projects from concept to completion and has also filled in as a last-minute replacement for fired directors. He wears his heart on his sleeve and has made deeply personal films while making other projects to earn a paycheck, providing dispassionate labor as a simple craftsman. We can reconcile some of these contradictions by considering the changing landscape of the film industry and unique factors surrounding each project. Schultz's work has not been produced in a vacuum; it has been heavily determined by outside context. Race played a major factor in determining his opportunities in Hollywood and informed the content of his films, even if audience members—such as the young Walter Gordon—were unaware of his identity.

BEGINNINGS

Born in Milwaukee on November 10, 1938, Schultz was encouraged by his mother, Katherine, to develop an interest in theater and literature to accompany his love for television and movies. An excellent student, he turned down an appointment at West Point following high school to attend the University of Wisconsin at Madison in 1956, where he pursued astronomical engineering. Schultz became entranced by European art cinema through campus screenings of *La Strada* (1954, Federico Fellini) and *Wild Strawberries* (1957, Ingmar Bergman), but pressing financial difficulties sent him back to Milwaukee, where he found work in a steel mill and on the assembly line at American Motors.[3]

Following a brief stint at a community theater, Schultz then enrolled at Marquette University, earning a scholarship by working as a lighting director in the theater department. Over the next few years, he was involved in a number of stage projects at Marquette and became a devoted pupil of Father John J. Walsh, a nontraditional member of the Jesuit faculty who often subverted the university's conservative ideology through his productions. Walsh had worked in New York with Elia Kazan before coming to Marquette and employed what Schultz terms "guerilla theater" techniques.[4] Walsh cultivated a sense of solidarity in the department, often staging productions in unauthorized areas of campus and utilizing unconventional resources for costumes and sets.

After graduating from Marquette in 1964, Schultz and a handful of his classmates headed to New York to try their hand at making it in the theater. Soon after arriving in the city, Schultz met the woman he would eventually marry, Gloria, an up-and-coming stage actress.[5] Working odd jobs along the way, he found work as a gofer on an off-Broadway production of *Benito Cereno*, which led to him eventually becoming the understudy of lead actor Frank Langella before being offered a job at Princeton University's McCarter Theatre by Arthur Lithgow. Schultz made his debut as a director at Princeton in 1966 on a production of *Waiting for Godot* before following Lithgow to Antioch College to direct Shakespeare the following summer.[6]

While Schultz spent his winters on the campus of Princeton directing Samuel Beckett and his summers in pastoral Yellow Springs, Ohio (home of Antioch), New York was ablaze in revolutionary rhetoric among African American playwrights and actors. While Larry Neal and Amiri Baraka were spearheading the Black Arts movement, Douglas Turner Ward, Robert Hooks, and Gerald Krone were laying the foundation for what would become the Negro Ensemble Company (NEC). Ward started the ball rolling with his 1966 essay/manifesto in the *New York Times*, "American Theater: For Whites Only?" In it, Ward pointed out the state of underrepresentation of blacks on the American stage and called for a new, revolutionary approach to theater in which black stage artists would be given the opportunity to speak to and for the African American community. Ward looked for a "theater of permanence, continuity, and consistency, providing the necessary home-base for the Negro artist to launch a campaign to win his ignored brothers and sisters as constant witnesses to his endeavors."[7] The article's erudite and impassioned call to action came to the attention of the Ford Foundation, which soon agreed to fund the NEC for three years.[8]

With financing secured, Ward and Hooks began to assemble actors, directors, and material. They placed an ad for talent in the *Village Voice* and enlisted Lloyd Richards to work with the actors. Months after responding to the *Village Voice* ad, Schultz received a visit from Douglas Turner Ward inviting him to become a major figure in the NEC. Ward hired Schultz to the NEC's first production, German playwright Peter Weiss's Singspiel *The Song of the Lusitania Bogey*, a play about the Portuguese oppression of Mozambique and Angola.[9] *The Song of the Lusitania Bogey* became a success both commercially and critically, and Schultz received the Obie Award as best director before moving on to his next NEC project, Wole Soyinka's *Kongi's Harvest*. It was an auspicious start for someone who had been working on an assembly line in Wisconsin just a few years earlier.

Although Schultz's work at the NEC matched his political and artistic interests, his ultimate goal was to direct feature films. "When I was going to college, I had no role models," Schultz later explained. "Gordon Parks hadn't appeared on the scene yet. Melvin Van Peebles hadn't appeared on the scene yet. But I knew that it was something I wanted to do, I just didn't know how to get a foot in the door. . . . I had a theory that if I made a reputation as a director in the theatre that someone would hire me to direct a movie."[10] When Schultz was offered the opportunity to direct a Broadway play, he jumped at it, seeing it as the logical next step toward his goal of directing for Hollywood. *Does a Tiger Wear a Necktie?*, a 1969 play set in a halfway house for heroin addicts, starred Al Pacino, Hal Holbrook, M. Emmett Walsh, and Schultz's wife, Gloria. It earned rave reviews and Tony nominations for Schultz, Gloria, and Pacino. The play lost out to *The Great White Hope* at the Tonys, but its success spurred local public broadcasting station WNET to offer Schultz his first opportunity to direct a film, a 16 mm television production of Lorraine Hansberry's posthumously produced play *To Be Young, Gifted and Black* (aired in 1972).

Adapted by Hansberry's widower, Robert Nemiroff, the play consists of separate sketches that illuminate Hansberry's autobiography and creative work. Schultz compiled a diverse and talented cast to portray various aspects of Hansberry's persona, including Blythe Danner, Roy Scheider, Al Freeman Jr., Claudia McNeil, and Ruby Dee. The sketches are framed through a table reading of the actors, showing what would become a central component to a number of Schultz's films. Schultz used his theater background in working with actors for film, holding rehearsals before shooting and cultivating improvisation and creative input from his actors. The finished film shows a director acclimating to a new medium, balancing the ambition to emulate his art-house heroes with the formal expectations and financial constraints of public broadcasting. Schultz used *To Be Young, Gifted and Black* and his next few projects as hands-on training to learn the craft of filmmaking.

INDEPENDENT MARGINS

Schultz made his first foray into commercial features with *Together for Days* (1972), a low-budget film about interracial romance. Produced by Robert Buchanan (whose only other film experience was producing the nature documentary series *Over Land and Sea*), the film is based on a story outline from Lindsay Smith, a young white woman chronicling her romance with a black man. Looking to add insight and artistry, Buchanan hired acclaimed black playwright William Branch to write the screenplay. Best known for his 1951 play *A Medal for Willie*, Branch went through a long and contentious process working with Buchanan and

Smith on *Together for Days*.[11] Buchanan and Smith's concept for the picture was aligned with white liberalism rooted in the civil rights years, whereas Branch's screenplay looked to infuse the film with a contemporary black consciousness and sense of realism.[12] This struggle for perspective carried over to finding a director for the film.

Buchanan initially targeted Gordon Parks, but Parks was busy shooting *Shaft's Big Score*. Unable to land him, Buchanan intimated that he would have to start looking for white directors to make *Together for Days*. Branch offered alternatives, hoping to retain an air of authenticity in the black thematic elements of the story through the perspective and lived experience of the director. He mentioned his friend and neighbor Ossie Davis, but Davis was making *Black Girl* at the time. Branch then mentioned Michael Schultz. He had never met Schultz, but he was aware of him through his stage work. Branch personally approached Schultz during the filming of *To Be Young, Gifted and Black* to pitch the film, and Schultz signed on to the project.[13]

Together for Days was shot in Atlanta over the course of a few weeks in 1971 with a shoestring budget of $600,000.[14] Clifton Davis and Lois Chiles play the young lovers, while stage mainstay Woodie King Jr. joined his friend Schultz in Atlanta to appear in a supporting role. *Together for Days* also serves as the screen debut for Samuel L. Jackson, a theater student at Morehouse College at the time. Jackson was cast thanks to Carlton Molette, a professor at Morehouse who was also serving as the art director on the film.

Following the contentious partnership in writing the film, William Branch was barred from the set by Buchanan, left helpless as a number of the scenes in his screenplay were reworked or replaced altogether.[15] With limited funding, the film was shot in a hurry, and Schultz headed to Los Angeles to direct Derek Walcott's play *Dream on Monkey Mountain* immediately after principal photography wrapped.[16] Schultz never saw a finished version of *Together for Days*, trusting Buchanan to find an editor and to distribute the film. This type of passive labor—not playing a role throughout all phases of production—would become a recurring theme for Schultz, and the fact of his outside commitments and lack of personal investment problematizes a unified reading of his body of work.

Very little information survives about the film itself. *Together for Days* never received a distribution deal, so rather than shelve the picture Buchanan decided to attempt to distribute the film himself. Borrowing the name from his nature documentaries *Over Land and Sea*, Buchanan christened his distribution company Olas Corporation, which existed for the sole purpose of releasing *Together for Days*.[17] Be it naïve ambition or an ironic juxtaposition,

Buchanan made the odd choice of holding the premiere at Atlanta's Peachtree Theater (previously called the Loew's Grand Theater), the site of the gala premiere of *Gone with the Wind* (1939, Victor Fleming) decades earlier.[18] *Jet* magazine later reported a screening in Chicago, while playwright Lonnie Elder claimed to have seen the film in Los Angeles, perhaps having been invited to the November 30, 1972, screening for *Variety*.[19] Aside from these screenings there is no evidence of *Together for Days* playing anywhere else in the United States. *Variety*'s review sealed its fate, calling *Together for Days* "a sincere, well intentioned" film that nevertheless was a "commercial and creative lightweight."[20] *Variety*, always mindful of a film's ability to make money, pointed out that the film failed "to predetermine the audience for which it is intended. . . . While lacking the energy that is demanded by black audiences, it inadvertently insults whites who might have been attracted to the liberal underpinnings of this romantic tract."[21]

The scathing *Variety* review, coupled with the film's lack of star power, budget, or easily marketable premise, ended any chance of *Together for Days* either being picked up by a major distributor or garnering interest from theater owners hoping to book the movie.[22] Very few people have seen the film, as it was limited to those three American screenings in 1972 and a nonexistent afterlife in retrospectives or home video. No known prints of the film exist, and neither Michael Schultz nor William Branch know of any extant copies or have leads on where one might be stored. Robert Buchanan died a number of years ago, and his Olas Corporation, needless to say, only survived long enough to get *Together for Days* on those three screens. Schultz used the film as a stepping-stone to further projects, however, approaching the project as on-the-job training to learn the particulars of making movies. The film was a useful addition to his résumé even if it never saw substantial theatrical release. The film's disappearance nevertheless speaks to the unsettling reality of the lack of preservation of blaxploitation-era films.

Shortly after *Together for Days* was completed, Schultz again found himself being courted by an independent film producer. Eager to make a name for himself by riding the wave of black-oriented movies, Jack Jordan approached Schultz to direct *Honeybaby, Honeybaby* (1974). Schultz was given a few weeks to make his decision before location shooting began in Beirut, Lebanon.[23] He accepted the project knowing little about Jordan or the film itself. Jordan had already signed Diana Sands to star in the film, assembled the rest of the cast, scouted shooting locations, and agreed on a final shooting script before hiring Schultz to direct. On the surface, *Honeybaby, Honeybaby* seemed to be a dramatic departure from the fly-by-night production of *Together for Days*. It had an established lead in Sands and an international locale. But like his first feature, *Honeybaby* suffered from having a novice producer and failed to find a major distributor; it played at only a handful of theaters in its initial run.

The film is modeled on a Hitchcock thriller and is centered on a beautiful woman from Harlem who wins a television contest for an all-expenses-paid trip to Beirut. While on vacation she becomes entangled in a complicated battle for microfilm between the Lebanese underworld and a revolutionary group from an unspecified African nation. The microfilm serves as the McGuffin, as it ends up being an irrelevant plot diversion by the picture's end, while the finale, set in a history museum, retraces Hitchcock's tendency to stage climactic scenes in notable locales, specifically invoking the British Museum sequence in *Blackmail* (1929). Like *Together for Days*, *Honeybaby* was panned in *Variety*, this time for having an "inane and highly confusing script, ineffectual performance by supporting cast and inadequate—indeed unprofessional—production values."[24]

Whether the failures of the film can be traced to Schultz is debatable. Schultz had no way of knowing how the project would turn out based on the information he was presented in 1972. Jack Jordan had yet to produce a film, but while he was working on *Honeybaby* he was simultaneously producing Bill Gunn's *Ganja & Hess*, a film ostensibly about vampires that replaces genre conventions for an impressionistic meditation on African American identity. Releasing the film under his own production and distribution company Kelly/Jordan Enterprises, Jordan drastically changed the form and function of *Ganja & Hess*, editing Gunn's final cut of 110 minutes down to an often indecipherable 78 minutes.[25] With *Ganja & Hess*, Jordan wanted a simple and formulaic retread of *Blacula* (1972, William Crain). What Gunn gave him was a highly nuanced and experimental formulation of a black aesthetic, continuing Van Peebles's avant-garde approach to *Sweetback* but with a more coherent worldview. As was the case with *Ganja & Hess*, the final product of *Honeybaby, Honeybaby* was far from the vision of the director, as Schultz was not involved in the editing of the film. Gunn's passion project was taken away and artistically mutilated, while Schultz lacked a personal stake in *Honeybaby*. Whereas Gunn struggled to retain his authorial stamp and ultimately became disenchanted with commercial filmmaking, Schultz left his film behind, moving to Hollywood to begin what would become a prolific career directing episodic television.[26]

Working on *The Rockford Files* and *Starsky & Hutch*, Schultz traded in the artistic ambition that informed his stage work for the dual opportunity to continue learning the craft of directing for the screen while also making a name for himself within the studio system (*The Rockford Files*, for example, was made under the television wing of Universal). "TV was an opportunity to play with bigger toys," Schultz later explained. "TV was a way to get experience that I wasn't able to get in the low-budget movie world."[27] While Schultz learned the rudiments of camera movement and *mise-en-scène*, he was also meeting the more basic need of providing for his growing family. Since their days in New York, he and Gloria had had two sons. For Schultz, directing was an occupation as well as a creative outlet, and he had no qualms with plying his craft for a paycheck. At the same time, he remained hopeful that financial stability and artistic expression could coexist in future projects.

THE RISE

Schultz's success directing for television brought him to the attention of Sam Arkoff, the head of American International Pictures (AIP). The most visible producer of blaxploitation films, AIP applied the same exploitation practices in the 1970s that Arkoff had used on past cycles of horror films, teen beach movies, and biker flicks by capitalizing on audience trends. AIP made its films fast and cheap, emphasizing sex and violence to appeal to drive-in and grindhouse audiences. Its hits, including *Slaughter* (1972, Jack Starrett), *Black Caesar* (1973, Larry Cohen), and *Blacula*, drew complaints from black civic leaders and became icons for the derisive repurposing of the term "blaxploitation."

Following a protracted conflict between AIP and the Coalition Against Blaxploitation, a militant splinter organization set off a car bomb outside of AIP's Beverly Hills offices on August 23, 1972, exploding studio executive Richard Zimbert's car.[28] Perhaps as a result, the tone of the studio's black-focused releases shifted in subsequent years, with Schultz's *Cooley High* (1975), *Cornbread, Earl and Me* (1975, Joseph Manduke), and *JD's Revenge* and *Monkey Hu$tle* (both 1976, Arthur Marks) appearing over the next few years. The studio began making a different kind of black-focused film. With Schultz on board, AIP hoped to avoid criticism: the company was employing a black director for only the second time in its history.[29] As a byproduct of AIP's shifting approach to black representation, *Cooley High* also employed a black writer, Eric Monte, using his semiautobiographical screenplay about growing up in Chicago circa 1964. Monte had come to prominence developing the television series *Good Times* for Norman Lear the year before, but he had found entry into feature films through the bizarre confluence of events at AIP that had prompted Arkoff to expand his approach to making black-focused films.

Following a group of friends from the Southside of Chicago, *Cooley*

High's coming-of-age tale quickly drew comparisons to the wildly successful *American Graffiti* (1973, George Lucas), causing AIP to label the film as "the black *American Graffiti*" in its advertising.[30] Both films incorporate music throughout, with Motown replacing the rock and roll of *American Graffiti*.[31] While Lucas's portrait of high school graduates in the San Fernando Valley relies heavily on feelings of nostalgia, *Cooley High* remains grounded in the realities of urban transformation and decline.

The teenage protagonists in both films take part in strikingly similar hijinks, ranging from landing the ever-elusive bottle of liquor to cozying up to local toughs, but the two films differ drastically in terms of consequence. The relatively privileged white teenagers in *American Graffiti* have a good laugh over their stunts, while *Cooley High*'s Preach (Glynn Turman) and Cochise (Lawrence Hilton-Jacobs) face punishment from their families, their schools, the police, and the hoodlums they once wished to befriend. In *American Graffiti*, the misadventures of one character, Curt (Richard Dreyfuss), with the local gang lead to little more than a colorful story to tell once he goes east to college. Cochise in *Cooley High*, on the other hand, pays with his life for a misunderstanding with local hoods. Lucas's suburban teens experience a loss of innocence by virtue of getting older. The innocence of the teens in *Cooley High* is threatened by the realities in which they live, as the inability to mature quickly is met with grave consequences. The films share structural and thematic similarities, but by labeling *Cooley High* the "black *American Graffiti*," AIP ultimately (and unknowingly) reinforced the dramatic differences in maturation and memory across racial lines that were evident in them.

Turning a steady profit without pandering to a specific demographic, *Cooley High* was an oddity among AIP's releases, eschewing action/exploitation narrative models and finding a multiracial audience. *Cooley High* has endured as a key text in African American cinema. It has been explicitly reworked in a number of subsequent films, most notably *Boyz n the Hood* (1991, John Singleton). Just as *American Graffiti* inspired the creation of the television series *Happy Days*, the success of *Cooley High* allowed Monte to use the film as a rough composite for the sitcom *What's Happening!!*[32] Schultz would direct a few episodes of that series, but they would turn out to be his final collaboration with Monte, who found himself shut out of Hollywood after a legal battle with Norman Lear over compensation for developing *Good Times*, *The Jeffersons*, and *What's Happening!!*[33]

For all of the talk about *Cooley High* being a "black *American Graffiti*," the incessant comparisons ultimately led to Schultz being embraced by his would-be rivals. Francis Ford Coppola, the producer of *American Graffiti*, had seen *Cooley High* and was impressed with the film. Recalling the particulars, Schultz says, "Coppola called up Lucas and said, 'You've got to see this movie. It's better than *American Graffiti*!'"[34] Lucas and Coppola invited Schultz up to the Napa Valley, where they talked about their respective films and established a friendship that would persist throughout the years, eventually turning into a professional partnership in 1994 when Schultz directed episodes of Lucas's television series *The Adventures of Young Indiana Jones*. Schultz had found himself being embraced by his peers and courted by the major studios, a remarkable turn of events after the failures of *Together for Days* and *Honeybaby, Honeybaby*.

Cooley High was a major turning point for Schultz. The acclaim for the film expanded his profile within Hollywood, with particular attention being paid to the way he handled pacing and music. The immediate result was Schultz being offered his first studio feature with Universal's *Car Wash*. The film was conceived by Gary Stromberg, an influential public relations manager in the music industry who was looking to break into Hollywood as a producer. Inspired by watching *Nashville* (1975, Robert Altman), Stromberg came up with a multi-character narrative that would serve as a platform for music.[35] Before finding a screenwriter or director, he contacted Motown producer/songwriter Norman Whitfield and persuaded him to sign on for the project and write all of the film's music. Stromberg emphasized soundtrack sales when he pitched the film to Universal, using a clear financial logic. "I researched and found that Whitfield never produced an album that sold less than a million copies," Stromberg later recalled, "so with a modest budget, the film couldn't lose."[36]

With music as the central component, Stromberg (now co-producing with Art Linson) signed Joel Schumacher to write the screenplay. Schultz, because of his handling of music and movement in *Cooley High*, was approached to direct. The film serves as the artistic high point in Schultz's film career, showing a virtuosic control of camera, *mise-en-scène*, performance, and sound to create a detailed world with layered social and political commentary. Schumacher's script, which, according to Schultz, was initially made up of "a series of jokes," was transformed into a complicated critique of late capitalism, using the car wash as a microcosm of urban America.[37]

Set in the span of a single working day at Los Angeles's Dee-Luxe Car Wash, the film features an elaborate web of characters, storylines, and action. Schultz convened the entire cast for weeks of rehearsals before shooting began, allowing the actors in the ensemble to explore their characters in depth and bring their own creative input to the project. With twenty central characters, the rehearsals helped Schultz and Schumacher find points of focus. Ultimately, the two characters that stand out as the

Lonnie (Ivan Dixon) and Abdullah (Bill Duke) in Car Wash.

emotional and political center of the film are the ex-convict Lonnie (Ivan Dixon) and Abdullah, a young militant played by Bill Duke. The interplay between these characters is the heart of the film, with generational tension giving way to a shared understanding and struggle.

Duke made his feature film debut with *Car Wash*, investing heavily into his character of Abdullah, so much so that he stayed in character throughout shooting, isolating himself from the rest of the cast and carrying his character's anger with him on and off camera for the duration of the production.[38] Duke, with his relative inexperience, was a counterpoint to Dixon, who had already had a successful career as an actor and had been one of the black directors to enter the fold of studio filmmaking during blaxploitation. From his performance in *Nothing But a Man* (1964, Michael Roemer) to his work as a director with *The Spook Who Sat by the Door* (1973), Dixon holds a distinct position as being a part of two of the most noteworthy black-focused films in the fifteen years prior to *Car Wash*. Keeping this meta-text in mind, the Lonnie character can be read as a composite of the two films, a quiet and unassuming Duff Anderson (in *Nothing But a Man*) who has been informed by the militant black nationalist politics of *The Spook Who Sat by the Door*. The final embrace between the two characters at the end of the film, with Abdullah tearfully telling Lonnie that "it's all falling apart," speaks both to the circumstances of the character and to the stalled momentum of revolutionary black politics by 1976.

Aside from Lonnie and Abdullah, the ensemble employs a wide array of types. The car wash has a Native American, a Mexican American, a nihilistic Vietnam veteran, a black conservative Korean War veteran, a numbers runner, an urban cowboy, a would-be comic-book hero, a prostitute (played by Schultz's wife, Gloria), a flamboyant cross-dresser, an ineffectual white liberal leftover from the heyday of SDS (Students for a Democratic Society), and an elderly shoeshine man played by Clarence Muse.[39] The mélange of characters set in a confined urban space allows Schultz to employ a broader commentary. With white flight a foregone conclusion, the dynamic between white and black is divided not only by class (rich/poor, employer/employee), but also in terms of residency. The urban space surrounding the car wash is the home of the ethnic working class, whereas the white customers only pass through during their workday. The members of the white upper class drive their freshly washed luxury vehicles back to their idyllic suburban homes at the end of the day, while the workers at the car wash rely on public transportation, shared rides, and secondhand scooters. *Car Wash*, in essence, is a microcosm of racial division and the disparity of wealth in postindustrial America.

Music, while not the sole focus of the film, is indispensable in creating the textured world of the microcosm. As Richard Dyer has pointed out, the characters' interactions with the music help organize the broader social critique of the film.[40] Instead of simply being associated with joy and leisure, music is interwoven into the working life of the employees at Dee-Luxe, with various styles and tones being incorporated to add dimension to the narrative. The music is largely incidental, coming in the form of radio broadcasts that are piped throughout the car wash. Nevertheless, these radio singles intersect with the characters' lives, embodying emotions and paralleling action. On a few occasions, the characters serve as the creators of the music. Examples include Abdullah's soulful saxophone lament, the Sam-and-Dave-styled routines of Floyd and Lloyd (Darrow Igus and DeWayne Jessie), and the full-fledged Hollywood musical number "You Gotta Believe" with Richard Pryor and the Pointer Sisters.[41] Although the rest of the film does not function as a musical in the strictest sense, the characters always make the Whitfield score central to their performance. The title song sequence most clearly illustrates the importance of the music, with the coupling of music and labor reconfiguring the southern work song into a contemporary urban setting. That connection is solidified near the end of the film with the recitation of the "it's quittin' time" slave dialogue from *Gone with the Wind*.

In many ways, *Car Wash* is the apotheosis of black-focused cinema in the 1970s. It transcends the limitations of the simple comedy and, in turn, is one of the most complex cinematic portraits black America put forth in the decade. The critical response in the United States, however, failed to fully recognize the layers of social commentary or the film's formal nuances. Ranging from dismissive brush-offs seeing *Car Wash* as a clichéd comedy to the briefly insightful assertions of Janet Maslin, who noted the tradition of *Nashville* and the employment of the microcosm, the film was largely seen as a disposable movie with little artistic relevance.[42] In contrast to its poor reception at home, *Car Wash* received accolades abroad. In 1977, it won the Technical Grand Prize at the Cannes Film Festival for its virtuosic camera movements and crisp editing, while also taking home Best Music honors.[43] In 1985, Schultz traveled with the film to the Soviet Union and screened *Car Wash* for a highly appreciative audience at the Moscow Film Festival. Viewers reveled in the film's sharp critique of class and racial divisions, reading it as a clear commentary on capitalism.[44]

While the French and Soviet festivals greeted the film warmly, British scholar Richard Dyer is one of the few academics to take the film seriously. Dyer later observed that the plot, structure, and tone of *Car Wash* uncannily prefigured Spike Lee's *Do the Right Thing* (1989).[45] But while Lee's film was immediately heralded as an artistic achievement and was added to the Library of Congress Film Registry in its first year of eligibility, *Car Wash* has languished in DVD bargain bins as if it were a disposable comedy. Perhaps this is a byproduct of Rose Royce's title track being a mainstay on radio (and in sports arenas), or part of the overall artistic devaluing of films made during the blaxploitation cycle. Critics and scholars shape legacies, and Schultz's socially mimetic approach was far less effective than Lee's didacticism in shouting out its own artistic worth. *Car Wash* requires a careful and thoughtful reader, whereas *Do the Right Thing*, unencumbered by genre expectations, places its commentaries in the foreground, where they are easily identifiable for even the most casual viewer.

Regardless of the critical slights in the United States, *Car Wash* was a major financial success, earning over $20 million at the domestic box office, an additional $3 million in foreign receipts, and a whopping $22 million in soundtrack sales.[46] The film established Schultz as a bankable director at exactly the same moment that many of his African American peers were disappearing from Hollywood. Gordon Parks's disappointment with Paramount's distribution of *Leadbelly*, and Ossie Davis's failure to find success with *Countdown at Kusini*, both came in 1976, effectively ending their directorial careers.

Meanwhile, Melvin Van Peebles, with a passion project for Warner Bros., looked to return to the studio fold at the same moment that the blaxploitation cycle was coming to an end. *Greased Lightning* (1977) was a true-life story about Wendell Scott, the moonshine runner who became the first black driver to compete in NASCAR. Van Peebles had written the screenplay himself, began assembling the cast in 1976, and soon moved to Georgia to begin production. Richard Pryor was cast as Scott, providing the comedian with his first opportunity to headline a studio film. Along with Pryor, Van Peebles brought in an interesting supporting cast that included Pam Grier, Beau Bridges, and Cleavon Little. Folk singer Richie Havens, Atlanta mayor Maynard Jackson, and Georgia statesman Julian Bond agreed to play minor roles. Van Peebles hoped to use these performances symbolically to tie Scott's legacy as a stock-car driver to the black freedom struggle.[47]

With about one-third of the film shot, however, Van Peebles had a falling out with the producers and executives. The studio was not granting him the creative autonomy he felt he had earned with *Sweetback* and his success on Broadway.[48] Warner Bros. fired Van Peebles from his own picture mid-shooting and began looking for a replacement director. With money already invested in period costuming and set pieces, not to mention salaries and film stock, Warner Bros. executives felt obliged to finish the picture and at least give themselves a fighting chance of recouping some of their investment. Pryor, with his first starring role in jeopardy, called on Michael Schultz to take over the picture. Schultz and Pryor had formed a relationship prior to working on *Car Wash* (see chapter 7) and had already agreed to work together on what would become *Which Way Is Up?* Schultz had made trips to Georgia to visit Pryor and work on the script during the filming of *Greased Lightning*, and one of Schultz's trips just happened to coincide with Van Peebles getting fired. Pryor was desperate for help, and now he had an obvious choice for someone to ask who might be able to save the picture.

"I had designed *Which Way Is Up?* as Richard's introduction to Hollywood as a leading man," Schultz later explained. Not particularly interested in the story or tone of *Greased Lightning*, he decided to take on the picture regardless. "What I didn't want was for Richard to be in a flop before *my* movie came out," Schultz recalled. "So I had very selfish motivation for going in and trying to save that movie."[49] With the singular voice of Van Peebles removed from the project, Schultz tried his best to remain faithful to the director's vision. However, Schultz allowed Warner Bros. the input during production that Van Peebles had so vehemently opposed, and once shooting wrapped, he left the studio in control of shaping the picture in postproduction.

Greased Lightning serves as an interesting side note to the cycle of car pictures being made at the time, with Pryor as a black counterpoint to the Burt Reynolds archetype of Gator McClusky in *White Lightning* (1973, Joseph Sargent). Scores of pictures about bootleggers flooded theaters in the late 1970s, but the white male fantasy of running moonshine through the South and *Greased Lightning*'s earnest attempts to put forth a tale of black accomplishment in the face of segregation were incongruous. The first half hour of the picture follows Wendell Scott outrunning the law while transporting whiskey, with comedic chase gags replacing the supposed political content in Van Peebles's initial script. Running from a bumbling sheriff, Scott's back-road exploits naïvely replicate the tone of Reynolds's movies, but under the specter of Jim Crow the adventures are fraught with an unspoken danger that is wholly absent from a film with a white protagonist.

What is evident is that Scott's backstory as a bootlegger fits in with the origins of NASCAR. His transition from dirt tracks and open entries into the era of corporate sponsorship and superspeedways represents the changing face of stock-car racing in the 1950s and 1960s. Eager to champion a hero rather than explore the complexities of the sport's structure, the film overstates Scott's accomplishments.[50] What is lost in the false triumph of *Greased Lightning* is the proper context through which to appreciate Scott's achievements. While Jackie Robinson's integration of Major League Baseball took place in northern cities, Scott's breaking of stock-car racing's color barrier took place in the Deep South, where black athletes were nonexistent in the separatist sporting culture that was focused on NASCAR and college football.[51] Scott faced greater odds and competed in more hostile venues than Robinson, having little to show for it at the end of his career. More disconcerting than the film's departure from Scott's lived reality was the mild reception to *Greased Lightning* at the box office, which ended Wendell Scott's hope of finally profiting from his racing exploits. His contract with Warner Bros. gave him a share in profits that never materialized.[52]

Schultz was disappointed with *Greased Lightning* and regretted having to replace his friend Van Peebles as the director, but with shooting completed, he quickly moved past the project and returned to California with Pryor in tow to begin *Which Way Is Up?* The film is an adaption of Lina Wertmüller's *The Seduction of Mimi* (1972), a comedy about a philandering metalworker caught between communist labor organizations and Sicily's anti-unionist mafia. Starring Giancarlo Giannini, Wertmüller's film traverses a wide spectrum of settings and storylines, but retains a sense of continuity in tone throughout. *Which Way Is Up?* instead shifts wildly from farce and slapstick to moments of dramatic reflection, mirroring the sharp contrasts in Pryor's comedy that Schultz was able to translate into one of the most engaging screen performances in the comedian's career. Pryor plays Leroy Jones, a poor orange-picker who is accidentally thrust into

Ramon Juarez (Luis Valdez) and Leroy Jones (Richard Pryor) in Which Way Is Up?

the center of a labor movement modeled on that of Cesar Chavez and the United Farm Workers. Leroy mistakenly finds himself in the middle of a protest march, where he is hailed as a hero by activists for bravely defying the corporate owners of the grove. Leroy's unwitting stance for unionized labor begins a chain of events in which he is threatened, prodded, and ultimately controlled by nefarious corporate power figures.

Aside from differences in tone and cultural idiosyncrasies, *Which Way Is Up?* remains faithful to the political ideology of Wertmüller's source material. Much like *Car Wash*, the film is teeming with ambition. Attempts are made not only to portray the workers movement, but also to comment on feminism, corporate power, the sexual revolution, organized religion, and Chicano identity. Schultz had been working with El Teatro Campesino, a stage troupe made up of farm workers founded by Luis Valdez, who plays Ramon Juarez in the film.[53] In adapting *The Seduction of Mimi*, Schultz chose to shift from the industrial focus of the original source—the factory setting is apparent in the film's Italian title, *Mimí Metallurgico Ferito Nell'onore*, which translates to "Mimi the Metalworker: Wounded in Honor"—to a unionization focus highlighting a struggle like that of the United Farm Workers.[54] Here, as with *Car Wash*, the concerns of the working class create a cross-cultural bond connecting blacks, Latinos, American Indians, and poor whites.

In addition to playing Leroy, Pryor takes on multiple other characters, donning a gray beard and wig to become Leroy's crotchety father, Rufus, for example, and channeling his Daddy Rich character from *Car Wash* to portray the conniving country preacher Reverend Lenox Thomas. Pryor's characters are integrated into the film through editing but always appear in separate shots when populating the same scene. By playing multiple characters, Pryor had his first opportunity on film to showcase the range of characters he could portray. His roles highlighted his standup routine and comedy records, turning the film into a performance spectacle.[55] The platform helped make Pryor a movie star, and once again Schultz connected with a crossover audience. *Greased Lightning* failed to generate business, but *Which Way Is Up?* surpassed *Car Wash* at the box office, with $15 million in domestic rentals and an additional $8 million in foreign rentals—approximately $46 million in global box office. According to the film's producer, Steve Krantz, it was the most profitable black film ever made.[56]

The irony of this success is that it came in 1977, in the immediate aftermath of the blaxploitation cycle and the concurrent disappearance of Van Peebles, Ossie Davis, and Gordon Parks from the ranks of working directors. Six years earlier, the dual success of *Sweetback* and *Shaft* had prompted an unprecedented investment in black-focused films and helped to foster the careers of a host of black filmmakers. *Which Way Is Up?* was never considered a harbinger of future success for black-focused films. Instead, it was seen as a promising sign for Pryor's transition to the big screen and proof that Schultz was a talented and bankable director. In the blockbuster landscape of Hollywood in the late 1970s, the next logical move was for Schultz to abandon black-focused stories to take on a big-budget studio film that could reach the largest possible audience.

THE FALL

Unfortunately, the first project Schultz made after *Which Way Is Up?* turned into a disaster both critically and at the box office. Schultz was hired to direct the big-budget musical *Sgt. Pepper's Lonely Hearts Club Band* (1978), a film produced by music impresario Robert Stigwood for Universal. The film tells a story loosely formed around the Beatles' seminal 1967 album of the same name. It features Peter Frampton and the Bee Gees in the place of the Fab Four, with the new stars singing the Beatles' iconic catalog. Following their soundtrack for *Saturday Night Fever* (1977, John Badham), the Bee Gees were arguably the most popular group in the world at the time, while the surprise success of the double live album *Frampton Comes Alive!* in 1976 had made Frampton a superstar seemingly overnight.[57] Using the most popular musical acts at the time to translate one of the most loved albums in rock history seemed to provide the film with all of the earmarks for a blockbuster success, but instead, *Sgt. Pepper* failed on almost every level.

Robert Stigwood, the Australian-born music promoter, had formed what was shaping up to be a media empire by 1978. After founding the Robert Stigwood Organisation (RSO) a decade earlier, he had expanded beyond managing musical acts, producing theater and establishing his own record label (RSO Records). The label especially showcased the Bee Gees and another of his clients, Cream.[58] In 1973 Stigwood entered into film production, overseeing the film adaptation of *Jesus Christ Superstar* (1973, Norman Jewison) as well as the Who's song cycle *Tommy* (1975, Ken Russell). Stigwood's crowning achievement came with *Saturday Night Fever* in 1977, which not only became a runaway hit at the box office but also established Stigwood's friends and clients the Bee Gees as superstars. On the strength of seven original Bee Gees compositions, the soundtrack to *Saturday Night Fever* became one of the best-selling albums of all time. Together with the film, the tracks brought the once passé disco craze back into the public consciousness, reinvigorating a cultural phenomenon that was otherwise tapering off by 1977.

Eager to capitalize on his cinematic success, Stigwood began preproduction on two big-budget musicals that he figured would be surefire hits. The first project was *Grease* (1978, Randal Kleiser), an adaptation of the Broadway musical starring John Travolta, fresh off his star-making performance in *Saturday Night Fever.* Looking for a director who could handle movement and music, Stigwood offered the picture to Schultz based on his work on *Cooley High* and *Car Wash*, but Schultz turned down *Grease* because of scheduling conflicts.[59] As a consolation, Schultz was offered Stigwood's other project, *Sgt. Pepper's Lonely Hearts Club Band*, a few months later. He was to replace Chris Beard, who had been fired during early stages of preproduction.[60] So once again, as in *Greased Lightning*, Schultz entered a picture as a replacement, only this time he had the chance to oversee all of the principle photography.

Schultz was presented with a number of givens to start the production. Stigwood was committed to Frampton and the Bee Gees (brothers Barry, Robin, and Maurice Gibb) playing the lead characters despite the fact that they were novice actors.[61] In addition, Stigwood had developed the story along with Henry Edwards (a screenwriter with no previous credits to his name) and was staunchly committed to seeing the screenplay followed to a tee. Schultz, rightly so, felt that the screenplay was weak and misguided—a flimsy story that existed only to connect the songs. "My vision for it was to do a long-form music video," Schultz remembers.[62] With a star-studded

Not the Beatles. The Bee Gees and Peter Frampton in Sgt. Pepper's Lonely Hearts Club Band.

supporting cast being assembled, Schultz hoped to convince Stigwood to abandon Edwards's screenplay and make a concert film of popular groups giving their take on Beatles classics. But he was unable to dissuade Stigwood. Not wanting to cause waves on his first big-budget assignment, Schultz fell in line with the producer's vision.

For Schultz, not only was *Sgt. Pepper* a unique opportunity to direct a big-budget picture, but it also carried with it a certain responsibility. In broad terms, Schultz was a test subject for African American directors in Hollywood. Feuding with producers or showing signs of being temperamental would have hindered his career and impacted opportunities for other black directors in the future. With Stigwood at the helm, Schultz was well aware that taking a firm stance in opposition to the producer's intentions would result in him being added to the list of directors fired from RSO projects. Rather than fight to have the script drastically altered, Schultz satisfied himself with winning smaller battles. Hoping to broaden the appeal of the film, Schultz suggested adding a few acts from outside of the rock and disco milieu that Stigwood oversaw. "I tried to add a little color in the movie by getting Earth, Wind & Fire and Billy Preston,"[63] Schultz remembers. In that effort he was successful. But while he was able to add breadth to the musical tapestry of the picture, Schultz remained powerless to combat the dreadful premise.

The nonsensical plot of *Sgt. Pepper's Lonely Hearts Club Band* tells the story of wholesome American kids trying to find a set of magical instruments. But in doing so, the film reconfigures the political and aesthetic dimensions of the Beatles' albums. It pulls exclusively from the post-1966 recordings, songs that are steeped in the geography of England, psychedelia, and late 1960s counterculture. Edwards's script creates a fantasy that is devoid of the intended context of the songs, putting forth an antithetical worldview. The film's tale of small-town American values (the central locale is named Heartland, USA) subverts and distorts the Beatles' catalog, superimposing a sort of conservative politics on decidedly antiestablishment music. Magnifying the problems of the narrative's concept, Edwards and Stigwood decided to attempt to tell the entire story through the song lyrics, so no dialogue was written for any of the characters. Essentially, *Sgt. Pepper* was meant to function like a silent film, with the action being conveyed through pantomime and title cards. By avoiding spoken dialogue, Stigwood hoped to minimize the lack of acting experience among his star actors. What he did not account for was that it would become a stilted two-hour spectacle that had no proper device for conveying a storyline.[64]

While the story itself became a main point of contention for critics, the musical numbers were supposed to be the *pièce de résistance* of *Sgt. Pepper*. Despite its star-studded cast, however, very few of the musical numbers come off very well, as the confines of the picture deny Frampton and the Bee Gees the essence of their appeal. Frampton's guitar playing and live performance are undercut by his having to lip-synch prerecorded tracks, and the nature of the project itself denied the Bee Gees' prowess as songwriters and producers. Instead, the makeshift band is hesitant and awkward, not at all resembling a fusion of pop's hottest commodities. The only standout musical moment by the lead actors comes with Robin's performance of "Oh! Darling," which takes the intrusion of the plot into the musical numbers literally when Robin is physically pulled away from the microphone and out of the frame in the middle of singing.[65] Not simply a problem in performance, the misguided story concept reduces songs with rich metaphorical subtleties to vapid exercises as the lyrics are expressed with mind-numbing literalness. When Barry sings, "I read the news today, oh boy," in "A Day in the Life," he is reading a newspaper. When the Bee Gees sing, "You gotta carry that weight," from "Golden Slumbers," they are literally carrying a heavy load, serving as pallbearers at a funeral. And when Frampton sings "The Long and Winding Road," he is walking down a very long and winding road.[66]

When Stigwood looked at the Beatles, he saw record sales, sold-out concerts, hit movies (*A Hard Day's Night* [1964, Richard Lester], *Help!* [1965, Richard Lester]), and related merchandise. Not caring to consider the deep emotional connection that Americans and Brits had with the Beatles would ultimately prove to be the picture's downfall. Looking back on the film, Schultz confided, "What none of us really understood was the sacrosanct feeling that American and British audiences had for the Beatles. And just to have anyone do the Beatles was heresy."[67] As Ian MacDonald

The not-so-subtle visual representation of "The Long and Winding Road."

has suggested, the Beatles' emotional hold over baby boomers went far beyond nostalgia. When the group came to America in early 1964, their visit served as a cathartic release for young people in the wake of John F. Kennedy's assassination.[68] As the decade progressed, the hysteria that accompanied their early records gave way to an artistic and intellectual connection that reflected and informed youth counterculture. By the time of their breakup in 1970, the Beatles had transcended the realm of rock stardom, becoming a mythologized ideal of the artistic and spiritual potential of the psychedelic era. *Sgt. Pepper* trampled on this legacy by depoliticizing and depersonalizing their songs, using the Beatles catalog for a tasteless jukebox musical.

Critical response to the film was universally harsh, with Frampton and the Bee Gees singled out for their stiff and incompetent performances. One strain that runs through the reviews in *Variety*, *Rolling Stone*, and the *New York Times* (to name a few) is the transparency of the financially exploitative motivation of the production. Stigwood, Edwards, and Schultz had little emotional investment in the Beatles material, giving the impression that they only saw their music as an opportunity to attract a mass audience to theaters and sell them merchandise on their way home. The soundtrack album included a mail-order flier for officially licensed clothing. Bookstores carried both pocket novels and picture books, while drugstores peddled *Sgt. Pepper's Lonely Hearts Club Band* Topps trading cards to the younger set. Janet Maslin described it best in her *New York Times* review when she said, "This isn't a movie. It's a business deal set to music."[69]

Unfortunately for Universal, the business deal never paid off. The film fared poorly at the box office (at least in North America and Great Britain), and the apparent success of its soundtrack album was a Pyrrhic victory. Although the album went double platinum, at the time Recording

Industry Association of American (RIAA) certification was calculated by how many copies shipped rather than by how many were actually purchased. RSO shipped out 2 million copies on the day the album was released, but received over 1 million unsold copies back from retailers.[70]

Despite all this, Schultz now looks beyond the film's overall failure and remembers the film for being one of the most financially rewarding projects of his career. Although no accurate figures are available for its foreign box-office take, Schultz claims that the film was very successful in markets outside of North America and Britain. Universal's distribution deal gave the studio the proceeds from North America and Britain, while Stigwood received the rest of the international gross. Schultz's contract stipulated he receive 2 percent of Stigwood's share, earning him an additional payday on top of his base salary. Deflecting the perceived catastrophe of the film, Schultz spins a silver lining when remembering *Sgt. Pepper's Lonely Hearts Club Band.* As he explained, "I made more money on that movie than three or four of my other movies combined."[71] His office in Santa Monica proudly displays the platinum album he was awarded.

Personal finances aside, *Sgt. Pepper* and the changing climate in Hollywood regarding black representation erased much of the opportunity for Schultz to pursue new projects. Talking about the aftermath of *Sgt. Pepper*, Schultz deflected the damage done by having his name attached to a high-profile flop. "It definitely had an effect," Schultz recalled, "but the studios appreciated my work."[72] And while the goodwill of the studios may not have been enough to grant him freedom to develop his own projects, it did allow him to remain within the Hollywood establishment. Eager to get behind the camera, Schultz accepted an offer to direct *Scavenger Hunt* at Twentieth Century Fox. *Scavenger Hunt* is a low-budget retread of *It's a Mad Mad Mad Mad World* (1963, Stanley Kramer) in which a large ensemble cast, composed of television actors and B-list celebrities Cloris Leachman, Richard Benjamin, Tony Randall, Richard Mulligan, and Dirk Benedict, scrambles across the California highways in search of fortune. The opening credits of the film speak volumes to Schultz's level of involvement (or lack thereof). Following the studio and production company credits, the title reads, "A Steven A. Vail Film . . . by Michael Schultz." Bucking an established tradition of assigning authorship to the director, Vail—a co-producer and screenwriter—is designated as the film's creative overseer. Schultz is merely a hired hand.

Scavenger Hunt entered and exited theaters within the span of a few weeks over the Christmas holiday of 1979. Critical response to the film was worse than what it had been for *Sgt. Pepper.* While the sheer spectacle and wealth of noteworthy celebrities in *Sgt. Pepper* had elicited curiosity from critics, *Scavenger Hunt*'s cheap look, awful screenplay, and uninspired performances were roundly drubbed. Schultz's direction became a focal point for most reviewers. The *Los Angeles Herald Examiner* pointed out that "Michael Schultz . . . simply places the camera in the actors' general vicinity and then encourages them to scream and leap about in senseless frenzy."[73] *Variety*'s review was even harsher, calling Schultz's direction "vapid" and stating that "Schultz seems unable to come up with any exciting visual gags, as most stunts revolve around people falling out of windows with their prizes." Adding insult to injury, the review continues, "*Scavenger Hunt* also has the dubious distinction of insulting most minorities, along with those who are overweight, have speech impediments or other physical deformities."[74] The charges of racism stemmed from the broad caricatures played by Scatman Crothers and Cleavon Little as well as an American Indian tracker who uses his keen sense of nature to follow the paths of cars on a highway.

How did someone who handled comedy and ensemble so deftly three years earlier with *Car Wash* make a film like *Scavenger Hunt*? The answer, clearly, can be found in his level of commitment on each of the films. Schultz had directed two studio features that he was uninvolved with during development and that were completely divorced from his black perspective. Not coincidentally, both had failed miserably. As the conservative 1980s dawned, Schultz would have to consider the privileges and pitfalls of being a nondescript filmmaker working on the margins of the major studios, on the one hand, or, on the other, pushing against Hollywood trends to reassert his creative voice and carve out a space for black representation.

STAYING ALIVE

Scavenger Hunt, much like *Sgt. Pepper*, found Schultz at odds with Hollywood. Bucking the trend of black directors being excluded from Hollywood by working at major studios, neither project spoke to Schultz's artistic or political sensibilities. His career was at a crossroads: he could either continue pursuing work at the majors, dispassionately directing projects in which he had little interest, or he could begin looking to make films outside of the studio confines that would be creatively invigorating. With 1981's *Carbon Copy*, he chose the latter. Released by AVCO Embassy Pictures, a distribution company that was mostly dealing with horror and quirky sci-fi in the early 1980s, *Carbon Copy* was an ambitious attempt at incorporating the brand of socially concerned comedy that producer

Norman Lear had used in television throughout the 1970s.[75] The film features George Segal as Walter, a sexually frustrated corporate lawyer living a plush existence in San Marino, California. His life is turned upside down when Roger (played by Denzel Washington in his big-screen debut), a brash seventeen-year-old, informs Walter that he is his long-lost son. Stanley Shapiro's script veers wildly from mindless insults and crass humor to sincere social criticism and introspection.

The film tells the well-worn tale of a reversal of fortune, with Walter learning the value of family and humility along the way, and his fall from grace serving as penance for abandoning his values. Walter can be seen as a stand-in for the white liberal of the 1960s who has long abandoned his commitment to social struggle by entering into the world of business and consumption. Through his son Roger, Walter grudgingly finds an inner truth and adopts the worldview he had as an idealistic student radical. Needless to say, in the final reel, Walter accepts Roger as his son, shuns an offer from his father-in-law to come back to work at his law firm, and vows to be a better man.

For 1981, *Carbon Copy* is notable for featuring a black actor in a lead role, not to mention having issues dealing with race central to its narrative. The ambition of the film is commendable even if its execution is sometimes lumbering. Perhaps the most telling example is a scene in which Walter attempts to scrounge up a few extra dollars by challenging a white and portly father and son to a game of basketball. Having never talked to Roger about the game or knowing anything about his abilities, Walter assumes that since he's black he must be good at basketball. Roger, in his own estimation, is "the only black kid in America who can't play basketball." Roger is hopelessly awkward on the court, and the five dollars that Walter bet on the game are soon lost. The scene hopes to bring Walter's racial essentialism out into the open, but in its execution it fails to do much more than paint Roger as an anomalous exception rather than as proof that not all black youth excel at sports.[76]

Washington's performance as Roger hints at the actor he would later become, but lacks the self-assurance he would develop on stage and television in the years to follow. While critical response to the film was neutral—neither burying Schultz, as had been the case with his two previous films, nor praising the film much beyond its well-meaning efforts at social commentary—the film does mark a crucial act of refusal on the part of Schultz. Rather than once again agreeing to function as an anonymous studio director, Schultz had moved to the realm of the minor distributors to work on a film where he found an artistic and political sense of connection. If *Carbon Copy* looked forward to Schultz reclaiming his creative

Walter (George Segal) and Roger (Denzel Washington) in Carbon Copy.

independence from the major studios, his move toward becoming a more personally invested director would, however, be deferred. Richard Pryor called Schultz and again asked him to save a failed project, and he accepted. As was the case with *Greased Lightning*, Schultz was to take over a project from another black director, this time Oz Scott on the film *Bustin' Loose* (1981), originally titled *Family Dreams*.

Pryor had developed the story concept and was co-producing the film, which he hoped would show a new side of his personality.[77] His intentions and efforts, however, failed to merge. The film was hampered by his chemical intake: as his wife, Jennifer Lee Pryor, would say years later, "One project he did care about was *Bustin' Loose*, and he was drunk and stoned the entire time."[78] The film also suffered a number of setbacks during production, most notably on June 11, 1980, when Pryor nearly died after lighting himself on fire in his Northridge home. It occurred before shooting was finished, leaving a before-and-after image on screen that forces the audience to suspend their disbelief in approaching the film's chronology. By the time production wrapped, the film had gone through numerous script drafts and two directors. The whole team had been forced into a three-month halt in production while Pryor recovered from his burns.

The film began shooting long before the Northridge fire and marked the film debut of theater director Oz Scott. Scott had had success on Broadway with Ntozake Shange's *For Colored Girls Who Have Considered*

Suicide When the Rainbow is Enuf, but he had no experience directing away from the stage. Scott's inexperience, as well as Pryor's erratic behavior, affected the project. When Pryor called Schultz, large portions of the footage (Schultz estimates as much as half of Scott's material) were unusable. Pryor's performance had been lethargic, and the plot lacked enough substance to compile a feature-length release. Sensing a surefire failure, Universal had shelved the picture in order to avoid a futile advertising campaign and keep Pryor's career from entering a downward spiral. Studio executives thought he would remain a marketable star only if they unloaded the burden of another box-office letdown.

Following the Northridge fire, the media onslaught that came in its wake, and the unforeseen success of *Stir Crazy* (see chapters 3 and 7), Universal changed its position, seizing the opportunity to release *Bustin' Loose* to a public that was ravenous for anything related to Pryor. Schultz later explained that "when Universal found out that [Pryor] wasn't going to die, they called him up and said, 'Richard, will you finish the picture?' You know, not 'Are you okay?' but, 'Will you finish the movie?' "[79] So it was that, recovering in Hawaii, Pryor contacted Schultz to ask him if he would take over. Reluctantly, Schultz agreed. He ended up re-shooting much of the film, adding an entirely new plot line, and attempting to mask the burns over much of Pryor's body. He also had to try to hide the noticeable physical maturation of the juvenile cast that had taken place during the long break in shooting. Using portions of Scott's footage and multiple script drafts, Schultz worked hard to make a coherent film out of odds and ends and make up for the gaps of coverage in wildly disparate locations. As Schultz remembers, "It was like making a puzzle out of pieces that were no good."[80]

The plot recalls elements of *The African Queen* (1951, John Huston), with Pryor's gruff ex-convict being forced to undertake a journey along with a prim and proper social worker played by Cicely Tyson.[81] The two take a group of orphans on a cross-country road trip, escaping the crumbling Philadelphia ghetto and a dysfunctional social welfare system and finding an idyllic and pastoral new home for the children on a farm in the Pacific Northwest. The combination of Pryor and the children, which may have seemed counterintuitive, adds a compelling dimension to the film. Pryor shows a gentle and caring side of himself when talking to the children, providing some poignant moments in which a genuinely troubled man empathizes with troubled kids. However, one such intervention is not as tasteful as the rest. In an unlucky coincidence, one of the children is a pyromaniac, causing Pryor to be set on fire, briefly and unwittingly reminding audiences of his real-life trauma.

Bustin' Loose was a hit at the box office, largely thanks to the renewed interest in Pryor and the timeliness of the release of the film, because it was his first starring vehicle after *Stir Crazy*. Schultz, however, was not particularly pleased with the project and opted to forgo taking screen credit on the picture, which reverted back to Oz Scott. The end of production on *Bustin' Loose* found Schultz at an emotional low point in his career. As with *Greased Lightning*, Schultz loathed having to take over another director's film. For all of his success on screen and stage, not to mention the possibilities explored in *Carbon Copy*, Schultz had once again become a hired hand for the studios, sent in to save a film that had become an opportunistic money grab. Universal found its payday with *Bustin' Loose*, happily exploiting Pryor's personal tragedy without regard for his artistic integrity or ambition, and grossing $31 million at the box office along the way.[82] While Pryor's post-fire involvement may have very well stemmed from his financial despondency, pulling his friend Schultz into the project made the director a seeming accomplice to a rather distasteful example of the bottom-line concerns of show business.

The malaise that followed the backlash from *Sgt. Pepper*, the uninspired *Scavenger Hunt*, the lack of box-office success on *Carbon Copy*, and the ethically troubling *Bustin' Loose* left Schultz reevaluating his role in Hollywood. Recalling his thoughts on being a director in 1980s Hollywood, Schultz remembers thinking, "My heart is really not in this business because it's a waste of time."[83] It had been a decade since he had gotten behind the camera for *Together for Days* with dreams of a brighter future for himself and black cinema as a whole. The dreams that were able to flourish in the halcyon years of blaxploitation had given way to a jaded pessimism that flowed from Hollywood's neglect of black themes and talent. As much as Schultz may have wanted to abandon the medium, though, being a director was part of his self-definition. Regardless of the climate in Hollywood, Schultz would have to adapt.

After finishing *Bustin' Loose*, Schultz returned to television for the first time since making his studio feature debut with *Car Wash*. He directed the TV movie *Benny's Place* (1982) with Lou Gossett Jr. and Cicely Tyson for ABC, and then made *For Us the Living: The Medgar Evers Story* (1983), starring Howard Rollins as the slain civil rights leader. Both projects allowed Schultz to reconnect with the sort of socially conscious dramatic depictions of the black experience that he had put forth on stage at the Negro Ensemble Company in the 1960s. His next television assignment, however, was the uninspired and misguided sequel *The Jerk, Too* (1984), a cheap retread of *The Jerk* (1979, Carl Reiner) without the benefit of Steve Martin reprising the lead role. Alternating between directing material where he could find artistic fulfillment and merely finding work on whatever projects were available had already defined his work in feature films. This give-and-take would come to define his television work in the coming years as well. He often leaned more to the side of projects that served as gainful employment rather than seeking a venue for artistic expression. Four years after returning to television, however, Schultz was offered a chance to direct a theatrical Hollywood release, this time on a project steeped in black culture and informed by the burgeoning hip-hop movement.

HOW MICHAEL GOT HIS GROOVE BACK

Schultz's return to feature filmmaking, 1985's *The Last Dragon*, may not explicitly draw from hip-hop in its narrative construction, but its postmodern mix of racial and cultural identity is deeply rooted in the origins of the movement. Written by Brooklyn native Louis Venosta, it playfully incorporates elements of hip-hop's aesthetics and mannerisms while paying homage to the kung-fu and blaxploitation pictures that flickered across the screens of downtown theaters in the 1970s. It joyfully embraces the structure and conventions of Bruce Lee films while providing a counterpoint to the blaxploitation antihero. Rather than recalling the nihilistic *Sweetback* archetype, *The Last Dragon* depicts a black hero who is unfailingly decent and kindhearted.

Venosta's script came to Schultz's attention through Motown executive Suzanne de Passe, with whom he had developed a friendship while working on *Cooley High* and *Car Wash*. "I read it," Schultz recalled, "and it was so much fun that I said, 'Suzanne, I have to do this movie.'"[84] Taking the lead in getting the picture off the ground, de Passe convinced her boss, Berry Gordy, to get on board. Over the course of production, control over *The Last Dragon* fell alternately in the hands of Venosta, Schultz, de Passe, and Gordy. Gordy's initial role in the film was marginal, but as production progressed he became more interested in the picture. Eventually, he removed de Passe from the picture in an effort to have more control as producer—hence the film's misleading screen title, *Berry Gordy's The Last Dragon*.[85]

No longer a major force in the music industry, Gordy's clout as president and founder of Motown had greatly diminished by the mid-1980s. Michael Jackson, Diana Ross, and Marvin Gaye (before his death in 1984) had all left the label, while acts like the Temptations, Smokey Robinson, and Stevie Wonder were clearly past their prime as writers, performers, and moneymakers. In 1985 Motown was riding the coattails of Lionel Richie, its lone superstar, while desperately trying to cultivate young acts in the mold of past Motown greats. Motown's decline as a record label notwithstanding, Gordy's past failures in producing feature films proved more debilitating in landing the best possible financing and distribution deal for *The Last Dragon*.

Making an initial splash into the motion picture business after moving Motown from Detroit to Los Angeles in the early 1970s, Gordy had hit pay dirt with *Lady Sings the Blues* (1972, Sidney J. Furie). With its success, Gordy hoped to turn Diana Ross and Billy Dee Williams into full-fledged movie stars, but their follow-up, *Mahogany* (1975, Berry Gordy), was ravaged by critics and tanked at the box office. Gordy attempted to right his ship with *The Bingo Long Traveling All-Stars and Motor Kings* (1976, John Badham), a dramatic comedy about a fictional Negro League baseball team starring Billy Dee Williams, James Earl Jones, and Richard Pryor.[86] While *Bingo Long* featured a compelling story and capable performances, Universal failed to locate an audience broad enough to recoup its sizable budget. With the disappointments of *Bingo Long* and *Mahogany* as precursors, Gordy's high-profile disappointment in *The Wiz* (1978, Sidney Lumet) ended his run as a major player in Hollywood. All told, Motown produced eight features after moving its operations to Los Angeles, with only *Lady Sings the Blues* turning a profit.[87]

Although Gordy's sway in 1985 was nowhere near what it had been a decade earlier, he was still able to secure a financing and distribution deal with TriStar. A far cry from the big budgets and saturation release deals Gordy had negotiated with Paramount (*Mahogany*) and Universal (*Bingo Long*, *The Wiz*), TriStar's modest budget for *The Last Dragon* caused Schultz and Venosta to retool the script, cutting forty pages (approximately forty minutes of screen time) of costlier scenes that would have sent the picture over budget. Returning to New York for the first time since making *To Be Young, Gifted and Black* (at least in a professional capacity), Schultz approached *The Last Dragon* as his opportunity to express his love for the city cinematically. The inexhaustibly rich visuals of the cityscape and the deep pool of talent made shooting in New York rewarding, but Schultz found the lack of African American inclusion in film unions stifling. "New York unions were ten years behind LA," Schultz later explained, "but I had too much on my plate at the time to fight that battle . . . so [I promised myself that] I'll come back to New York and shoot with an all-black crew just to prove it could be done."[88] The racial

Leroy (Taimak) and cross-cultural identities in The Last Dragon.

imbalance of his union crew may have troubled Schultz, but he placed his energy into making a family-friendly ode to black heroism, something that was wholly absent from movie screens in 1985.

The Last Dragon centers on Leroy Green (Taimak), an earnest young martial artist searching for the mystical "final level" in his quest to become a kung-fu master. Referred to as "Bruce Leroy" with equal amounts of respect and mocking derision, Leroy inhabits an interior universe in which the kung-fu matinees he frequents bring sublime insight and motivation. He dresses in traditional Chinese peasant garb, speaks in soft tones with a pace that suggests he is quoting the *I Ching*, and even eats his movie-theater popcorn with chopsticks. Along his path to enlightenment, Leroy struggles to merge his African American identity with a wholehearted investment in Chinese art and culture. His family, friends, and foes put forth notions that ethnicity and culture are fixed and static, labeling Leroy as "weird" for dressing like a Chinese "coolie" and performing an Asian identity.

Through the film's New York setting, however, Schultz and Venosta problematize notions of fixed identity and suggest a cultural cross-pollination in its place. The film is teeming with characters that blur traditional designations of ethnicity and culture, creating a postmodern articulation of the melting pot. Leroy's father, for instance, makes a living running a pizza shop, while three young Chinese men who run a fortune-cookie factory perform blackness, staging a James Brown revue, shooting craps, and speaking in a black slang. The Chinese "soul brothers" even code-switch into a mocking stereotype of broken Chinese-English

Sho-Nuff (Julius J. Carrey III), the "Shogun of Harlem."

when they talk to Leroy, turning the tables on identification to "speak his language."

The most compelling cross-cultural performance, however, can be found in Leroy's over-the-top nemesis Sho-Nuff (Julius J. Carrey III), the self-proclaimed "Shogun of Harlem." Meeting Leroy at a matinee screening of *Enter the Dragon* (1973, Robert Clouse), Sho-Nuff challenges the young kung-fu prodigy in hopes of proving once and for all that he is the "real master." Sho-Nuff does not suppress his black identity through speech patterns or mannerisms like Leroy, but he does don an elaborate samurai-influenced costume replete with rising sun symbols. Sho-Nuff's adopted fashion identity—a modern-day articulation of imperialist Japan—runs counter to the noble Chinese peasantry with whom Leroy aligns himself. Invoking the historicized Japan-China conflict of *Chinese Connection* (1972, Wei Lo), Leroy comes to embody the oppressed everyman, while Sho-Nuff functions as the cruel tormentor.

The film's sincerity and sense of fun are balanced with practical concerns, as Gordy shoehorns the promotion of Motown acts in ways big and small, ranging from incidental music to the choice of Vanity as Leroy's love interest.[89] Despite these competing motives, *The Last Dragon* proved to be a success with audiences, earning $25 million at the box office and receiving surprisingly positive responses from critics despite its kung-fu plot, young target audience, and offbeat humor.[90] Beyond the successful theatrical release, the film found a second life on pay cable and home video, where it built a sizable cult audience. Although Schultz has had bigger box-office successes, *The Last Dragon* remains the film he speaks about with the greatest sense of pride. Explaining his intentions, Schultz has said, "I knew that kids would look at this movie over and over and over again."[91] Whether it is his own son Brandon, who appears in the movie and still lists it as one of his all-time favorites, or the countless members of Generation X and Y who have approached Schultz on the street and quoted lines of dialogue to him, *The Last Dragon* resonates with people more than any of his other films. It lingers in the minds of those who have seen it at a young age in a way that is far more profound than simple nostalgia. Schultz set out to capture a wholesome and heartfelt black hero and succeeded in creating a source of inspiration for African American spectators that was also inclusive, inviting similar passions across racial and ethnic boundaries.

Schultz's biggest regret relating to *The Last Dragon* was his inability to affect change in the racially exclusionary New York unions. But his chance to return to the city and make a film on his own terms came much sooner than he expected, with *Krush Groove* (1985). At the invitation of producer George Jackson, Schultz and a handful of associates attended a concert at the Long Beach Auditorium to check out a number of acts that had been featured in the *Wall Street Journal*, which had run a short series about New York's burgeoning rap scene and the significant dent it was making in the northeastern music market. Knowing little about the budding genre, Schultz was astonished to see 19,000 young fans at the concert. Going backstage after the show, Schultz floated the idea of making a documentary chronicling hip-hop's growing appeal. Approaching Run-DMC, Kurtis Blow, and the Fat Boys with his idea, Schultz was surprised to hear that they were not interested in being the subject of a documentary. "They wanted to be real movie stars," Schultz explained. "They said, 'We want to ride the horse. Shoot the gun. Kiss the girl.'"[92] Seizing the opportunity, Schultz, Jackson, producer Doug McHenry, and screenwriter Ralph Farquhar began putting together a loose narrative that would showcase the talents of rap's leading performers.

Assuming the role of co-producer for the first time in his career, Schultz pitched the project to Warner Bros. Records president Mo Austin. The only requirement from Austin was that Sheila E—whose 1984 Warner Bros. album *The Glamorous Life* had been a hit—be given a leading role in the film.[93] Like Vanity, Sheila E had experienced a rapid rise to fame that was largely due to her close association with Prince, who had produced her debut album. Prince's role as Svengali was more pronounced (and more short lived) with Vanity, whose physical beauty was emphasized to hide her negligible singing talent. Sheila E, in contrast, was an accomplished percussionist. Prince valued and respected her talents and creative input, although his influence was clearly evident in both her sound and image. With Prince being Warner Bros.' hottest commodity, Mo Ostin felt it best to keep the artist happy by supplying his protégé with an unparalleled opportunity for exposure.

Based loosely around the life of Def Jam Records founder Russell Simmons, the film features Run-DMC, Kurtis Blow, the Fat Boys, and Sheila E in leading roles as well as the Beastie Boys, New Edition, and a very young LL Cool J (to name a few) making peripheral appearances. Initially titled *Rap Attack*, the film chronicles rappers on the road to success as they learn to deal with the temptations and pitfalls of the record industry without losing their sense of community.[94] Although its cheerful ending in which everyone is happy may seem forced and fanciful, the outcome for the parties involved was far more prophetic than they could have imagined, as within a few years most of the featured artists would sell millions of records. Def Jam (dubbed "Krush Groove Records" in the film) would become a billion-dollar industry juggernaut.

Krush Groove follows a long tradition of films made for teen audiences with the sole purpose of showcasing musical acts whose appeal is specific to youth culture. Like *Jailhouse Rock* (1957, Richard Thorpe) and *A Hard Day's Night*, the film employs a narrative framework that exists merely to connect musical numbers. Critiquing *Krush Groove* for its poor storyline and dramatic performances—as most reviewers did—misses the point of the film. The appeal rests with the film's success in capturing the performances without sacrificing authenticity or immediacy. It is important to note that in 1985, MTV was mostly closed to black artists (with Michael Jackson, Prince, and Lionel Richie being the few exceptions), while BET and most black radio stations remained conservative and shunned rap. *Krush Groove* was a much-needed vehicle for hip-hop performers and an important visual artifact of an otherwise under-documented moment in music history. With the exception of the Fat Boys' "All You Can Eat" and "Don't You Dog Me," none of the songs in *Krush Groove* fit the metadiegetic model that is traditional to the film musical. Instead, Schultz roots the musical numbers in his original concept by shooting them in documentary fashion as they are performed on stage or in the studio, perhaps learning from the failures of *Sgt. Pepper*.

Although the box-office returns were modest, with the film earning $11 million, *Krush Groove* has lasted as a cultural landmark largely through Schultz's good fortune of being in the right place at the right time.[95] Not only did Run-DMC, the Beastie Boys, LL Cool J, and the Fat Boys transition into crossover stars, but the film also featured appearances by a number of future music impresarios. Def Jam's founders Russell Simmons and

Rick Rubin (Simmons plays a club manager, while Rubin plays himself) cut ties in 1988, with Simmons taking full control of Def Jam and expanding the company into a force across media, while Rubin started his own label, Def American, and became the most important record producer of the past twenty years before becoming co-president of Columbia Records in 2007.[96] Lyor Cohen, then a low-level Def Jam employee who made a brief appearance as an extra in the film, eventually went on to become CEO of Warner Music Group, while Dr. Jeckyll & Mr. Hyde rapper Andre Harrell went on to found Uptown Records before becoming president of Motown in the 1990s. Odd as it may have seemed to Schultz in 1985, the small business that was run out of Rick Rubin's New York University dorm room would not only produce hit records in subsequent years but also generate a dynasty of music-industry power brokers.

Aside from creating a kinetic documentation of hip-hop culture when it was on the threshold of becoming a worldwide phenomenon, Schultz was also able to use *Krush Groove* to address issues with New York's film unions that had troubled him during the production of *The Last Dragon*. With the exception of Blair Underwood (who made his film debut in *Krush Groove* playing the thinly veiled Russell Simmons character), the cast was composed of non-actors. By hiring a nonunion cast, Schultz was able to avoid the high cost of employing Screen Actors Guild members. He also assembled a nonunion crew. Ultimately, 80 percent of the crew members on *Krush Groove* were African American, and a number of them—including cinematographer Ernest Dickerson—would become Spike Lee's crew members in the years that followed. Although he was not hired, Lee himself applied for an assistant director position on the film, hoping to take advantage of an unprecedented opportunity to work on a Hollywood picture.[97]

The push among black filmmakers to open up New York unions to black crew members dates back to Gordon Parks's *Shaft*, where he was able to convince MGM to back his demands for a more racially representative crew. With *Krush Groove*, Schultz realized Parks's initial objective and became a model for future black filmmakers. Spike Lee's insistence on having a representative crew for his New York shoot of *Do the Right Thing*, for example, was built on work of the previous generation of directors. Simply getting a picture made was not enough. For Schultz, being a truly conscientious black director meant taking all the political factors of film production into account; he wanted to portray the black experience on film without accepting bias and discrimination behind the camera.

HIP-HOP CINEMA AND BEYOND

In terms of box-office success, *Krush Groove* may have been the victim of bad timing, featuring as it did a pop-music movement that had not yet entered mass consciousness. In 1986, a year after *Krush Groove*'s release, rap broke through on the charts in a major way. Run-DMC's *Raising Hell* went triple platinum, and Def Jam's release of the Beastie Boys' *License to Ill* sold 5 million copies, becoming the first rap album to top the *Billboard* chart. Hoping to capitalize on rap's newfound popularity and the inroads he had made with *Krush Groove*, Schultz pitched Warner Bros. the slapstick Fat Boys vehicle *Disorderlies* (1987). While the non-acting cast of *Krush Groove* had left much to be desired dramatically, there had been a bright spot: the performances of the Fat Boys. Seeing the three of them off camera—Mark "Prince Markie Dee" Morales, Damon "Kool Rock Ski" Wimbley, and Darren "Buffy" Robinson—Schultz had been amazed by their quick wit and ability to turn ordinary situations into high comedy. In the back of his mind, he believed the Fat Boys could become a modern-day version of the Three Stooges.

Schultz's enthusiasm for *Disorderlies* vanished shortly after production began. The Fat Boys may have excelled at joking around off set, but the rigors of slapstick comedy proved to be beyond their capabilities. "They couldn't repeat it," Schultz later said, referring to their off-camera antics.[98] Rather than capturing their comedic energy, *Disorderlies* makes the Fat Boys seem like stiff, uncomfortable amateurs. While Run-DMC and the Beastie Boys may have beaten them to the punch by reaching platinum status, the Fat Boys were clearly the most marketable rap group at the time. In the innocent years before the birth of gangsta rap, Run-DMC was perceived to have a hard edge, while the manic and mindlessly rebellious Beastie Boys had an aura of frat-boy danger and debauchery. Both groups had audiences that could only be defined in rather narrow terms—namely, males in their teens to twenties. The Fat Boys had a softer image that made them palatable to younger fans, and, more importantly, their parents. Their first three albums on Sutra Records were musically on par with their peers (Run-DMC, Whodini, UTFO, et al.), but the group had largely turned into a clumsy marketing gimmick by the time *Disorderlies* was released.[99]

Young and impressionable, the Fat Boys acquiesced to their management's limited vision, releasing novelty singles that failed to reflect their talent as rappers. Their major label debut, *Crushin'* (1987, Polygram), supplied much of the music that was used in *Disorderlies*, a conscious attempt to court a white suburban audience.[100] Sales of *Crushin'* were boosted by their hit single "Wipe Out," a collaboration with the Beach Boys, but to hip-hop fans the attempt at crossing over to a pop market was transparent and disingenuous.[101] Trading in their legitimacy as a rap group in hopes of striking it rich, the Fat Boys thought that *Disorderlies* would pave the way for a long and lucrative career in movies and music. Unfortunately, the film marked the beginning of the end, as their novelty singles and their overt courting of a suburban audience were out of place with the ethos of rap's golden age. The Fat Boys became both a punch line and a cautionary tale.

Stylistically, *Disorderlies* is a return to Schultz's worst films, using the same comedic dissolves and overly obvious sound effects that he had used in *Sgt. Pepper*, *Scavenger Hunt*, and *Carbon Copy*. The film was ravaged by critics and fell flat at the box office. As the Fat Boys slipped into obscurity, Schultz's career stalled after *Disorderlies*. With the climate for African American directors shifting in Hollywood, Schultz found himself, perhaps unwittingly, retreating from feature films. Spike Lee and Robert Townsend were making names for themselves, while Schultz was earning a paycheck directing the less-than-ambitious TV movies *Rock 'n' Roll Mom* (1988) and *Tarzan in Manhattan* (1989). Schultz's next theatrically released project, *Livin' Large!* (1991), would solidify his sense of unease with the changing landscape of feature filmmaking.

Part of a wave of black-focused comedies that flooded the market following the success of *House Party* (1990, Reginald Hudlin), *Livin' Large!* also coincided with the beginnings of the ghetto action film cycle and an emphasis on blackness in popular culture.[102] While cheap and hastily made comedies like *Strictly Business* (1991, Kevin Hooks) and *Mo' Money* (1992, Peter MacDonald) received some degree of credibility by starring cast members from TV's sketch comedy program *In Living Color* (which aired on Fox), *Livin' Large!* went largely unnoticed by critics and audiences. With the sudden influx of black-oriented films it was easy to get lost in the shuffle. For *Livin' Large!* the problem was compounded by the film's striking similarity to the better-financed and well-advertised *True Identity* (1991, Charles Lane), a comedy that also features its black lead donning whiteface. Without the ability to distinguish itself from other black-oriented features at the time, be it through advertising or content, to audiences *Livin' Large!* seemed to be a halfhearted entry in Hollywood's mad dash to turn a once-neglected African American filmgoing audience into a cash cow.

Schultz exercised some form of power in the 1970s and 1980s, but in the 1990s the ability to get a project green-lighted by a studio resided with a handful of young film-school-trained directors and, more pervasively, successful rappers. Rather than struggle to insert himself into a cinematic era that valued youth over experience, Schultz moved full-time to television. Returning to the small screen to direct episodic television may have seemed like a step down for someone who had worked making feature films for so long, but Schultz was able to prolong his career via television and avoid the undesirable capitulations that may have been necessary to remain working in black-focused films at the height of the 'hood cycle.

Schultz had used the opportunity to direct episodic television in the 1970s as a springboard to bigger and better things, learning the craft of filmmaking along the way. Following *Car Wash*, he had done feature-length projects instead in his television work. Schultz therefore had ostensibly remained a film director, with only the venue for exhibition being altered. Following *Livin' Large*, he directed his first episodic television series since the mid-1970s. Beginning with the CBS drama *Picket Fences* in 1992, he became a regular at the networks, working on over thirty different series, including *Ally McBeal*, *Felicity*, *Chuck*, *Everwood*, *The O.C.*, *The Practice*, *Charmed*, and *JAG*. Although the breakneck shooting schedules and producer control inherent in these series did not fully utilize Schultz's creative abilities, the turn to directing episodic television accentuated his expertise in working with actors. The ability to walk onto a new set and get the most out of an unfamiliar cast without compromising the tone and consistency of the series has made Schultz one of television's most reliable directors.

After a decade working in television, and with no expressed interest in returning to feature filmmaking, Schultz was then offered the chance to direct *Woman Thou Art Loosed* (2004), one of the first mainstream Christian features targeted toward African Americans.

Based on the Reverend T. D. Jakes's seminar-turned-stage-play, *Woman Thou Art Loosed* is part secular self-help manual and part evangelical soul saving. Jakes's ministry pays special attention to the plight of women, giving voice to issues such as spousal abuse, the trials of raising children without a spouse, and patriarchal control, mixed in with a classic prosperity doctrine that Schultz had previously lambasted via Richard Pryor's performances in *Car Wash* and *Which Way Is Up?* Ambivalent about Jakes's sincerity and financial motivation, Schultz distanced himself from the religious rhetoric of the story, instead focusing on the female protagonist. Without abandoning Jakes's message, Schultz restructures the tone and mood associated with the project's gospel theater foundation, inserting his own creative voice within given parameters rather than defaulting to a voiceless director for hire.

After premiering at the Santa Barbara International Film Festival, where it won for Best American Film, *Woman Thou Art Loosed* received a distribution deal from art-house distributor Magnolia Pictures. The film received mixed reviews, with the most positive notices emphasizing Schultz's directing. Placing the film within the context of Schultz's career, Dave Kehr of the *New York Times* noted, "Never backing off from big, emotional moments, but also fleshing out the necessary transitions between them, he has realized his finest movie. It's a renaissance for Mr. Schultz, who seems to be speaking with his own voice after all these years."[103] Less favorable reviews took umbrage with Jakes, rather than critiquing the film itself. Kris Wilton of the *Village Voice* wrote, "Interspersed with weepy confessionals and Jakes' own preaching . . . [the film] feels part reality show, part mockumentary, part Jakes promo video."[104]

In retrospect, the most striking aspect of the film was the role it played in paving the way for the type of faith-infused black dramas and comedies that would make Tyler Perry so successful. Perry had actually been recruited by Jakes in 1999 to help write and direct the stage play of *Woman Thou Art Loosed*, which was modeled on the sort of urban circuit gospel theater popularized by Perry, Shelly Garrett, and David E. Talbert.[105] Perry does not receive screen credit on the film version of *Woman Thou Art Loosed*, but the sensibilities most associated with him are earmarked throughout Schultz's film. Oddly enough, Schultz's return to feature directing kicked off an entirely new cycle, as gospel cinema has served as the only consistent model of black-focused films to find a place in multiplexes over the past decade.

In many ways, *Woman Thou Art Loosed* is a culmination of Schultz's experience making movies that were not produced on his own terms. When he was offered the light and comedic script for *Car Wash*, his initial reaction was to turn it down. His friend Suzanne de Passe said, "Are you kidding? This is a Hollywood movie! If it's not what you want it to be, take it and make it into what you want."[106] This advice seemingly resonated with Schultz nearly two decades later. Today, with an understanding of the realities of Hollywood formed by decades of experience, Schultz is simultaneously skeptical of the film industry's willingness to expand its definitions of black experiences and hopeful for the future of African Americans in cinema. His work as a director at times suggested new possibilities for black involvement in feature filmmaking, though at other times it revealed how confining Hollywood could be for black screen artists. Schultz has been a latter-day articulation of expressive directing during the studio era, and he found an authorial entry point on films that were strictly defined in terms of size, scope, audience, and genre.

The death of his close friend Lloyd Richards in June 2006 gave Schultz the impetus to reflect not only on his career, but also on the deeper questions of meaning behind a life's work. Richards, a true luminary of the American stage, became the first black director on Broadway in 1959 with *A Raisin in the Sun*. He then became the dean of the Yale School of Drama, bringing playwright August Wilson (among others) to national attention. Returning to New York for the funeral and memorial service, Schultz took on what was one of the most heartfelt projects of his career. Filming personal tributes from friends, family, and colleagues—including Sidney Poitier, Ruby Dee, Laurence Fishburne, and Charles S. Dutton—Schultz was able to express his emotions through the act of filming, editing, and exhibiting rather than through direct address.

Richards and Schultz became close friends during their time together in the Negro Ensemble Company, and the success of Richards provided a model for Schultz concerning the possibilities of a black director. Richards's passing seems to have had a profound impact on how Schultz views his own career. Perhaps seeing himself through the lens of his departed friend, Schultz quickly moves past discussions regarding much of his work in film and television, instead lingering on his time spent in the theater during the 1960s. While he does not regret the path he chose, Schultz has developed an understanding and appreciation for just how special it was to be a part of the creative nexus of African American theater in the 1960s, a time defined by ambition and idealism, and free from the financial obligations and compromises of Hollywood filmmaking.

During the height of Schultz's career, Hollywood never fostered a similar community of black artists. Instead, Michael Schultz often worked in isolation as the most prolific and oftentimes only working black director in Hollywood. Schultz has created a body of films that are often filled with vibrant and thoughtful reflections on the black experience. With *Which Way Is Up?* and *Greased Lightning*, he became one of the few directors to capture a more meditative side of Richard Pryor. On *Krush Groove*, he was the only person in Hollywood with the forethought to document a pivotal moment in hip-hop, capturing what would become a dominant force in global culture at the very moment it was codifying its commercial expression. *Cooley High* and *The Last Dragon* remain viable articulations of black adolescence, both achieving cult status and renewing themselves with subsequent generations of young spectators. *Car Wash*, Schultz's finest achievement as a film artist, is a deeply textured social commentary that deserves to be considered alongside the best American films of the 1970s. His body of work is sometimes contradictory and occasionally compromised, but it demands to be considered with the same attention afforded to fellow black filmmakers such as Oscar Micheaux and Spike Lee.

CHAPTER THREE

Writing His Second Act

SIDNEY POITIER'S MOVE BEHIND THE CAMERA

JOHN GUARE'S 1990 PLAY *SIX DEGREES OF SEPARATION* provides a perfect summation of Sidney Poitier's legacy. The play reiterates the central role that his image has played in shaping and sustaining a popular liberal consciousness, with his iconic performances in the 1950s and 1960s serving as a clear extension of the civil rights movement. At the same time, the play also touches on Poitier's fall from the public eye and the declining artistic significance of his film work in the 1980s.

Six Degrees of Separation is a fictionalized account of David Hampton, a real-life con artist who posed as the son of Sidney Poitier to win over Manhattan socialites.[1] As Sidney's nonexistent son "Paul Poitier," he regales a white family with tales of his father and recounts what he purports to be the inside story of his father's busy schedule directing a big-budget film adaptation of the Broadway musical *Cats*.[2] The ridiculousness of the lie, geared toward a knowing New York theater crowd, is a biting commentary on just how far Sidney Poitier's reputation had fallen by the end of the 1980s, when the idea of him directing a film version of *Cats* was not wholly implausible. This brief sequence, more than any other moment in the play, speaks to how Poitier was perceived by critics and the general public by the end of the 1980s. After two decades working behind the camera, Poitier's legacy remained rooted in his performances from the 1950s and 1960s, and his directorial career could serve as mere fodder for a punch line.

The Poitier icon is premised on the repetition of particular images: slapping the face of a white plantation owner in *In the Heat of the Night* (1967, Norman Jewison), reaching out for Tony Curtis's hand at the end of *The Defiant Ones* (1958, Stanley Kramer), or perched atop a ladder, Christ-like, in *Lilies of the Field* (1963, Ralph Nelson). As a director, his films are bereft of similar iconography—Poitier's body was no longer being used as a clear stand-in for a supposedly singular black experience. The films also lack the underlying social context of being made and released in the midst of the civil rights movement. However, the notion that Poitier's work as a director is somehow less important than his acting is problematic and speaks to recurring limitations in how blackness in cinema is addressed. Such a notion focuses largely on representation while ignoring or undervaluing African Americans as cultural producers.

Along with Michael Schultz, his only other contemporary working along a similar trajectory at major studios, Poitier helped sustain the presence of black filmmakers in Hollywood in the aftermath of the blaxploitation cycle. Just as Poitier carried the burden of representing black actors (and black Americans at large) throughout the 1950s and 1960s, his work behind the camera in the 1970s and 1980s played an important role in the continuum of black representation and involvement in the American film industry. More importantly, his directorial work challenges notions of a politically and aesthetically monolithic "black community," as his perspective diverges from that of other black screen artists both creatively and commercially. Nevertheless, his work as a director is rarely invoked in summaries of his accomplishments in Hollywood. This oversight is partly due to a desire to keep Poitier frozen as a symbol of the black freedom struggle, an aim necessitating the omission of a directorial career that produced a group of films that contemporary critics felt had little social or artistic value.

The prevailing opinion that Poitier's directorial output is of low artistic quality, or even an embarrassing blemish to his legacy, must be balanced by the context in which these films were made. Particular attention must be paid to the changing landscape of the US film industry, Poitier's age and level of influence in Hollywood, and the dramatic shifts then taking place in the social, cultural, and political climate. To make sense of Poitier's work as a director, we must first recognize the limitations of how various aspects of "quality" are most commonly assigned, and challenge the methodology of film history, particularly as it relates to using film criticism as an authoritative source. There are a number of reasons why mainstream critics were largely unreceptive to Poitier's films, with responses ranging from indifference to open hostility.

Part of the critical aversion to his films can be traced to Poitier's actors-first approach. His heavy use of long takes and loose narrative structure allows for improvisation, but it also gives his films an odd rhythm and pace that violate the slick and studied approach to film language that was being normalized by a new generation of film-school-trained directors in the 1970s. Poitier also strayed from making the types of films that critics champion in terms of genre and intended audience, lacking self-important messages geared toward white liberal audiences or consciously highbrow fare for the art-house circuit. He instead initially directed films about black experiences geared specifically for a black audience, and later attempted to make popular entertainment for mainstream America. The fact that his films received poor to tepid reviews from contemporary critics means little today, largely because the response was so predictable. What is more telling is the varying legacy of his work, with some films now hailed as cornerstones of African American screen culture and others relegated to the dustbin of history.

In the 1970s, Poitier utilized his celebrity to create new projects that focused on black themes and employed black writers, performers, and crew members. As time progressed, his approach to making films became less subversive of studio policies and more closely aligned with the status quo of commercial entertainment. Poitier's universalist self-conception, and his stated goal of fostering African American inclusion within the film industry, reflects the changing social and industrial context, as his films in the 1970s speak to and for African Americans with a decided political edge, while his 1980s films either negate blackness or imagine an assimilated and apolitical world. Regardless of these contradictions, Poitier's directorial career exhibits a similar sense of exceptionalism to his decade-long run in the 1960s as Hollywood's lone black star.[3]

Beginning with his first film, *Buck and the Preacher*, in 1972, and ending with *Ghost Dad* in 1990, Poitier directed nine films over the span of nearly two decades. His films in the 1970s show Poitier striving to cultivate a cinematic space rooted in black culture and politics that was separate from the black action vehicles that became synonymous with the blaxploitation cycle. Although his film *Uptown Saturday Night* (1974) garnered a crossover audience, Poitier was making movies with black audiences squarely in mind, using his own performances to give voice to a black perspective. Beginning with *Stir Crazy* (1980), Poitier began working exclusively as a director, no longer appearing in his own (or any other) films. This move allowed him the freedom to make films without having to shape his own image, but it also made his contributions less evident. Regardless of his lack of visibility, Poitier played a central role in fighting Hollywood's exclusion of black artists behind the camera, directing pictures at major studios and facilitating inclusion in crews and unions. Poitier also played a key role as a member of the Directors Guild of America (DGA) in bringing a lawsuit against the major studios, charging them with exclusionary hiring practices.[4]

There is a running tension to Poitier, both as an actor and as a director, in which he alternately views himself as a black artist serving a black audience *and* as an artist free of any racial, political, or national affiliation. Reiterating his dialogue from *Guess Who's Coming to Dinner*—where his John Prentice character tells his father, "You think of yourself as a colored man. I think of myself as a man"—Poitier told *Jet* magazine in 1980, "I can't allow myself to be circumscribed as simply a black director."[5] Before then, Poitier had said that black audiences were his primary concern, and he had used his status as producer and director to open doors for African Americans, not only working with black actors and writers, but also insisting on black inclusion in film crews.[6] These contradictions are difficult to reconcile, but they are an extension of a complicated man whose life has been oversimplified in the public's imagination.

Poitier's turn toward directing was initially an outgrowth of his frustrations as both an actor and a de facto symbol for African Americans. In interviews throughout the 1960s he often expressed interest in taking a more active role in controlling his own image.[7] His conflicted participation in *Porgy & Bess* (1959, Otto Preminger) was instrumental in reshaping Poitier's approach to navigating Hollywood, as he felt pressured to take the role, believing that he would become ostracized by the industry if he refused.[8] Poitier has harbored regret over participating in *Porgy & Bess* for years, indicating that it was one of two projects he wishes he had not made.[9] While he would spend the following decades working to create projects on his own terms, in the 1960s he began to refuse projects he felt were either unappealing or offensive. This approach led to a spate of films that reflected his political outlook, which was deeply connected to the civil rights movement.

Poitier's iconic integrationist archetype catapulted him to the upper echelons of Hollywood in the 1960s.[10] But this box-office success and the enduring tone of the characters Poitier portrayed starkly contrasted with the drastically shifting social climate in black America. The civil rights hero that Poitier embodied was suddenly out of step with black youth and became the subject of scorn among a vocal faction of African American artists and intellectuals. The tone of discontent is best summarized in the title of black playwright Clifford Mason's 1967 *New York Times* editorial "Why Does White America Love Sidney Poitier So?"[11] Although a close and careful look at the performances, including *In the Heat of the Night* and *To Sir, with Love* (1967, James Clavell), undercuts popular notions of the static, agreeable, passive, and asexual tendencies of his characters, the backlash embodied in Mason's article brought about immediate change on the part of both Hollywood and Poitier. The cultivation of Jim Brown as a film star can be read as a direct reaction to Poitier, with Brown's athletic, virile, and sexualized image functioning as an inversion of Poitier's perceived deficiencies as a screen image of black masculinity.[12]

THE PRODUCER

As the backlash to his roles in the late 1960s took shape, Poitier began to work behind the scenes to develop his own projects and help forge a different climate for black film artists. Poitier had been planning on starting his own production company as early as 1962, and throughout the decade he had looked at optioning material for the screen.[13] In 1967 he started E&R Productions and signed a distribution deal with Columbia.[14] Poitier received story credit on *For Love of Ivy* (1968, Daniel Mann), produced *Brother John* (1971, James Goldstone) with E&R, and used his leverage as the star of Universal's *The Lost Man* (1969, Robert Alan Aurthur) to ensure that 50 percent of the film's crew was black.[15] By 1970 he was starting his second production company, Verdon Cedric Pictures, part of an ambitious venture with his Hollywood peers. Along with Barbra Streisand and Paul Newman, Poitier founded First Artists Pictures.[16] The company afforded the stars a greater level of power and autonomy than they could obtain working for a salary at the studios and allowed them to choose their own projects with financing secured beforehand. First Artists began with a financing and distribution deal with National General, later transferring to Warner Bros.[17] Suddenly Poitier had a wealth of opportunities to control his image and get new projects off the ground.

In addition to his First Artists deal and other starring roles in studio features, Poitier also had a three-picture deal with Columbia to distribute his E&R releases, the last of which was a western. Poitier's first job as a film director came by accident rather than design when he was pressed into action on the western *Buck and the Preacher*, which he was producing and starring in opposite Harry Belafonte.[18] After three days of principal photography, Poitier and Belafonte decided to fire white director Joseph Sargent, finding the dailies they were viewing incompatible with the political and aesthetic qualities they wanted the film to express. Without time to find a replacement for Sargent, Poitier took over the film at the urging of Belafonte. He delivered a picture that reflected the tradition of Hollywood westerns, but filtered through a black political perspective.[19]

Buck and the Preacher illustrates the central tension in how Poitier would think of himself as a black director, but it also exhibits the style and approach to filmmaking that he would employ throughout his career. While the film was a disappointment at the box office (and ultimately cost him a production deal with Columbia), it did have some good qualities. Its most notable success is Belafonte's performance, which is full of humor and manic energy, far removed from the cold and debonair characters Belafonte played in the 1950s.[20] Poitier privileges Belafonte's performance often at the expense of his own character, Buck, who is the ostensible protagonist of the film but is rarely given the same expressive space and freedom as the Preacher character. The film also captures elements of the off-screen relationship between Poitier and Belafonte, which was rife with tension and misunderstanding, yet defined by mutual respect and the realization that they were inextricably linked.

Although Poitier was not involved in the initial concept development for the film, *Buck and the Preacher* carries with it a number of the hallmarks that would come to define him as a director. His heavy use of close-ups and loose editing, with long takes rather than crisply edited sequences, are primary examples of how he crafted films around his actors. Close-ups allow actors to maximize the emotional value of a subtle expression. Poitier's penchant for long takes gives actors room to improvise (limiting the editor's options as well). Rather than more traditional shot / reverse shot during conversations, Poitier mostly uses long shots that include all of the characters in the frame, trading in the downside of a single, static long take for an organic interplay between actors that is rooted in the stage. Primarily concerning himself as a director with performance rather than using montage or organizing *mise-en-scène*, Poitier pulls from his theater background, translating the style of stage directors like Lloyd Richards to the realm of cinema. Most of the critical aversion to Poitier as a director can be traced to this actors-first approach, as can the reasoning for the gulf that separates Poitier's best and worst films.

Apart from the stylistic earmarks that would come to define Poitier's directorial philosophy, *Buck and the Preacher* is notable for being one of the most focused and unapologetically political films of his career, as either an actor or a director. Although the film serves as an allegory of issues central to the civil rights movement (namely, housing discrimination), its tone and content show Poitier responding to and embodying the sentiments of Black Power and thus becoming part of a broader political and aesthetic movement among black filmmakers. The film is set in the Old West immediately following the Civil War, and Poitier plays a wagon master escorting ex-slaves across the plains as they escape the South for opportunities in newly opened territories. The wagon master, Buck, struggles to protect black families from white night-riders and bounty-hunters who, despite the legal abolition of slavery, are employed by southern plantation owners to retrieve their former chattel. Westerns often serve as allegories for contemporary issues. Here, the persistent racism that followed the 1964 Civil Rights Act is spelled out in a conversation between a white bounty-hunter and a local sheriff. As the conversation suggests, racism is denounced by the government, but propped up by lack of enforcement. The tenuous settlements of African Americans along the plains function as a stand-in for the resistance met by black families hoping to move into all-white neighborhoods in the early 1970s, despite the Fair Housing Act of 1968.

The film does not simply use the past as a device to comment on contemporary issues; it also employs the western to explicitly redress the exclusion of African Americans from history. Over sepia-toned images that suggest historical documentation, the film begins with a prologue saying, "This picture is dedicated to those men, women and children who lie in graves as unmarked as their place in history." As film scholar Mia Mask has pointed out, Poitier engaged in a revolutionary political project, using the film to assert Black Power, forge a united front with American Indians, and write blacks into the fabric of the American experience.[21] Poitier had broken from his passive and nonthreatening 1960s archetype, with Exhibit A being his character slapping a white woman across the face. The film crafts a triumphant final shootout against the racist aggressors that would not be out of place in blaxploitation fantasies.

Poitier the actor takes a backseat to the director in *Buck and the Preacher*, disappearing at times into the margins of his own film. As would be the case with his subsequent comedies in the 1970s, his discomfort with directing himself is masked by the abundance of the talent that surrounded him. Without a gifted cast, his performances become awkward. Starring opposite Esther Anderson in the romantic drama *A Warm December* (1973), Poitier's lead character comes off as stiff and calculating, while the demands made on Anderson as an actress exceed her experience. Building a directorial philosophy on improvisational performance requires both a talented cast and a script that provides room for an actor's interpretation, rather than a project emphasizing the director's close crafting of visual information and dialogue.

Despite its artistic shortcomings and box-office disappointments,

A Warm December helps explain Poitier's conceptions of race and his desire to create a political platform. The film follows Matt Younger (Poitier), a respected physician and widower traveling with his daughter in London, who becomes romantically involved with Catherine (Esther Anderson), the daughter of an African diplomat suffering from sickle cell anemia. Much of the film revolves around a black diasporic cultural exchange as the couple visit a museum collection of African art and spend their night out in London among the city's African and Caribbean community. Poitier expands notions of his blackness beyond an American context, carving out a space through allusion to his oft-forgotten Bahamian identity.

Moving away from allegory and into the realm of explicit and didactic politics, *A Warm December* shows Poitier using the narrative as a platform for social causes. A dramatic shift in understandings of sickle cell anemia was then taking place in the United States as a direct outgrowth of black political enfranchisement.[22] A number of black celebrities had helped to bring sickle cell into the public consciousness: it had been championed as a cause by boxers Joe Frazier and Muhammad Ali, baseball's Willie Stargell and Dock Ellis, and actor Bill Cosby, becoming by the 1960s a focal point of national health-care debates.[23] Poitier now added to the debate. As was the case with *Buck and Preacher*, *A Warm December* strives to fill in gaps of knowledge about black experiences, in this case sickle cell anemia, which, in the words of historian Keith Wailoo, "seemed to embody the problem of unrecognized pain in the African American community."[24] The film goes to great lengths to explain the disease to the audience, with Poitier having a frank conversation with his daughter about the nature of the "black disease," providing her with statistics and using correct terminology related to sickle cell ("trait," "crisis," etc.).

Although Poitier may have intended for the film to shed new light on the disease, its release in 1973 came at a time when sickle cell had already been politically co-opted by the Nixon administration. Government programs and treatment had become a political ploy to appease African Americans by addressing a single, visible issue.[25] The fragmentation of black politics left sickle cell as a unifying cause among African Americans and a perfect topic for political posturing on the part of both Democrats and Republicans who were too weary to address other complicated fissures in the black political landscape. By the time *A Warm December* made its way to theaters, sickle cell had already been used effectively in Nixon's reelection campaign. It had also been dramatized on television. *To All My Friends on Shore* (1972, Gilbert Cates), a CBS television movie starring Bill Cosby as the father of a son with sickle cell anemia, was followed by special episodes of *M*A*S*H* and *Marcus Welby, M.D.*, focusing on the disease, all of which aired in 1972.[26] The context surrounding *A Warm December* muted its impact, as sickle cell was removed from the exclusive political domain of black pride and had entered the mainstream.[27]

UPTOWN

A Warm December failed to find an audience, and his drawing power as an actor was fading, but Poitier was still able to direct films of his own choosing. His saving grace in the early 1970s was the partnership with First Artists, which guaranteed financing on his projects. And Poitier unexpectedly chose to make his first comedy, *Uptown Saturday Night* (1974), which breathed new life into his career. He parlayed its success into the quasi-sequels *Let's Do It Again* (1975) and *A Piece of the Action* (1977).

The decision to make a comedy with *Uptown Saturday Night* and eschew the dramatic persona that had been so bankable in the 1960s did not come without resistance. Warner Bros., the company that distributed films under the First Artists banner, tried to persuade Poitier to abandon the project. However, the terms of the contract with First Artists granted Poitier creative autonomy, and he went ahead with *Uptown* despite studio protests.[28] He also used his leverage to secure a film crew that was 25 percent black, a vast improvement over the nearly all-white crews on most studio pictures.[29] More than a move in a new direction in terms of genre, the project was a perfect match for Poitier's directorial philosophy.

Uptown Saturday Night focuses on a pair of working-class friends played by Cosby and Poitier who become entangled with the underworld in an attempt to retrieve a lost lottery ticket. The plot is secondary to performance, serving as a framework for comedic gags. The focus on performance and improvisation rests not only on the abilities of his cast but also in the flexibility embedded in the screenplay, which allows for scenes to take unexpected turns. Written by black playwright Richard Wesley, the first two Poitier-Cosby comedies are rooted in the tradition of folk humor and feature almost exclusively black casts, a departure from the traditional dramatic fare that had defined Poitier's career, often with Poitier being the only black actor in an otherwise white cast.

Wesley had come to prominence in 1971 with his play *The Black Terror*, a piece informed by the Black Arts movement that focuses on revolutionary characters seriously engaging race, class, and gender relations. Poitier, along with Harry Belafonte, met Wesley backstage following one of his plays and asked if he would be interested in writing a new project for them.[30] Wesley had done preliminary work on unrealized film projects before, but *Uptown* was the first that came to fruition and would carry his name on the credits.[31] He wrote the script in six weeks while staying at Poitier's house in the Bahamas, with the director serving as a sounding board during the script's development, structuring the picture as an ensemble piece that showed the previously unseen breadth and talent of African American performers. According to Wesley, Poitier's primary goal was to get "as many top black comedians as he could get."[32]

The cast he assembled spoke volumes to the respect Poitier had among his peers. *Uptown* featured Harry Belafonte, Bill Cosby, Richard Pryor, Roscoe Lee Browne, Flip Wilson, Calvin Lockhart, Rosalind Cash, Paula Kelly, and Harold Nicholas. The film provided a breakthrough role for Cosby on the big screen and increased his already high profile from television, comedy clubs, and records. The pairing of Poitier and Cosby follows the tradition of comedy teams like Bob Hope and Bing Crosby, or Dean Martin and Jerry Lewis, with Poitier playing the straight man for Cosby's more dynamic comic characters. Poitier had been hesitant to act in the films he directed, and his initial concept for *Uptown Saturday Night* was to team stand-up comics Redd Foxx and Richard Pryor in the roles he would eventually fill alongside Cosby.[33] However, Poitier was required to star in the films he produced in order to get funding through his First Artists contract, and it was this part of the agreement that turned him unwittingly into a comedic straight man.[34] Despite his misgivings about taking on a leading role, *Uptown Saturday Night* became a hit at the box office. Its $12 million take placed it on par with the biggest successes of the blaxploitation era and spawned a quick follow-up.[35]

In *Let's Do It Again*, Poitier and Cosby play factory workers who try to save their lodge (a complex black institution that is a strange hybrid of the Nation of Islam and the Shriners) by going to New Orleans to fix a boxing match, soon becoming entangled with gangsters. The ensemble approach follows the mold of *Uptown*, with Cosby, Poitier, and Lockhart returning, and Ossie Davis, Denise Nicholas, Billy Eckstine, boxer George Foreman, John Amos, and Jimmie Walker joining the cast.[36] The ensemble cast is given a chance to shine, and Poitier's performance is much stronger than it was in *Uptown*, showing a growing confidence with comedy. For example, in one scene he poses as a gangster in a sartorial display inspired by *Super Fly*'s Youngblood Priest, wearing a caped jacket, bell-bottoms, and a wide-brimmed hat. Here, Poitier makes a reflexive commentary on his star persona and the widespread backlash, accepting the fact that his personality strays from the antiheroes of the blaxploitation era. He allows the comedy

Sidney Poitier posing as a blaxploitation-era gangster in Let's Do It Again.

of the scene to come at his expense by showing just how ridiculous it looks for him to take on the trappings of the hustler. The humor is self-effacing and satirical, never mean-spirited.

The wide appeal of his comedies forced a reconsideration of the rhetoric that had propped up the backlash against Poitier in the late 1960s, as *Let's Do It Again* outperformed *Uptown Saturday Night* at the box office, grossing $15 million.[37] Whereas Poitier was charged with catering to white liberal sensibilities in the 1960s, his comedies in the 1970s were unapologetically geared toward a black audience. While he never claimed to be a comedian, his ability to bring black folk humor to the big screen in a manner that was tasteful and lacked condescension speaks volumes to his skill as a director. Poitier's most lasting contribution as a director came with his approach to comedic performance. *Uptown Saturday Night* and *Let's Do It Again* point toward a major shift in American screen comedy—coinciding with the growing importance of Chicago's Second City and the debut of *Saturday Night Live*—where improvisational performance takes precedence over punch lines or visual gags.

For all of his newfound acclaim as a comedian, Poitier still hoped to make serious commentaries from the director's chair. He looked to follow Ossie Davis's lead in creating a pan-African production model, hoping to use First Artists financing to make a film in and about Africa.[38] The proposed film, *Cabral*, was to be shot in Tanzania, recalling the life of Amilcar Cabral, the African nationalist who helped Guinea-Bissau achieve independence before his assassination in 1973. Unable to secure financing, the project never came to fruition, however, and Poitier returned to working as a hired actor in *The Wilby Conspiracy* (1975, Ralph Nelson) instead, starring opposite Michael Caine in a sort of anti-apartheid reworking of *The Defiant Ones* (1958, Stanley Kramer) set in South Africa.

Poitier made his final appearance as an actor-director in his fifth film, *A Piece of the Action*, which blends the social consciousness of his first two directorial efforts with the outer trappings of his far more successful comedies opposite Bill Cosby. This attempt to combine two seemingly incongruous tendencies touches on Poitier's growing confidence as a director, which is evidenced in the film's more clearly developed narrative and technical aspects. But Poitier in this film also gives his most self-assured performance of the decade. The growing pains of his first four features did not come as a surprise, as Poitier was hesitant about his ability to direct himself from the outset, and made the transition to working behind the camera before he deemed himself ready to take on the responsibility. Remembering the day he took over the production of *Buck and the Preacher*, Poitier later wrote that he was "putting on a hat I had no intention of wearing for at least another three or four years."[39] Now, five years later, he had finally found a level of comfort acting in his own films, and no longer defaulting to his costars.

In *A Piece of the Action*, Poitier teams up once again with Cosby, but the film moves away from the tone of their first two films together, reflecting Poitier's personal politics via a screenplay from Charles Blackwell. Poitier's story concept (which is credited to his pseudonym "Timothy March") looked to address his growing disconnect from black youth. Straying from the folk humor of its predecessors, the narrative instead functions as a sort of morality play about personal and community responsibility. In contrast to Richard Wesley, who wrote *Uptown* and *Let's Do It Again* through the prism of Black Power politics, Blackwell brought with him the generational sensibilities of Poitier and Cosby, informed by the civil rights movement and middle-class aspirations.

Poitier and Cosby play career criminals (a con man and a safe cracker, respectively) who get blackmailed by a police detective (James Earl Jones) to volunteer at a community outreach center in Chicago for troubled black teenagers. Poitier takes over in the classroom, reworking elements from *Blackboard Jungle* (1955, Richard Brooks) and *To Sir, with Love*, delivering impassioned speeches on the importance of self-respect and good manners. The plot is an inversion of *Uptown* and *Let's Do It Again*, with Poitier and Cosby playing criminals who are forced to give back to the community rather than everyday working-class people forced to navigate the underworld. With its dramatic weight and straightforward message, *A Piece of the Action* is a departure from the two previous films, so that notions of a Cosby-Poitier trilogy are cosmetic, at best.[40] Although the interplay between Cosby and Poitier provides a few comedic moments, they share preciously little screen time. The tone and content of the film are more aligned with the social messages of *Buck and the Preacher* and *A Warm December* than with the previous Cosby comedies. The result is an often didactic statement on black youth that functions as a denunciation of the mythology of blaxploitation and what Richard Majors would later term the "cool pose."[41]

The title of *A Piece of the Action*, as explained in the film, uses the terminology of street hustling and applies it instead to becoming a member of the middle class. The film looks to reverse the blaxploitation construct of the street-hustling antiheroes evident in *Super Fly*, *The Mack* (1973, Michael Campus), and *Black Caesar* (1973, Larry Cohen) by reforming both the teacher and their students into productive, perfectly assimilated members of society. While a number of blaxploitation-era films looked to revisit the racial-uplift message of the 1950s or paint a sociological portrait of the black urban underclass, *A Piece of the Action* exhibits a generational divide that is shown through the eyes of older, more conservative black characters.[42]

The film presages Cosby's more recent comments regarding the hip-hop generation, but ultimately expresses his shifting persona in the 1970s, where his focus on education began to dominate his work, forming a pedagogic black conservatism that would eventually resonate with a mass crossover audience on television.[43] Coming at the end of the blaxploitation cycle, *A Piece of the Action* shows Poitier's sensibilities aligning with Hollywood as he attempted to make peace with the pervading themes of the era by offering a new vision of middle-class idealism and assimilation. As Hollywood moved away from black-focused narratives in the following years, Poitier also transitioned to working solely as a director, making films with multiethnic casts.

THE DIRECTOR

In 1978 Poitier signed a four-year deal with Columbia to write, direct, *and/or* star in films of his choosing.[44] The Columbia deal came at just the right time for Poitier, as First Artists began to fall apart after a string of failures. Between 1972 and 1980, First Artists produced nineteen features, but with the exception of Barbra Streisand's *A Star Is Born* (1976, Frank Pierson) and Poitier's comedies, it had few successes at the box office.[45] Poitier had been the only member of the collective to dedicate himself first and foremost to First Artists; he acted in only one outside project and brought his best and most profitable projects along with him to the company. His partners, on the other hand, enjoyed their greatest successes outside of the company and used First Artists largely as a tool for financing projects with little box-office potential. Paul Newman made *The Sting* (1973, George Roy Hill), *The Towering Inferno* (1974, John Guillermin), and *Slap Shot* (1977, George Roy Hill) outside of First Artists. Streisand made *The Way We Were* (1973, Sydney Pollack) away from the company, and Steve McQueen joined the company only a few years before his death. In the final year of the company, Dustin Hoffman made the little seen *Agatha* (1979, Michael Apted) for First Artists while starring in *Kramer vs. Kramer* (1979, Robert Benton) for Stanley Jaffe and Columbia. The division between successful ventures made outside of the company and box-office disappointments within led to First Artists being liquidated at the end of 1979, also ending the contractual obligation for Poitier to star in his own projects.[46]

The dissolution of First Artists coincided with Hollywood stepping away from black-focused features and the cultivation of comedic stars like Richard Pryor and, later, Eddie Murphy as prominent exceptions to the marginalization of African Americans on screen. The films of Pryor and Murphy, in many respects, revisit Poitier's roles of the 1950s and 1960s, inhabiting screen worlds populated almost exclusively by whites. Ironically, the highest-grossing film of Poitier's career as either an actor or a director would come with *Stir Crazy*, the first film he directed but did not also appear in as an actor. Following the successful (albeit brief) pairing of Gene Wilder and Pryor in *Silver Streak* (1976, Arthur Hiller), *Stir Crazy* reworks the buddy formula Poitier had employed in *Uptown* and *Let's Do It Again*, this time with a biracial pairing and a shifting responsibility between Wilder and Pryor to play the straight man.

The first line of dialogue in *Stir Crazy* arrives in the form of a question that is spoken off-screen during the opening montage sequence. Over shots of the Brooklyn Bridge and the Manhattan skyline, Gene Wilder's protagonist asks, "Who needs Hollywood?" In 1980, Sidney Poitier may have very well been asking himself the same question. What motivation was left for someone who had succeeded as an actor, a director, and a producer to continue working in Hollywood, particularly considering that despite his efforts and influence, the film industry had reverted back to the same limited investment in black screen artists that had defined his acting career in the 1950s and 1960s? For Poitier, the answer came in the challenge of directing without the benefit of having himself in front of the camera. Thanks to his track record at the box office, his new contract with

Gene Wilder and Richard Pryor play tough for prison in Stir Crazy.

Columbia allowed him the freedom to step away from acting and devote all of his attention to directing.

Unlike many of his peers, who found themselves shut out of the industry after the fall of blaxploitation, Poitier was still working in film. He observed that, "fortunately for me, I was not at the mercy of the marketplace."[47] In the 1970s, Poitier had been able to utilize his celebrity to create new projects that focused on black themes, not to mention employing black writers, performers, and crew members. In the 1980s, his perspective dramatically changed. His approach to making films was no longer premised on subverting studio policies, and instead became more closely aligned with normative commercial entertainment.

In terms of box-office appeal, his first film working exclusively as a director would prove to be the biggest success of Poitier's career. *Stir Crazy* is built around the performances of Gene Wilder and Richard Pryor, who play two friends wrongfully convicted of armed robbery and sent to prison. A classic escape narrative, with a subplot involving prison rodeos, the story serves a secondary function to the comedic improvisation, using a screenplay that was more of a loose outline than a polished blueprint.[48] Poitier used three camera setups to provide Pryor and Wilder freedom to move and improvise, nurturing the same creative spontaneity as he had with the Cosby comedies, but with a more dynamic visual end product, as the extra coverage allows for inter-cutting between a single performance, instead of keeping him tied to a lone, static take. Poitier's growing competence in handling comedy, and his decision to provide space for Pryor and Wilder to work off of each other, pays off in a number of scenes. Reworking the most famous scene from *Silver Streak*, where Wilder dons blackface to pass as a Rastafarian, *Stir Crazy* opts for a more genuine (and less offensive) take on performing blackness—for example, when Pryor coaches his white friend as they arrive in prison. Light and playful in its use of comedic improvisation, the scene also has an undercurrent of seriousness in its suggestion of incarceration being an increasingly normalized extension of the black experience.

Columbia likely had modest ambitions for *Stir Crazy* from the outset, but as fortune would have it, the film became a surprise blockbuster, surpassing $100 million at the US box office to finish behind only *The Empire Strikes Back* (1980, Irvin Kershner) and *Nine to Five* (1980, Colin Higgins) among the films released that year.[49] *Stir Crazy*'s crossover success went beyond anything seen before by a black director, causing the *Washington Post* to ask, "What acceptable excuse could there be for perceiving Poitier as an exclusively 'black' filmmaker after 'Stir Crazy' gets around?"[50] Although Poitier was not the first black director to make a film that was not populated primarily with black actors or geared toward a multiethnic audience, the success of *Stir Crazy* seemed to signal his eventual ascendancy as a director in the new blockbuster climate of Hollywood.[51]

A critical look at the reasons for *Stir Crazy*'s success, however, helps to explain why Poitier was never able to duplicate it. His work as a director played little role in the film's box-office returns. Although the Wilder and Pryor pairing had been successful four years earlier in *Silver Steak*, much of the clamor for *Stir Crazy* came from the media blitz that followed Pryor setting himself on fire in his Northridge home just weeks after shooting wrapped.[52] While Poitier oversaw editing and prepared for the film's release, Pryor found himself elevated to another level of stardom as he recovered from his injuries. His release from the hospital in late 1980 and a round of candid television interviews regarding the incident proved far more effective than any studio marketing scheme. Largely because of his erratic behavior during shooting, Pryor's performance is minimized in the final cut of *Stir Crazy*, turning him into a supporting character for Wilder instead of a star on equal footing.[53] Nevertheless, Pryor shared top billing in the promotion of *Stir Crazy*, and the notoriety of the Northridge fire helped transform the film from a modest comedy into a Hollywood blockbuster, skewing perceptions for critics and audiences alike. Initially, *Stir Crazy* seemed to point toward a bright future for Poitier as a director, but it actually marks his final success behind the camera.

Although the 1980s started with the promise of *Stir Crazy*, giving Poitier confidence in his decision to step away from acting and focus exclusively on directing, his subsequent efforts failed with critics and audiences.

Columbia financed his next film with a generous $14 million, a major improvement from the budgets of his 1970s films and a sign of confidence in Poitier's bankability as a non-acting director.[54] *Hanky Panky* (1982) reteamed Poitier with Gene Wilder in a Hitchcock-inspired thriller about an architect who accidentally stumbles into a complicated plot to cover up a murder. The film veers wildly from suspense to slapstick comedy, and although it marked the beginning of an off-screen relationship between Wilder and costar Gilda Radner, the chemistry they shared on set is largely absent on screen. For Poitier, the film is most notable for lacking an identifiable racial element. In interviews Poitier had expressed his desire to work as a director on projects that would be offered to any other director, and his work on *Hanky Panky* is ultimately a reflection of this aim, as it is bereft of any outwardly recognizable personal vantage point. The film may be unremarkable and dry, but it is a standard Hollywood release, which may have been exactly what Poitier aspired to direct.

Despite his ability to find work in Hollywood, Poitier remained mindful of the climate for African American artists in the film industry. He recognized that in spite of his own success, the studios were more closed than ever to black creative talent. In 1983 Poitier testified before Congress, charging the studios with conspiring against minority-owned firms.[55] Earlier in the same year, the Directors Guild of America had filed suit against Warner Bros., citing discrimination against its minority and female membership. The DGA expanded its suit in 1985 to include two additional studios.[56] Poitier's role as a spokesman for the DGA and black filmmakers showed him to be just as committed to using his celebrity to foster the inclusion of African Americans in Hollywood in the 1980s as he had been in the 1970s, despite the fact that the content of his films no longer addressed black spectators directly. His advocacy would seem to suggest implementing a system akin to affirmative action in Hollywood, but Poitier's public statements were complicated (and possibly contradictory) as he began to call for black filmmakers to pick themselves up by their bootstraps.

Writing in 1980, Poitier saw a new set of roadblocks as well as opportunities for black filmmakers. That year, *Stir Crazy* was the only American film with a black protagonist to receive a distribution deal (and with Wilder receiving the lion's share of screen time, its being considered a black-focused film is tenuous, at best). Poitier preached the same sort of lesson of self-determination that he had delivered in *A Piece of the Action*, telling his fellow black screen artists in his autobiography *This Life* that "we're going to have to make the most of our films. I think we should no longer expect the white filmmaker to be the champion of our dreams."[57]

In some ways, this statement is overly simplistic, glossing over cinema's capital-intensive nature and the limited access to financing for black filmmakers. But he also noted the changing landscape of media industries, looking toward cable and the home video market as new opportunities.[58] The success of Spike Lee and the black film explosion in the 1990s benefited from VHS and (to a lesser extent) cable. Box-office grosses and the ability of a distributor to secure a large number of screens were no longer the be-all and end-all for a film's bottom line.

These changes were a decade away, though, and in the meantime, Poitier continued his move toward the mainstream in Hollywood. With one film remaining on his contract with Columbia, Poitier attempted to pull off an ambitious musical project that he hoped would connect with a youth audience. *Fast Forward* (1985), however, would be his low point as a director both at the box office and with critics. Working with a cast of dancing newcomers, the film is an inept attempt to pander to the MTV generation that shows little knowledge of popular culture.

Reworking themes from some of the more successful films of the 1980s—namely, "the three Fs": *Footloose* (1984, Herbert Ross), *Flashdance* (1983, Adrian Lyne), and *Fame* (1980, Alan Parker), as well as the breakdancing films *Breakin'* (1984, Joel Silberg) and *Beat Street* (1984, Stan Lathan)—the story revolves around a group of teenagers from the Midwest trying to make it big as dancers and singers in New York. The plot is formulaic and the acting reflects the cast's lack of experience, giving the film a stilted quality that is not helped by song and dance numbers egregiously out of touch with contemporary trends. Ending with a triumph at a big talent show, the film carries an intended message about the culture industry, greed, and the crafting of image, but the overriding optimism in the film mutes most of its critical commentary.

The musical numbers in *Fast Forward* come across as staged showtunes, using balletic choreography masquerading as street dance. The film attempts to incorporate elements of hip-hop, reworking the dance-crew battles from *Beat Street* and *Breakin'*, but the choreography of Broadway veteran Rick Atwell fails to convey any semblance of the style, form, or function of breaking. An impromptu performance in Midtown Manhattan emphasizes the difference between hip-hop and *Fast Forward* in geography alone. The musical numbers are similarly disconnected from hip-hop and rock, with songs that have a show-tune sensibility that is more reflective of a 1980s Las Vegas revue than anything that would appeal to the MTV generation.

The film would seem to suggest that Poitier was completely out of step with the 1980s, but the backstory of the production helps explain the film's

Street dancing, far removed from the style and sensibilities of hip-hop, in Fast Forward.

failures, redeeming the director's understanding of pop culture as well. Poitier began work on the story with a simple concept based around his own experiences as an aspiring actor in New York, focusing on young people struggling to find success and eventually succeeding despite long odds. Instead of a cast of unknowns, however, Poitier originally intended for the film to star Michael Jackson, fresh off of the success of *Thriller*.[59] Jackson verbally agreed to appear in the film, and Richard Wesley went forward with the screenplay with him in mind, leaving space for improvisation and for the bountiful dance numbers and songs that Jackson would perform while bringing his charisma to the project. As production drew nearer, with shooting scheduled for the summer of 1984, Jackson unexpectedly dropped out of the project to join the *Victory* concert tour.[60]

Now without a star for his film, Poitier's troubles became magnified by his contractual status with Columbia. With the expiration date on his three-picture deal approaching, Poitier was left with the decision to either go ahead and make *Fast Forward* that summer or forfeit studio financing. The film looks like a rushed and poorly planned effort largely because it was. Poitier had to assemble the cast, have songs composed, and get the choreography done just a few weeks before shooting began to take advantage of his Columbia contract before it expired.

Speculating on the picture that might have been may be imprudent, but the trajectory of Poitier's career would have likely changed had his initial concept for *Fast Forward* as a Michael Jackson vehicle been realized. Jackson was at the height of his stardom and had a fascination with movies that led him to break new ground in music video, largely in col-

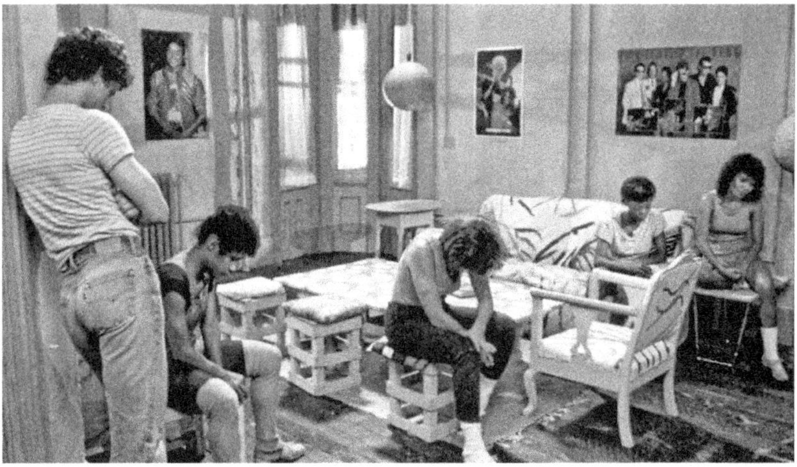

The Michael Jackson poster to the left of the frame serves as a reminder of the film that could have been.

laboration with well-known filmmakers.[61] But although he had costarred in *The Wiz*, Hollywood had yet to fully capitalize on his talents, although Jackson's cinematic ambition would play out over the next year with the 3-D Disneyland attraction *Captain Eo* (1986, Francis Ford Coppola), which had the pop star piloting a spaceship alongside a crew of puppets. However, though the theme-park attraction was well received, it made Jackson appear more alien and inaccessible than ever. He had forfeited the chance to humanize himself with the stripped-down character he had been slated to play in *Fast Forward*.

With a cast of newcomers in Jackson's place, *Fast Forward* was a difficult film to sell. Compounding the scathing reviews was the unfortunate coincidence of opening opposite *The Breakfast Club* (1985, John Hughes) at the box office.[62] John Hughes uncannily tapped into the mood of youth culture in 1985 (albeit from a decidedly Anglophilic perspective), while Poitier could not have looked more out of step. Hughes's films were informed by new trends in music—he often turned his characters' bedroom walls into an index of fashionable pop bands. The walls of the flophouse apartment in *Fast Forward*, on the other hand, are populated by posters of seemingly random musical acts, including Prince, Rod Stewart, the Police, Duran Duran, the Thompson Twins, U2, Men at Work, and Huey Lewis & the News. In a cruel (and possibly intentional) irony, a poster of Michael Jackson is placed in the center of the living room, suggesting the film that *Fast Forward* could have been.

Fast Forward became the undoing of Poitier as a director and a financial disaster for Columbia. The film was emblematic of the studio's decline and mismanagement in the 1980s under the control of Columbia's new parent company, Coca-Cola. Its budget reached a reported $17 million, but it only earned $2.7 million at the box office.[63] The *Boston Globe*'s review of the film echoed the prevailing sentiment, saying that Poitier "should leap back to the other side of the camera before his well-deserved reputation is completely tarnished by his directorial career."[64] With *Shoot to Kill* (1988, Roger Spottiswoode) and *Little Nikita* (1988, Richard Benjamin), he did just that, becoming a for-hire actor once again. His capital as a director was all but gone, and without a contract guaranteeing financing for his films, Columbia canceled Poitier's directorial project *Hard Knox* in 1988.[65] The last film he directed came with 1990's *Ghost Dad*, a regrettable Bill Cosby vehicle that lacks any of the energy of their earlier collaborations. It was a limp attempt to capitalize on its star's television success.

The comedian Poitier had worked with in the 1970s had been transformed through the success of *The Cosby Show* into a superstar, but he was now associated with a specific character that began to bleed into his personality outside of the sitcom. He had a string of successful books behind him and had become a pitchman for Coca-Cola, Jell-O, Kodak, and Ford Motors.[66] Cosby's initial attempt to translate his superstardom to the big screen came with the disastrous *Leonard, Part 6* (1987, Paul Weiland), a family-friendly spy comedy that got universally bad reviews and flopped at the box office. *Ghost Dad* was the second attempt to parlay the success of *The Cosby Show* into feature film, this time playing on the Cliff Huxtable character by casting Cosby as a career-obsessed widower who unwittingly becomes a neglectful father. Dying in a car accident, he comes back as a ghost to become the father he never was in real life to his three children.

Although *The Cosby Show* was criticized as a safe and uncomplicated vision of the black middle class, it regularly addressed issues of race through frank discussions of ancestry and culture. The show itself often served as a repository for otherwise forgotten or neglected black performers, with Cosby using his status to pay tribute to artists who had never received ample opportunities or recognition.[67] *Ghost Dad*, on the other hand, carries with it none of the nuance of Cosby's television work and instead envisions a suburban family living in a postracial world. A modest success, earning $25 million at the box office, the film was a critical disappointment, and it failed to connect the Poitier-Cosby partnership to the mood of their three films from the 1970s.[68]

Following *Ghost Dad*, Poitier returned to working in front of the camera as an elder statesman, acting in two more theatrical features, *Sneakers* (1992, Phil Alden Robinson) and *The Jackal* (1997, Michael Caton-Jones), as well as a number of made-for-television movies. The biggest career shift for Poitier did not come with his return to acting, but instead was an extension of his reconsideration of the power dynamics of Hollywood. Poitier was appointed as president of the Walt Disney Company in 1994 following the death of Frank Wells, and his role as a board member at Disney carried with it far more power in terms of green-lighting films and expanding opportunities for black screen artists than his two-decade run as a director had.[69] Unfortunately, he entered a company in flux, and the departure of Jeffrey Katzenberg and a host of disappointments at the box office limited his opportunities to effect change at the company.[70] Under CEO Michael Eisner, Disney reached new heights of success before becoming notoriously dysfunctional. Poitier's ability to make a major impact on the film industry as an executive was undercut by the boardroom power plays and ongoing litigation that defined Disney in the second half of Eisner's run as CEO.[71]

Poitier entered semiretirement following his departure from Disney in 2003. Through the reflection of his memoirs, the numerous honors he has received, and many retrospectives, conferences, and publications, Poitier's work as an actor has been celebrated, contextualized, and recontextualized. Aram Goudsouzian's definitive biography, *Sidney Poitier: Man, Actor, Icon*, provides a detailed account of his career and places it in conversation with the civil rights movement, while Percival Everett's postmodern novel *I Am Not Sidney Poitier* dissects the meanings and legacy of Poitier's screen image through satire.[72] He has received a cavalcade of lifetime achievement awards and honorary degrees based on his work as an actor and as a living symbol of the civil rights movement. His work as a director, however, has received scant attention. Finally, in 2001, he also received a Lifetime Achievement Award from the Directors Guild of America.[73] The award came from an active campaign by DGA's African American Steering Committee, with Michael Schultz, the only director who could fully appreciate the struggles Poitier had faced in the post-blaxploitation era, delivering one of the tributes at the ceremony. The DGA award may be the only public recognition Poitier has received as a director to honor his contributions in maintaining black involvement in Hollywood following blaxploitation.

Poitier has helped to shape his own legacy as a celebrated memoirist, providing a personal perspective on his life and career. In his books he is introspective and open, yet he rarely talks about his approach as a director, at least from an artistic standpoint. Directing, one would believe by reading between the lines of his statements (and omissions), is largely a tool for control in Hollywood and not a creative enterprise on par with acting. Whether it be directing or writing under the assumed name of Timothy

March, Poitier strived to find his creative voice on film outside of performance, yet his work as a writer and a director never seemed to effectively articulate his perspective. In many ways, his directorial career can be read as a transitional experiment separating his acting career and his later incarnation as a memoirist and folk philosopher.

CHAPTER FOUR

Think Locally, Act Globally

FRED "THE HAMMER" WILLIAMSON, LOW-BUDGET GENRE FILMMAKING, AND THE STRUGGLE FOR SELF-DEFINITION

NO BLAXPLOITATION-ERA STAR MADE AS MANY FILMS or helped shape the cycle more than Fred "The Hammer" Williamson. Crafting his own unique hypermasculine screen persona, Williamson was able to flex his muscles playing gangsters, detectives, and cowboys. With his ever-present thin cigar, bulging biceps, and phallic firearms, the Hammer became the archetype of male power in a cinematic era that was primarily based around reclaiming black masculinity. Never graced with the singularly transcendent roles afforded Richard Roundtree or Ron O'Neal, Williamson was nevertheless the biggest star of the era.

From 1972 to 1976, no other black actor made more films, grossed more money at the box office, or made as many inroads with mainstream Hollywood as Williamson. More importantly, no one else was as successful at cultivating an image on the screen so full of strength, bravado, and sex appeal. Not simply a "black John Wayne," Williamson was instead a decidedly 1970s version of the western hero, trading in the political conservatism of Wayne for a self-gratifying attachment to the sexual revolution and a selective engagement with Black Power politics.[1] Williamson is perhaps the clearest articulation of the blaxploitation era in terms of its iconography, aesthetics, and political sensibilities. At the very least, he is one of the first names a casual fan of the era might think of when trying to provide an example of a blaxploitation hero.

Yet Williamson never saw himself as being part of the cycle, and he continues to distance himself from both the blaxploitation label and other stars from the era. "I didn't fit the mold," Williamson explains. "I never fit into the category of 'let's get whitey.'"[2] On one level, Williamson is correct, in that his characters often were defined outside of an urban American milieu—although his most iconic roles of the era were predicated on violently overthrowing white power figures. The more telling difference between Williamson and his peers from the 1970s can be found in his relationship to the Hollywood system. Williamson was never a passive participant in his film career, at the mercy of studio whims or opportunities created by other people. "Everything I ever did in my life always had a plan," he explains, pointing out that all of his success has come from his own determination and ability to lead.[3] Acting in studio projects at the height of the blaxploitation cycle was part of his plan, and he used the star-making power of the film industry to gain complete independence a few years later. Whether it was rooted in a desire for creative and financial autonomy or a distrust of corporate studios, Williamson's planning was instrumental in helping him survive the purge of black creative talent that affected the majority of participants in the blaxploitation cycle after 1976.

At the height of the black film explosion, a handful of black stars transitioned from veritable unknowns (at least in the acting world, as a number of them had previously starred in professional sports) to bankable box-office draws. Williamson, along with Jim Brown, Bernie Casey, Jim Kelly, Ron O'Neal, Richard Roundtree, Billy Dee Williams, and Pam Grier, succeeded in carrying multiple films into theaters, turning low-budget efforts into moneymakers for major studios and independents. Far from being rewarded for success, most of these blaxploitation stars soon returned to the margins of Hollywood once the cycle had ended, struggling to find work in an industry they had helped to keep afloat just a few years earlier. Williamson was able to escape the fate of his peers largely by making his own films, never allowing the logic of major studio executives to dictate the terms of his career. His transition to directing coincided with the decline of blaxploitation: in the final year of the cycle, 1976, he directed five features. Under this blistering schedule, he went from being a first-time director to a seasoned veteran behind the camera in a matter of months. He would direct an additional six films by the end of 1986. All of these films were made outside of the American studio system, with small budgets that utilized financing strategies that were unheard of for projects featuring an African American star.

Unlike the other big stars of the era, Williamson had taken the initiative during the blaxploitation cycle to become more than a star, serving as a writer, director, and producer. More than just learning the trade, he developed an understanding of financing and distribution that allowed him to bypass Hollywood studios by scraping together money for production costs and looking for distribution deals in foreign markets. In some respects Williamson became a modern iteration of Oscar Micheaux, turning himself into a hustler in the name of low-budget independent film, and along with this financial prowess he had a strictly defined narrative sensibility and the single-minded goal of having his films reach an audience.

This audience, however, was not solely conceived as being African American. His pursuit of foreign financing and distribution was an extension of a broader self-conception, as Williamson considers himself a global citizen and has tried to cultivate a screen persona that transcends the limitations of race within an American context. His goal was to be an international action star alongside people like Sylvester Stallone and Charles Bronson, though he never was able to attain their level of success. Nevertheless, the Hammer's legacy internationally is perhaps the most important aspect of his film career, as he was able to find a model for financing and distribution that completely defies Hollywood's self-imposed limitations on black-focused films.

Often Williamson's directorial efforts are read as an attempt to hold on to the past—as desperately trying to preserve his blaxploitation screen persona long after the cycle's demise. But the Hammer has always looked toward the future and taken the initiative to set new trends. He made inroads outside of the United States that exposed Hollywood's false notion that black-focused films could only make money domestically. Whether he was stuck in the past or ahead of his time, Fred Williamson's directorial career is as idiosyncratic as the man himself.

HERE COMES THE HAMMER

For the first generation of black directors in Hollywood—those who landed projects from 1969 to 1976—entry into the position was rarely conventional. Hollywood pulled from a number of different mediums, with backgrounds in theater, television, acting, writing, photography, and editing all leading for different people to directing features. No director, however, had as improbable a route to the director's chair as Fred Williamson.

Born in Gary, Indiana, on March 5, 1938, and eventually moving with his family to Chicago, Williamson excelled in track and field and football, eventually earning a scholarship to Northwestern, where he became a star athlete while earning a degree in architecture.[4] He began his professional football career in 1960, playing eight seasons as defensive back for the Pittsburgh Steelers, Oakland Raiders, and Kansas City Chiefs.[5] Playing in an era before million-dollar contracts, he put his college degree to use and earned a living in the off-season working as an architect for the

Bechtel Steel Corporation.[6] As an architect, Williamson became a model of upward mobility, being featured in *Ebony* magazine as one of the country's most eligible bachelors alongside prominent physicians, lawyers, and academics.[7] As a football player, he developed a brash persona through his hard-hitting tackles (earning him the nickname "The Hammer") and braggadocio in interviews, becoming a prototype for players decades later like Deion Sanders and Terrell Owens.[8]

Following his retirement from football in 1968, Williamson moved away from the stability of being an architect and instead went to Los Angeles to pursue an acting career, quickly landing a small role in an episode of the television series *Ironside*.[9] Williamson often relates a story about his big break as an actor that happened shortly thereafter. Watching Diahann Carroll's cavalcade of boyfriends on her NBC show *Julia*, Williamson pitched himself to the show's producers as a candidate to be her first long-term boyfriend, sneaking onto the lot at Twentieth Century Fox, conning his way into the office of producer Hal Kanter, and talking his way onto the show.[10] For twelve episodes he played Julia's boyfriend Steve Bruce, an ex-football player that Kanter had written into the show specifically for Williamson. While working on *Julia*, Williamson transitioned to feature films, with a small role in *M*A*S*H* (1970) after a chance encounter with director Robert Altman in the Fox commissary.[11] Williamson worked with acting coaches while filming *M*A*S*H* and earned praise from Altman, who said, "Fred's a lot better than pretty good. He has everything to make it big, including the drive, and he comes off great on the screen."[12] According to Williamson, he not only acted in the film but also choreographed and codirected the football scenes in the film alongside Altman.[13] Again, his scenes were predicated on his background in football, but Williamson was beginning to gain traction in Hollywood.

After *M*A*S*H*, he landed another supporting role in *Tell Me That You Love Me, Junie Moon* (1970, Otto Preminger). Following Jim Brown (and Woodie Strode a decade earlier), Williamson was part of a wave of former black football players who pursued acting careers in the late 1960s and early 1970s. Surpassing his peers, however, Williamson became one of the few whose success on screen eclipsed his accomplishments on the gridiron. He was neither the most notable on the football field (Jim Brown) nor the most talented dramatic actor (Bernie Casey), but he was by far the most prolific film star coming from football, largely as a result of his outsized ambition. Before he ever starred in a movie, Williamson began developing his own material, writing the original story for *Julian Drake*, an unrealized feature that was supposed to be his first starring role as a sort of James Bond type involved in an interracial romance.[14] Hollywood may not have exactly been Williamson's for the taking in 1970, but the climate would change by the end of the following year.

Williamson's charisma, self-confidence, and athletic physique positioned him perfectly for stardom in the wake of *Shaft* and *Sweet Sweetback's Baadasssss Song*. Fueled by ego and a keen understanding of Hollywood's failure to deliver a viable black star, Williamson actively sought out heroic roles. As a star, he established a credo for his screen image that followed a basic three-rule system, which he supposedly presented to producers and directors before signing on to make a picture.[15] As Williamson would explain to producers and directors, "One, you can't kill me. Two, I win all the fights. And three, I get the girl at the end of the movie, if I want her."[16] This combination of physical force and unapologetic sexuality made him a crystallized representation of blaxploitation's project of recuperating black masculinity onscreen. He headlined two features during the first year of the blaxploitation cycle, beginning with Paramount's *The Legend of Nigger Charley* (1972, Martin Goldman), a western about a group of fugitive slaves. With its provocative title reflecting Melvin Van Peebles's in-your-face sensibility, *Nigger Charley* sold itself as a Black Power statement while also aspiring to achieve historical accuracy and reflection. The tagline on the poster reads, "Somebody warn the West, Nigger Charley ain't runnin' no more," a clear reprise of the ending text to *Sweetback*.[17] Williamson is only credited as an actor, but along with Larry G. Spangler he helped conceive the film, making *The Legend of Nigger Charley* the first in a long line of self-generated projects.[18]

The majority of Williamson's projects during the blaxploitation era found him in a more traditional role, working as an actor for hire. He starred in the boxing/crime film *Hammer* (1972, Bruce D. Clark), with a title that explicitly attempts to cash in on his football celebrity. The following year, he made his signature film of the era, playing gangster Tommy Gibbs in AIP's *Black Caesar* (1973, Larry Cohen). In the hurried sequel *Hell Up in Harlem* (1973, Larry Cohen) released later that year, he reprised his Gibbs character, and he made another sequel that same year with *The Soul of Nigger Charley* (1973, Larry G. Spangler). Establishing himself as the most prolific black star in Hollywood, Williamson looked to be on the brink of bigger and better things. Universal financed *That Man Bolt* (1973, Henry Levin and David Lowell Rich), a big-budget feature in terms of blaxploitation's economic model that hoped to turn the globetrotting Jefferson Bolt character into a James Bond styled franchise. He earned his biggest paycheck to date, making a reported $1 million to star in the film, and Universal was planning two *Bolt* sequels before the first film hit theaters.[19]

Instead of starting an action franchise, however, *That Man Bolt* underperformed at the box office and played a role in convincing executives at Universal to abandon their investments in black-focused features.[20] Williamson's private detective feature for Warner Bros., unfortunately titled *Black Eye* (1974, Jack Arnold), also fared poorly at the box office. The dwindling interest on the part of the major studios in black-focused features was becoming apparent, but Williamson had success with the independently distributed *Three the Hard Way* (1974, Gordon Parks Jr.), teaming with Jim Brown and Jim Kelly in one of the most elaborate political fantasies of the blaxploitation era.[21] While Williamson's celebrity had grown through his film work, extending to a spread in *Playgirl* magazine and a brief stint in the booth for ABC's *Monday Night Football* telecasts, the changing approach to black-focused films by the major studios began to limit his options in Hollywood, with only minor distributors carrying his films after 1974.[22]

PO BOY

The 1976 federal Tax Reform Act may have brought an end to the blaxploitation cycle, but the contours of the film boom had started changing a few years earlier. Major studios had already begun to step away from black-focused features, and low-budget independent productions were becoming the primary option for black actors. The number of black-focused films remained relatively steady in 1975 and 1976, but they were more marginalized in terms of financing and distribution and lacked the machinery of the majors. Never short on confidence, though, Williamson looked at the changing landscape as an opportunity to be more proactive in cultivating his opportunities. In 1975 he made films that would mark new beginnings, serving as the foundation for the next twenty years of his career.

In that period Williamson traveled to Italy to make two spaghetti westerns, *Three Tough Guys* (1975, Duccio Tessari), with Isaac Hayes and Italian actor Lino Ventura, and *Take a Hard Ride* (1975, Antonio Margheriti), in which he teamed up again with Jim Brown and Jim Kelly in a quasi-sequel to *Three the Hard Way*. *Three Tough Guys* would mark the first of more than twenty features for Williamson in Italy, where he took advantage of alternative options in financing for films that fell outside of the exclusive exhibition realm of urban American theaters. Later in the year, he returned to the western genre with the American-made *Boss Nigger* (1975, Jack Arnold), featuring his first credit as a screenwriter. He finished out the year starring in AIP's *Bucktown* (1975, Arthur Marks), a film about racial tensions in a small southern town that was one of the studio's more thoughtful blaxploitation-era releases, and one that Williamson also co-produced.[23] While blaxploitation stars like Ron O'Neal, Richard Roundtree, and Jim Brown saw their options becoming limited in Hollywood, Williamson was transforming his career by developing his own projects and looking toward Europe for work. With his run of success developing projects outside of the confines of Hollywood and working behind the scenes, he furthered his transition into directing, founding Po Boy Productions to handle his projects.

Po Boy was not akin to the traditional movie star's production company. Rather than serving as a studio-financed subsidiary or a traditional independent production company making films for intended distribution by the majors, Po Boy was intended to bypass Hollywood altogether. Williamson's fame as an actor allowed him to be independent from the Hollywood system, and his charisma helped him land deals. Talking about his ability to draw attention and control a room, Williamson recently explained, "If I have that presence then I don't need anyone else to sell my film."[24]

Po Boy became a one-man show, with Williamson writing, directing, starring, and producing all of his own films. Understanding the limitations of American financing, he instead used a European model for gathering production budgets and selling distribution rights. Williamson went to Cannes for the first time in 1973 and over the next twenty-plus years became a mainstay at the Marché du Film, the business-oriented event that takes place alongside the Cannes Film Festival.[25] Although critics, filmmakers, stars, and the social elite screen and discuss films in competition at Cannes, Cannes also hosts the busiest international cinematic marketplace, where financing and distribution deals are struck for projects ranging from art films to pornography. Williamson gained financing for all of his projects at Po Boy through Cannes, where each film was presold to international distributors. While this limited the scope of his productions, with budgets never topping $500,000, it also insulated him from the restraints and vacillations of American financiers. African American film production has been cyclical, subject to changing tastes and industry practices, and one of the biggest limitations has been the self-fulfilling logic in Hollywood that there is no foreign market for black-focused films. The scale of Williamson's projects may have been small, but he proved that a black filmmaker could succeed outside of America.

Williamson's first film as a star-director-writer-producer was the low-budget action vehicle *No Way Back* (1976). Originally titled *Journey to No-*

where, *No Way Back* was shot for under $100,000, a fraction of most independent blaxploitation fare, much less a studio feature.[26] The film is representative of the majority of Williamson's directorial work in terms of its narrative sensibilities and aesthetics, both of which were born out of the budget. As he would throughout his career, Williamson used a basic stationary camera rather than taking the time to set up tracking shots or spend money renting cranes or a Steadicam. His shooting schedules were expedient, rarely lasting over two weeks for an entire feature-length film. Quick camera setups and nonunion crews helped keep costs down, turning Williamson into something of a guerrilla filmmaker. He would shoot unannounced in public, often with gawking onlookers visible in the frame.

His stories are often equally threadbare. In *No Way Back*, he plays Jesse Crowder, a detective / bounty hunter hired to find a missing businessman who has fled town with a beautiful young woman and a briefcase of stolen money. Beginning in San Francisco before moving down the coastline to Los Angeles and San Diego and then finishing in the California desert, *No Way Back* prefigures the cinematic travelogues of most of Williamson's films, making a point of imaging him as more than a physically imposing strongman. Crowder is cultured, charismatic, and irresistible to women, and the role is both an obvious attempt at cultivating a star persona and a cinematic exercise in wish fulfillment, with Williamson creating a character that represents his ideal self.

As with Williamson's subsequent films, the conflict of *No Way Back* is very basic, with clearly defined "good guys" and "bad guys," to use Williamson's own terminology for talking about his characters. The details of the plot are less clear, with little explanation for the story. Fistfights, gunplay, and chase sequences are justification unto themselves, with action taking priority over motivation. Williamson's films tend to lack narrative progression and instead function as a collection of loosely connected scenes. Chases on foot and by car, scenes of violence, and sexual encounters function much in the same way that gags do in a silent screen comedy, with the spectator's joy located in the isolated moment. The plot becomes secondary to the pleasure of the Hammer's physicality.

Williamson's screenplays were written quickly—he churned out five screenplays for 1976 alone—leaving little time to flesh out nuanced plots or characters. From a broader perspective, his cheap and quick approach to filmmaking became a hallmark of his directorial style. Regardless of genre categories or value judgments—whether or not he makes "good" films—Fred Williamson movies are idiosyncratic at their core. He took *No Way Back* to Cannes in 1976, and presold the film to international distributors, but he chose to release the film himself in the United States, forming the short-lived Atlas Distribution solely to handle Po Boy releases. With a small budget and no need to split money with any collaborators, he quickly turned a modest profit with *No Way Back*. Although there are no reliable numbers for the film's box-office gross or international distribution fees, it would only take a modest return to support Williamson's claim that all of the films he produced during his career earned a profit.[27]

No Way Back was just the first in a flurry of productions at Po Boy: Williamson served as a multi-hyphenate on six features in little over a year. He reprised the Jesse Crowder character for *Death Journey* (1976), another action travelogue in which the private eye escorts a witness from California to New York to testify against a mafia boss, fighting off hired assassins along the way. The scope of the location for *Death Journey* is remarkably ambitious for a film with such a limited budget and short shooting schedule, using car, train, plane, bus, and even air tram as modes of transportation connecting location shooting in Los Angeles, Palm Springs, Apple Valley, Kansas City, St. Louis, Chicago, and New York. Some of the cities are better utilized than others, with a well-developed fight sequence on the Palm Springs Aerial Tramway mismatched with the brief shots of train stations and airport terminals in other cities. The use of the respective cityscapes, or lack thereof, gives the impression that *Death Journey* was filmed haphazardly during an actual cross-country trip, with Williamson setting up the camera during pit stops.[28] Both of the Crowder films show Williamson in his comfort zone, playing a tough-guy urban character who complies with Williamson's three rules for screen representation. His other 1976 releases provide points of departure in tone and setting.

Mean Johnny Barrows (1976) is the most direct attempt at social commentary of Williamson's career. In it he moves past the one-dimensional tough-guy role in a story about a down-on-his-luck Vietnam veteran who becomes a hit man for the mob. The film defies Williamson's stated rules for his own characters, with Barrows losing fights and living on the streets. He is not particularly popular with the ladies, and the film ends with Barrows lying alone in the desert with a gunshot wound to the chest. Williamson's decision to bend his own rules for the sake of narrative impact is the best indicator of his sincerity and ambition with *Mean Johnny Barrows*. The mood is a drastic departure for him. The film has a somber ending with a humbled character who is defined by moral self-questioning. *Mean Johnny Barrows* at times functions like a social-message film, but it predates the more popular and critically respected efforts to address the difficulties of Vietnam veterans returning home, including *Rolling Thunder* (1977, John Flynn), *Coming Home* (1978, Hal Ashby), *The Deer Hunter* (1978, Michael Cimino), and *First Blood* (1982, Ted Kotcheff). Williamson goes so far as to end the film with a prologue-like statement, which reads, "Dedicated to the veteran who traded his place on the front line for a place on the unemployment line. Peace is hell."[29]

Mainstream Hollywood's unwillingness to deal with Vietnam until well after the fall of Saigon tells only part of the story of cinematic responses to the war. Some films, such as *Kelly's Heroes* (1970, Brian G. Hutton) and *The Wild Bunch* (1969, Sam Peckinpah), dealt with the war through allegory, and others, like *Taxi Driver* (1976, Martin Scorsese), made vague references to the vet experience. Films made outside of the normative Hollywood model, such as documentaries and foreign productions, were able to deal with Vietnam more directly. Two films dealing with African American experiences relating to the war came out of Sweden, of all places. The documentary *Terry Whitmore, for Example* (1969, Bill Brodie) chronicles the experiences of a black war deserter living in Sweden, while the fictional narrative *Georgia, Georgia* (1972, Stig Björkman)—based on a screenplay by Maya Angelou—deals with an interracial romance between a black singer (Diana Sands) and a white war deserter (Dirk Benedict). There were also more traditional blaxploitation releases, including *Gordon's War* and *Brotherhood of Death* (1976, Bill Berry), dealing explicitly with the black vet experience—returning home to crumbling cities and a heroin epidemic in the North, or to persistent racism and the remaining presence of the Ku Klux Klan in the South.

Mean Johnny Barrows frames the vet experience more through class and psychology than through race—Barrows is only able to survive by embracing the way his mind has been altered by the war. Rather than focusing on posttraumatic stress, the film reflects on the dehumanizing nature of being trained as a combat soldier. "Soldiers became victims of what they had learned," Williamson explains. "He [Barrows] learned to kill people."[30] Although the film maintains elements of the action fantasy, with ample violence and a revenge theme, there is a vulnerability to the character and a sincerity of purpose that separates the film from the Jesse Crowder vehicles. Williamson strives to make a profound commentary on the human toll of war within the confines of a low-budget production.

The other two films that Williamson made during Po Boy's first year in existence lacked the political ambition of *Mean Johnny Barrows*, but they signaled their difference by departing from the contemporary urban milieu. Returning to the western genre, this time as a director, Williamson traded in the cityscape for desert expanses in *Adios Amigo* (1976) and *Joshua* (1976). But although the films share genre classification, they vary dramatically in terms of style, tone, and meaning. The comedy *Adios Amigo*, costarring Williamson alongside Richard Pryor, uses the Old West loosely as a stand-in for urban experience and a site for comedic sketches, while *Joshua* is self-consciously styled within the traditions of the genre to tell a sincere and contemplative story.[31]

The films also differ in how they have been remembered. Because of Pryor's involvement, *Adios Amigo* has been lumped in with scores of other disappointing screen vehicles for the comedian. In *Adios Amigo*, Williamson had a budget of $500,000, much more than he had had at his disposal for *No Way Back*. It marked Pryor's first starring film role as he moved away from his brief supporting roles in films like *The Mack* and *Uptown Saturday Night*.[32] Williamson attempted to create space for improvisation, allowing Pryor the freedom to create memorable scenes much in the same way Sidney Poitier would approach working with him a few years later on *Stir Crazy*.

"The script was only twelve pages," Williamson explains, "and Richard just did his thing."[33] Unfortunately, Williamson's first foray into comedy failed to translate Pryor's unique humor onto the screen, and the film was poorly received by critics (although it did earn a profit). Pryor himself expressed embarrassment with the film and tried to distance himself from the project. Asked in an interview to explain his involvement to disappointed fans, Pryor said, "Tell them I apologize. Tell them I needed the money."[34]

The shortcomings of *Adios Amigo* are rooted in Williamson's approach to filmmaking. His breakneck shooting schedules and minimal budgets often led to technically crude films lacking narrative focus. *Joshua*, conversely, provided a perfect match for his mode of production. Borrowing heavily from Sergio Leone and John Ford, the film stands apart from Williamson's previous westerns (as an actor and director), locating the aesthetics in genre tradition and avoiding the formulaic conventions of most blaxploitation-era westerns, which tend to serve as thinly veiled allegories for the black urban experience in the 1970s. Light on dialogue and heavy on sweeping shots of a strong and striking Williamson riding through Monument Valley, *Joshua* uses its meditative tone to add a deeper sense of pathos and purpose for the title character, a former Union soldier looking to avenge his mother's murder by a group of white outlaws. Like all Williamson films, *Joshua* exhibits shortcuts, the most noticeable being a looping five minutes of music rather than a full score. Yet, given his limited budget, the end product is remarkable in both its scope and its quality.

When asked to choose the one film he's most proud of from his body of work as a director, Williamson chose *Joshua*.[35] What is odd about this choice is that the final film is not actually credited to Williamson, but to Larry G. Spangler. While Williamson wrote the screenplay and produced the film, the initial shooting began with Spangler behind the camera, as Williamson and Spangler returned to the fruitful relationship they had cultivated with the *Nigger Charley* films. Spangler dropped out early in production, however, and Williamson directed the majority of the picture himself.[36] Out of respect to Spangler he kept his name on the film, failing to take credit for the film he is most proud of directing. This seeming contradiction between Williamson's bravado and his acts of selflessness only partly explains the complicated nature of the man. "As long as the film gets made, what do I care who gets the credit?" Williamson asked, striking an oddly humble tone for someone who has made a career out of self-promotion.[37] Regardless of who is credited, the film shows Williamson at his best as a performer and a director.

The proposed follow-up to *Joshua* was less successful. Looking to make another western, this one titled *Greed*, Williamson struck a deal with the government of Chile after officials offered to provide financing, travel accommodations, free use of locations, and three hundred Chilean soldiers to use as extras for an anticipated cavalry battle scene.[38] When word got out about the arrangement, Williamson came under fire by a number of human rights groups, with the Philadelphia Chile Emergency Committee proposing a boycott of his films.[39] Williamson was simply looking for a good business opportunity, and that is what he had found, with the Chilean government covering much of the production cost free of charge. But his involvement with Chilean dictator Augusto Pinochet and the country's poor human rights record made the choice of location hard to defend. Williamson was admittedly politically unsophisticated, and he decided not to film in Chile after learning more about Pinochet's regime for himself.[40] Soon after leaving Chile, he announced that the production of *Greed* would be moved to Mexico, and eventually he abandoned the film altogether.[41] Williamson looked toward foreign production as an alternative to his American features because of his low budgets, and he had been caught off guard by his lack of knowledge of global politics. Unfortunately for Williamson, returning to the low-budget model he had used in the United States as a producer was no longer an option.

Although Po Boy Productions secured financing internationally and was insulated from the fallout caused by the Tax Reform Act of 1976, Williamson's output in the following years shows how much the climate for independent black-focused films had changed. Williamson had announced a number of projects that were slated to be produced in 1977 and 1978, most of which were abandoned. The tax credits that had allowed for risk-free investments in low-budget films seem to have also impacted opportunities for distribution and exhibition: a black-focused film made in the post-blaxploitation landscape was now marked by difference and orphaned in the marketplace. The flurry of activity at Po Boy came to a quick halt, and Williamson retreated to Europe, not for financing, but simply to find work.

INGLORIOUS

After his run directing his own features, Williamson returned to Italy, costarring in the World War II action film *The Inglorious Bastards* (1978, Enzo G. Castellari), a low-budget retread of *The Dirty Dozen* (1967, Robert Aldrich). Taking on a smaller role as part of a large ensemble cast, Williamson started a lucrative side career with this film. He acted in supporting roles in a number of Italian genre films, earning enough money to live comfortably. However, he did not abandon his ambition to be a standalone star, so, securing financing through Po Boy, he took his weekends off from shooting *The Inglorious Bastards* to pursue another action vehicle, writing the script for *Mr. Mean* (1977). He even worked on this project on weekdays while on set with Castellari.[42] Like his previous efforts, *Mr. Mean* lacks a strong sense of narrative continuity—the basic story outline connects a series of fights, foot chases, and romantic interludes. And like Jesse Crowder, Mr. Mean is an ex-cop working in an unspecified profession somewhere along the spectrum of private detective and soldier of fortune who is flown to Rome and hired by rival families to kill a mafia boss.

The film has a few scenes shot in Los Angeles as bookends, including one in a nightclub with the Ohio Players performing the title song, but the rest of the footage shows Williamson maximizing the scenery of Rome. He uses a much wider visual scope than in his American films to capture recognizable landmarks of the ancient cityscape, including the Colosseum, the Spanish Steps, and picturesque piazzas. These images make good use of the film's low budget and static camera. The film mirrors some of the exploitation tendencies of his previous films in postproduction as well, with the use of prerecorded, looped intervals of music lasting only a few minutes to avoid the need to hire a composer to write a score. Although *Mr. Mean* offers little to differentiate itself from his previous efforts on *No Way Back* and *Death Journey*, it also showed that Williamson was just as capable of making a low-budget action vehicle overseas as in the United States.

Williamson initially conceived *Mr. Mean* as a way to maximize his time in Italy while acting in *The Inglorious Bastards*, rather than as a blueprint for a new career path. He thought he would return to the United States, where he had big plans for the remainder of the 1970s with Po Boy, beginning in 1977, when he was going to make use of the rights he had purchased to five remaining *Dirty Harry* scripts after Clint Eastwood chose to step away from the character.[43] Williamson envisioned using the screenplays to help further develop his Jesse Crowder character, this time with top-flight Hollywood screenplays rather than stories he had written himself. Williamson also signed jazz singer Nancy Wilson along with Lola Falana and the Reverend Cleophus Robinson to act in his unrealized film *Blues for a Hundred Yards*, a tale of an ex-football star that Williamson described as a tear-jerker made "for the ladies."[44] The film was going to chronicle the real-life romance between Dick "Night Train" Lane and Dina Washington. But indifference to black-focused projects in the United States and the limited appeal internationally for a subject related to American football made financing the picture impossible.[45] The only indication Williamson gave that he might be returning to Europe was that he began touting a plan to make a $2 million picture there along with Ursula Andress and Anita Ekberg in 1978.[46] This film would be a departure from the low-budget action fare he was known for. But the promised production budget fell through after a lover's spat between a rich financier and one of the leading ladies, leaving Williamson with yet another stalled project. The world of opportunities he saw for himself in the late 1970s was quickly vanishing.

Williamson appeared again as Jesse Crowder, but it was a far cry from the more mainstream Hollywood vehicle he had envisioned when he had purchased the rights to the Dirty Harry screenplays. Reprising Crowder in *Blind Rage* (1978, Efren C. Piñon), Williamson basically has a small walk-on role, appearing only in the last ten minutes of the film—although he was advertised as the film's star on posters. He took no part in writing, directing, or producing the film, which was shot and financed in the Philippines, a country whose film industry was synonymous with exploitation cinema. Why Williamson decided to use the Crowder character for a small walk-on role in a Filipino film is unclear, but the fact that he resorted to taking small roles in foreign exploitation fare shows how limited his opportunities had become.

Like so many of his blaxploitation peers who had been discarded by Hollywood, Williamson struggled to find work, and he grew disillusioned with the opportunities he was afforded in the United States. While black actors became mainstays at the unemployment offices in and around Hollywood, Williamson scraped together a few jobs while charting out a new plan for Po Boy Productions. He landed roles on television in 1978 and 1979, appearing in episodes of *Fantasy Island*, *Supertrain*, and *CHiPs*, as well as the miniseries *Wheels*. He returned to film acting with *Fist of Fear, Touch of Death* (1980, Matthew Mallinson), one of the countless low-budget attempts to posthumously cash in on the life and legacy of Bruce Lee. The film intercuts archival footage of Lee into a confused plot about a martial arts tournament.

Professionally, Williamson was at his lowest point. He had gone from starring in major studio films to earning a paycheck as a bit player on TV and doing low-budget films in a matter of years. Looking to kick-start his career and explore new opportunities, he decided to leave the United States. He filed for Canadian citizenship in 1979 and planned to move Po Boy's offices to Montreal so he could focus his productions more on European markets and financing.[47] Williamson saw Canada and its subsidies for national filmmakers as an opportunity to return to a financial situation that resembled US independent production before the 1976 Tax Reform Act and Hollywood's conservative turn. Williamson was still hoping to film *Blues for a Hundred Yards* once Po Boy made the move to Montreal and his Canadian citizenship was finalized, but by the time he was due to become a full citizen of Canada in 1982, he had already left the country, taking Po Boy Productions with him.[48]

Rather than a functioning company, with a staff and offices, Po Boy became a nominal extension of any project Williamson chose to pursue. As he told Roger Ebert in 1982, "Po Boy Productions is a telephone, a calculator, a typewriter and a dog named Hammer. I don't even have an agent. I sold my house in LA because I was never there and I didn't have anyone to bring in the mail. I live in hotel rooms. I love room service. I'm a real lone wolf."[49] Williamson took on what amounted to black buddy roles in Italian science fiction films to earn a living, reuniting with Enzo Castellari, the director of *The Inglorious Bastards*, for *1990: The Bronx Warriors* (1982). The film was a combined retread of *The Warriors* (1979, Walter Hill) and *Escape from New York* (1981, John Carpenter). Much like he had during the making of *The Inglorious Bastards*, when he had used weekends to shoot *Mr. Mean*, he decided to pursue his return to directing during his next acting job. Having already accepted a supporting role in *Vigilante* (1983, William Lustig), Williamson was going to use his time shooting the film in New York to make his own film on the side.[50]

Jim Kelly, Fred Williamson, and Jim Brown in 1974 in Three the Hard Way.

HAMMER RETURNS

Self-definition was a major reason why Williamson had looked to a career in movies in the first place. He had wanted to craft a life that eschewed the limitations of coaching, being a television commentator, or functioning as a walking symbol of nostalgia for fans' childhoods, the three main avenues available to most ex-athletes. Now that he was an actor for hire, playing supporting roles in marginalized films, he began to push toward the same independence he had enjoyed in the 1970s. Acting in *Vigilante* and the Castellari films provided him with the financial security he needed to pursue his own film projects without risking his personal well-being—a far cry from the all-in bets of independents like Spike Lee and Robert Townsend a few years later.

Returning to the United States to shoot *One Down, Two to Go* (1982), Williamson assembled a cast of his blaxploitation-era peers, bringing back Richard Roundtree and his costars in *Three the Hard Way*, Jim Brown and Jim Kelly. Everyone was to earn a share of the film's profits. Shot in New York (mostly on Staten Island to stay under the radar of unions), the film was made with Williamson's usual expediency: it was shaped around the limitations of the fifteen-day shooting schedule.[51] Before production began, he raised half of the budget, preselling the film to European distributors at Cannes, with the remainder provided by a loan from a London bank.[52]

One Down, Two to Go was not much of a departure for Williamson, merely providing the recently forgotten black screen heroes the oppor-

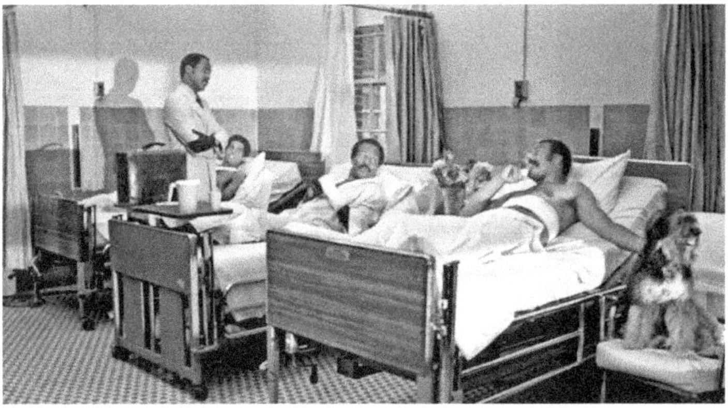

Kelly, Brown, and Williamson, joined by Richard Roundtree, circa 1982 in One Down, Two to Go.

tunity to "do their thing."[53] As Williamson put it, "Jim Kelly brought the karate to the film, Jim Brown brought the brawn, I brought the suave, and Roundtree brought the coolness."[54] The plot is basic, with the mafia trying to fix a karate tournament and kidnapping one of the contestants (Kelly), and three of his friends (Roundtree, Brown, and Williamson) taking on the mob to win his freedom. Using the 1970s black action formula in the 1980s, stars on the cusp of middle age act out a collective apprehension toward growing old, hoping to hold on to their youth as well as their careers. The final scene pokes fun at aging, as the stars lie battered and bruised in hospital beds, no longer able to easily endure the physical toll of their action exploits.

The film may not differentiate its stars' characters much from the iconic roles they played in the 1970s, but the reception of *One Down, Two to Go* was markedly different. In light of Hollywood's abandonment of black themes in the early 1980s and the scores of unemployed black screen talent, the film was championed by the same black middle-class publications and civil rights leaders who had targeted similar films in the 1970s for trafficking in racial stereotypes. Jesse Jackson had been one of the most outspoken members of the Coalition Against Blaxploitation in the 1970s, but by 1982 his opinion of black action vehicles had changed. The Chicago premiere of *One Down, Two to Go* served as a benefit for Operation PUSH, Jackson's nonprofit social justice organization.[55] Williamson also appeared alongside Brown and Roundtree on the cover of the conservative magazine *Black Enterprise*. There, camera in hand, he serves as a prime example of entrepreneurial determination.[56]

An underserved black audience and coverage in the black press helped

Williamson avoid spending money on advertising, because he knew there was a built-in audience for the film. Like Oscar Micheaux in the 1920s and 1930s, Williamson now traveled from city to city with the film, opening first in New York, then moving to other cities in the Northeast, the South, the Midwest, and finally, the West Coast. The director made a number of personal appearances at schools and local organizations to promote the film and pitch himself as a model of success for urban youth.[57] Though he was a decade removed from his first starring role as an action hero, Williamson was just as committed now as he had been then to cultivating his heroic image.

Williamson then signed on to direct another film outside of the confines of Po Boy Productions and his own self-made star vehicle while still in New York. Perhaps because of his experience making films quickly and under budget, or possibly based solely on his winning personality and ability to make fast friends, Williamson was hired to direct the boxing film *The Last Fight* (1983) by Jerry Masucci—he had met the producer while making *Vigilante. The Last Fight* was Masucci's first time spearheading a feature film, but the story touched upon his experiences in music and boxing. Masucci was also a former cop and lawyer, and in the 1960s he had founded Fania Records in New York with Dominican bandleader Johnny Pacheco.[58] Fania became a groundbreaking record label, popularizing salsa music with a roster of artists including Pacheco, Celia Cruz, Héctor Lavoe, Willie Colón, and Rubén Blades. Fania's success in the 1970s made Masucci wealthy and allowed him to branch out and explore other interests. Selling the label in 1980, he had briefly tried his hand promoting prizefights with Don King while also starting to make movies.[59] Masucci had produced two concert films for Fania acts, *Our Latin Thing* (1972) and *Celia Cruz and the Fania Allstars in Africa* (1974). The latter had been filmed in Kinshasa, Congo, capturing the concert series being held as part of Don King's promotion for the title fight held there between George Foreman and Muhammad Ali.[60] The use of music from the Fania label led to Masucci receiving executive producer credit on *Vigilante*, after which he began developing his own story concept for *The Last Fight*.

Williamson wrote the screenplay and directed *The Last Fight*, but the film breaks with the movie-making tradition of assigning authorship to the director, instead using the opening credit "A Jerry Masucci Film," identifying the producer as the key creative voice.[61] The final film is a strange hybrid of action formula, with Williamson reprising his role as Jesse Crowder for the final time. It is also a star vehicle for Fania artists Rubén Blades and Willie Colón. An extension of Masucci's interest in boxing, it features cameos from Don King, sportswriter Bert Sugar, and ring announcer Don Dunphy.[62] The most interesting aspects of *The Last Fight* revolve around its relationship with Fania's artists and its aesthetic legacy. The film plays with the gangster imagery of the label's 1970s album cover art and retains aspects of the social consciousness that defined much of the music. For Williamson, however, the film is an anomaly, in that his personal style and sensibilities are not pronounced in the end result. In the same way that he began making ends meet by acting in projects simply for a paycheck, he now became a director for hire. This point explains his lack of authorial credit. Not only does the film not reflect his style, but his Crowder character is often displaced in the narrative.

Williamson wasted little time in putting together another action vehicle explicitly suited to the Hammer persona, however, heading to his hometown of Chicago to make *The Big Score* (1983). Williamson plays Detective Frank Hooks, a brutal cop on the trail of a local drug dealer. The narrative contains all of the usual police movie clichés: Hooks, for example, is forced to return his badge to the captain, only to doggedly pursue the case on his own. What separates *The Big Score* from the rest of Williamson's films as a director is the conventional tone of the screenplay and the professional cast. Instead of writing the film himself, as he had on all of his previous films as a director, he used one of the Gail Morgan Hickman *Dirty Harry* screenplays that he had purchased in 1977, with a few minor tweaks to character names and setting. As a result, the narrative has far more coherence than his earlier Jesse Crowder films.[63]

The tone from his previous films also dramatically shifts, with the film trading in the confident, physically imposing ladies' man that he usually portrayed for a frustrated cop reaching middle age. He angrily delivers Dirty Harry dialogue such as, "You know who the law protects? Goddamn law breakers." In this respect his rebellious antihero of the 1970s had become an irritable conservative of the 1980s. Williamson was now using independent filmmaking to promote conformist values. From its established cast and expanded use of special effects to its politics, *The Big Score* functions as a mainstream film made on a shoestring budget.[64] Rather than pointing to a transition into Hollywood filmmaking, however, *The Big Score* marked the last American-based production for Williamson before he decamped to Italy.

VOYAGE TO ITALY

After finishing *The Big Score*, Williamson was slated to do another feature in the United States titled *Silent But Deadly* with his longtime friend and collaborator D'Urville Martin. Martin's sudden death of a heart attack in 1984, however, put an end to the project.[65] Martin, who had directed *Dolemite* (1975) and *Disco 9000* (1976), had been looking to rejoin the ranks of black directors that year with a film called *Stonehawk*, but died before production could begin.[66] Rather than attempt to continue working as a director in the United States, Williamson returned to Italy, this time choosing to live in Rome full time, making a living picking up small acting jobs in American and Italian productions. He used his earnings and new connections with European financiers and distributors to make new films under the Po Boy banner.

Following the examples of Orson Welles and John Cassavetes, Williamson would act in a wide variety of vehicles to earn a living, using the time between films to put his own projects into motion. Unlike Welles and Cassavetes, who acted in mainstream studio fare to fund their independent projects, however, Williamson had to find demand for his acting services outside of the United States. Italian genre film became a perfect match for him because of his experience working in the country throughout the 1970s and the wave of new films that Italian directors were making for international audiences. The country's love for Hollywood and the flexibility of its own genre films made an American star finding a second chance in Italy seem natural. For Williamson, one might expect this effect to be complicated by race. This was not the case, though it may seem counterintuitive to envision a country with very few African descendants welcoming a black star. Italians have often thought of themselves as being colorblind.[67] As Williamson explained it, to Italians he was no different from Charles Bronson, Chuck Norris, or any other American action star. He was not a *black* action hero, but simply an American action hero. "When they play my film, they play it in the same theater where they play Stallone or where they play any action star," he said, "because there are no ghettos [in Italy]."[68]

Dating back to the silent super-spectacles and continuing into the art cinema of the neorealists and later the art-house auteurs (Fellini, Antonioni, Bertolucci), Italy had proudly clung to a sense of independence from, and superiority to, foreign cinemas. But Italy also has a long tradition of genre filmmaking that is under-explored by film scholars, including peplum films, spaghetti westerns, and the horror films of Dario Argento and Lucio Fulci. Now, its art films were diminishing in quality and quantity. Facing a barrage of imports in the 1980s from Hollywood and the decline of its national directors—be it through the quality of their films (in the case of Fellini) or their departure for America (Antonioni and Bertolucci)—Italian studios looked toward genre films to remain sol-

Williamson in 1990: The Bronx Warriors, *one of his many supporting roles in Italy.*

vent. The futuristic knockoff films in which Williamson appeared flourished for approximately a decade: low-budget "trash films" became the dominant model of Italian production in the 1980s. Playing supporting characters in Italian science-fiction films may not have been what Williamson envisioned for himself—years later he said he "felt kind of stupid doing them"—but it was steady work, and it afforded him the opportunity to live comfortably in Rome while transitioning into a practice of filmmaking that was not dependent on American audiences.[69]

Williamson saw his appeal to Italian and European audiences as a testament to the lack of racial barriers there like the ones confronting him in America, yet these films still limited him to supporting roles in films with white leads. Typically, he was placed off-center in the narratives next to leading white American and Italian actors. And although his initial opportunities in Italy were not far removed from the small parts that actors like Bernie Casey, Ron O'Neal, and Richard Roundtree were being offered in Hollywood—they played marginal characters in films like *Revenge of the Nerds* (1984, Jeff Kanew), *Red Dawn* (1984, John Milius), and *City Heat* (1984, Richard Benjamin)—he never had the intention of basing his career solely on his supporting roles. But buddy characters became the hallmark of his work in Italian films, moving Williamson further away from his blaxploitation heyday with each additional outing.

Williamson appeared in a pair of similarly titled films with postapocalyptic settings, *Warrior of the Lost World* (1983, David Worth), an Italian/US co-production, and *Warriors of the Wasteland* (1983, Enzo G. Castellari), a wholesale imitation of *Mad Max* (1979, George Miller). The following year, he costarred in the dystopian *The New Gladiators* (1984, Lucio Fulci) before making a brief appearance in *White Fire* (1984, Jean-Marie Pallardy), a co-production between Turkey, France, and the United Kingdom. He then attempted to find work in England, only to be denied a British work visa to shoot the TV movie *The Dirty Dozen: The Next Mission* (1985, Andrew V. McGlaglen). The denial followed an uproar among underemployed black members of England's actors guild when they protested the hiring of a non-British black for the role.[70] Instead, Williamson returned stateside to make *Deadly Impact* (1984, Frabrizio De Angelis). Costarring with Bo Svenson, another American actor making a living on European action films, *Deadly Impact* was shot in Phoenix and Las Vegas, but had European financing and was made by an Italian filmmaker.

Although Williamson's primary residency was Rome, he pursued other opportunities in the United States following *Deadly Impact*. He did television work in 1985 on two episodes of *The Equalizer*, and he joined fellow ex-football players Bubba Smith and Dick Butkus on *Half Nelson*, a short-lived midseason replacement on NBC starring Joe Pesci.[71] That same year, Williamson took on his most visible role since the blaxploitation era, starring as himself in commercials, becoming the pitchman for Anheuser-Busch's King Cobra malt liquor, which was launched in 1985.[72] Using his self-consciously cool persona, the ads used the Hammer to sell an idea of urban sophistication and masculinity. Each spot ends with Williamson reminding the viewer, "Don't let the smooth taste fool you," implicitly suggesting that King Cobra may taste like a regular beer, but it is far more potent.[73]

Williamson became the face of the successful product launch, with King Cobra garnering 9 percent of the malt-liquor market share by 1990, as opposed to the 3 percent share Miller had taken when it introduced its malt liquor Magnum in 1981.[74] More importantly, Williamson's role as the primary spokesperson for King Cobra marked a swift reframing in how brewing companies marketed malt liquor. They shifted from focusing on white middle-class consumers in the 1960s and a multicultural working-class demographic in the 1970s to an exclusively black male target consumer in the late 1980s. Shortly after Williamson's King Cobra ads, Colt 45 turned to Billy Dee Williams, another black film star from the 1970s, with the commercial catchphrase, "Colt 45, works every time," an obvious response to Williamson's ad campaign. In the following years, malt liquor's association with black males and the inner city would become ubiquitous as a part of hip-hop's iconography. Consciously or not, Williamson's work as a pitchman for King Cobra had helped to pave the way.[75]

Finding work in series television and commercials in the United States was only a brief detour in Williamson's career. Returning to Italy, he set about working on films for Po Boy again after a two-year hiatus behind the camera, quickly making two films in less than a year as star, producer, and director. *Foxtrap* (1986) and *The Messenger* (1986) return to the format of his Jesse Crowder films, where he plays private detective types out for revenge.[76] Both films also incorporate his trademark travelogue style, and again Williamson used his own personal travel to add scope and production value to his films. There are scenes filmed in Rome, Cannes, Los Angeles, Las Vegas, and Chicago. The films also contain the other usual trademarks of a Hammer action vehicle, with fights, chase scenes, and sex in abundance.

But Williamson's age (forty-eight at the time) had begun to show. He noticeably struggles to meet the physical demands of his action sequences, slowly climbing over railings and laboring when running. Williamson counters this loss of dynamic physicality with a sense of himself as a man of the world. Whether he is pronouncing Italian words with flair or proving how comfortable he is in the south of France, he becomes in these roles an extension of the debonair man he wanted to be off-camera. The films also strengthen his desire to align his screen persona with Hollywood action-hero norms. The rugged individualism of *The Messenger*, and its clear association with President Ronald Reagan's "War on Drugs" policy, for example, emulates the contemporary action vehicles of Chuck Norris, Charles Bronson, and Sylvester Stallone, giving his Italian production an American ethos that could be sold across the globe in the same fashion as films starring the higher tier of action stars. In this respect, *The Messenger* and *Foxtrap* began the next chapter in Williamson's career—the *Wall Street Journal* called him a "low budget Bronson."[77]

Global audiences, particularly in developing countries, remained extremely loyal to their favorite action stars—including Bronson and others soon to emerge, such as Steven Segal and Jean-Claude Van Damme—while American tastes for their films waned. Williamson was the most prominent black action star to take advantage of this trend. As Spike Lee was changing the landscape for black-focused cinema in the United States with *She's Gotta Have It*, Williamson was separating himself from the construct of African American cinema. "My idea was always that I could bring something to the table and become colorless," he explains. He was striving for the same broad definition in the film industry as he had enjoyed as an athlete and an architect.[78]

Over the last quarter of a century, Williamson has remained as busy as ever. He has directed ten features since *The Messenger*, remaining committed to a vision of himself as a screen hero. He continues to act, both as a low-budget action star and in small supporting roles on television and in film. Williamson continued to work overseas into the mid-1990s, furthering his Hammer persona in films like *Black Cobra* (1987, Stelvio Massi)

Built-in production value. Shooting on location at Cannes in Foxtrap.

and its two sequels.[79] As always, his films were made cheaply, mostly shot in Italian parking garages and shipping docks in the Philippines to pass for an urban New York, Chicago, or Los Angeles. The eventual collapse of the Italian genre film business and the changing climate for independent production (with the burgeoning direct-to-video market and the affordability of shooting on video and digital stock) brought Williamson back to America, where he has continued to direct and star in self-financed action vehicles. He has done some supporting work as an actor in a few mainstream features, making appearances in *From Dusk Till Dawn* (1996, Robert Rodriguez) and *Starsky & Hutch* (2004, Todd Phillips), while also capitalizing on the brief resurgence of interest in blaxploitation stemming from the ghetto action film cycle of the 1990s. *Original Gangstas* (1996), a re-teaming with *Black Caesar* director Larry Cohen that enlisted former blaxploitation stars Jim Brown, Pam Grier, Richard Roundtree, and Ron O'Neal, can be read as the 1990s version of *One Down, Two to Go* in its goals and sentiments.

Williamson continues to sell a mythology about his career, emphasizing his integrity and resourcefulness. Discussing his transition from the US to the Italian film industry, Williamson explained it as follows: "My goal was never to be part of Hollywood, because I knew that Hollywood was not going to let me attain what I called success—let me attain the hype—because I was too far ahead of my time."[80] His ability to sell his films internationally is noteworthy, as they still outpace most films with black stars or themes, and his smooth transition into the direct-to-video market foreshadowed a dominant model of feature production, which for black-themed film moved away from the theatrical focus of the late 1990s toward low-budget video and DVD releases strictly targeted to black consumers.

Williamson's career in the decade following blaxploitation is a mixed bag between determination and compromise. His greatest accomplishment was becoming a self-sufficient actor and director. Williamson is the first to tell someone of his importance and aptitude, remaining a firm believer in his star image: "I'm good at what I do, which is selling me," he said. "If you see a Fred Williamson movie, there ain't gonna be no singing, no dancing, and I'm gonna kick some ass, I'm going to have some pretty ladies, and I'm gonna do my thing and I'm going to ride off in the sunset."[81] To be able to say that thirty years removed from the height of his film career is a testament to his lasting independence and ambition in navigating the film industry.

CHAPTER FIVE

Outside of Society

JAMAA FANAKA, THE LA REBELLION, AND THE COMPLICATIONS OF INDEPENDENT FILMMAKING

In March 2010 at the annual conference of the Society of Cinema and Media Studies in Los Angeles, a panel of black independent filmmakers convened to talk about their work for an audience of scholars. The special session, featuring filmmakers who had come out of the University of California at Los Angeles over the span of two decades—including Charles Burnett, Julie Dash, Billy Woodberry, Barbara McCullough, Zeinabu Davis, and Cauleen Smith—focused on the tradition and legacy of the loose collective that has come to be known as the "LA Rebellion." The panelists shared stories about their time at UCLA, highlighting the shared political and aesthetic spirit that helped to create a body of work operating outside of the commercial film industry. They discussed their own films as well as contributions from other UCLA filmmakers not in attendance, such as Haile Gerima, Larry Clark, Ben Caldwell, Alile Sharon Larkin, and Ntongela Masilela. Gerima was credited as the catalyst for developing something of a unifying philosophy for the group, while Burnett's *Killer of Sheep* (1977) was framed as the LA Rebellion's paramount achievement, having been added to the Library of Congress's registry of historically significant films in 1990. *Killer of Sheep* has also enjoyed a renewed interest with its long-delayed release in theaters and on DVD in 2007. One name that was not mentioned by any of the panelists, moderators, or audience members, however, was Jamaa Fanaka.

Fanaka's connection to the LA Rebellion is at once tenuous and undeniable. He attended UCLA and was in constant contact with Burnett, Gerima, and other members of the group, yet his stylistic sensibilities and approach to the business side of filmmaking have been viewed as a curious side note to the LA Rebellion. While his peers made noncommercial films that explicitly convey revolutionary black politics using formal techniques borrowed from Italian neorealism and Cinema Novo, Fanaka looked to make popular films catering to audiences at single-screen grindhouses and drive-ins. Fanaka found commercial distribution for his films and attempted to make inroads in Hollywood at the same time that his peers at UCLA were trying to distance themselves from the industry. Selling his student films to small commercial distributors, Fanaka took the opposite approach to his classmates. The films made by the LA Rebellion were a conscious counterpoint to the blaxploitation cycle, and Fanaka's commercial ambitions, with his focus on genre films and grindhouse aesthetics, were largely denounced by his peers. His work was seen as apolitical and exploitative, and ultimately as reinforcing the same stereotypes the LA Rebellion was fighting to redress.

But Fanaka's films do not fit easily into any box, as they equally defy the expectations of art-oriented and commercial genre filmmaking. Fanaka is a wholly unique and independent voice whose films found success at the box office while eschewing any semblance of narrative or thematic convention. A number of compelling issues in his work and in the production and exhibition of his films complicate the division between Fanaka and his peers at UCLA, problematizing the usual thinking about the LA Rebellion's approach to making films and conceptualizing audience.

The work of the LA Rebellion is difficult to generalize, as the filmmakers associated with it span decades, nationalities, gender, and filmmaking practices. The work includes everything from features to shorts and documentaries. At the risk of discounting the wide range of work from black directors at UCLA, one can start with the assertion that Fanaka's career is best understood alongside the handful of LA Rebellion filmmakers who were able to complete full-length narrative features in the 1970s and 1980s. This list is regrettably short, consisting of Haile Gerima, Charles Burnett, Larry Clark, and Billy Woodberry. Ultimately, these four filmmakers have made a handful of visually and politically intriguing films that few people have seen. Scholars and critics often view their work through the lens of textual analysis, paying scant attention to the contradictions of a revolutionary cinema that failed to find an audience outside of academics and cinephiles. While the LA Rebellion attempted to function outside of the film industry, it also failed to create an innovative or creative mode of distribution or exhibition. Their films have played at film festivals, university film societies, and community centers, but have been absent from first-run theaters, television, and mainstream video stores.

The LA Rebellion's roots lie in the late 1960s, when affirmative-action legislation began dramatically altering the makeup of college campuses, opening doors for black students and furthering a move toward the establishment of black studies departments. Informed by Black Power politics and cultural outgrowths like the Black Arts movement, as well as popular expressions of dissent through black musical idioms, literature, and theater, the students at UCLA looked toward cinema as their own mode of expression. Of course, what ends up on the screen is only part of the equation, as cinema is a troublesome medium for unfettered expression. Capital-intensive and largely profit-driven, cinema requires not only financial investment just to get a film made, but also a certain level of cooperation and mutual interest on the part of distributors and exhibitors to locate an audience.

The arrival of the group of young black filmmakers at UCLA coincided with the film industry's noticeable shift in its level of investment and interest in black-oriented cinema. The handful of Sidney Poitier vehicles being produced and the occasional independent feature made by white liberals (*Nothing But a Man*, *Putney Swope*, etc.) gave way to the full-blown explosion of blaxploitation. Many of the UCLA filmmakers, with Gerima being the most vocal, fell into the same camp as an older generation of the black middle class and black intellectuals who took offense at Hollywood's images of blackness and formed groups like the Coalition Against Blaxploitation. The LA Rebellion may have been informed by a different set of political and aesthetic concerns, but its proponents were equally suspicious of the blaxploitation cycle's output.

Rather than using film school as a springboard into Hollywood, the LA Rebellion found the black-focused features coming from Hollywood in the 1970s to be little improvement over the industry's previous exclusionary practices. Noting the lack of serious political discourse and the oversaturation of "negative" stereotypes within blaxploitation films, the members of the LA Rebellion looked to make films wholly separate from the mainstream. They therefore worked outside of traditional channels of financing and distribution and adopted a unique film language and aesthetics. As Ed Guerrero put it, "the 'black independent cinema movement' inspired by the films of university-trained black filmmakers of the 1970s laid a clear political, philosophical, and aesthetic foundation for an ongoing cinematic practice that challenges Hollywood's hegemony over the black image."[1] With a political point of view framed by the writings of Frantz Fanon and Amilcar Cabral, the LA Rebellion conceived the plight of African Americans along the lines of colonialism rather than in terms of legal and cultural marginalization. Gerima, for example, argued that filmmakers of African descent should refrain from using the language of the colonizers in their films.[2] In turn, the LA Rebellion filmmakers conceptualized the classic Hollywood narrative style as inherently hegemonic; in their effort to make truly revolutionary films, they chose to draw from other cinematic traditions.

Film scholar Clyde Taylor, summing up the legacy of the LA Rebellion, said that "what separates the new black cinema from these other episodes [Hollywood depictions, race films, blaxploitation] is its freedom from the mental colonization that Hollywood tries to impose on all its audiences, black and white."[3] Here, the use of the word "colonization" is important. Taylor was reflecting the rhetoric of Gerima, who sees African Americans as an internal colony within the United States and looks beyond the state apparatus to conceive colonization in terms of cultural and psychological control. The LA Rebellion merged American black nationalism with the brand of revolutionary national culture that Cabral and Fanon called for in Africa, attempting to engage a black audience, activists, and filmmakers in a collaborative political project. Seeing mainstream American cinema as a cultural and economic extension of white supremacy, the UCLA filmmakers attempted to function outside of the realm of the film industry, designing new distribution and exhibition practices that would bypass Hollywood altogether and revolutionize long-established social practices.

The conviction and sincerity of the LA Rebellion artists is admirable, but their decision to make films outside of established production and distribution norms limited their access to black spectators and made the task of making a living as filmmakers next to impossible. Gerima managed to complete four narrative features in the span of a decade, beginning with *Child of Resistance* (1972), which was followed by *Bush Mama* (1975), *Harvest 3000 Years* (1975), and *Ashes and Embers* (1982).[4] *Bush Mama* solidifies a number of the key elements of the LA Rebellion's aesthetic trademarks, from its nonlinear storytelling to a performance and visual style indebted to the Italian neorealists. Moreover, Clyde Taylor refers to *Bush Mama* as a "recoding" of Hollywood narrative conventions, which in this case brings to mind *Claudine* (1974, John Berry), Twentieth Century Fox's drama about a down-and-out welfare mother.[5] Seven years later, *Ashes and Embers* would recode Hollywood films like *Coming Home* (1978, Hal Ashby) and *The Deer Hunter* (1978, Michael Cimino), focusing on a Vietnam veteran suffering from posttraumatic stress disorder. Gerima's ambitions were tempered by his difficulty finding an audience outside of the festival and film society circuits, despite his efforts to take control of the distribution of LA Rebellion films by founding Mypheduh Films.

Limited audiences and the ongoing struggle to secure financing were problems shared by Charles Burnett. Although Burnett's first feature, *Killer of Sheep*, has grown in stature over the years, his approach and the distribution limitations under Mypheduh relegated the film to a select audience of cinephiles and academics. Although the film traveled internationally to festivals, and has been continually cited by critics and scholars as one of the most important independent films in the history of American cinema, it remained largely unknown and out of reach for American audiences. Instead, it became what the *New York Times* would call "an object of cinephilic fetishism."[6] Seen only in festivals and film societies initially, *Killer of Sheep* established its reputation despite a scarcity of prints and the lack of an official home video release, with bootleg VHS copies circulating among film buffs and academics. Possibilities for a commercial release, of course, were hampered by Burnett's use of popular music throughout the film without licensing the rights. Burnett's second feature, *My Brother's Wedding* (1983), was even more challenging, had even more limited screenings, and lacked the groundswell of critical praise that accompanied *Killer of Sheep*.

Billy Woodberry's *Bless Their Little Hearts* (1984), which Burnett wrote and served on as cinematographer, mirrors other LA Rebellion films. Stylistically, it borrows from neorealism to capture the struggle and emotion of family life in the Los Angeles neighborhood of Watts. As far as exhibition of the completed film, *Bless Their Little Hearts* never transitioned past a limited scholarly audience with Mypheduh distribution. The intention was never to find commercial success with these films, but at the same time there was a failure to reach the black working-class audience that served as the focal point for LA Rebellion narratives.

Perhaps no filmmaker symbolizes the LA Rebellion's problematic approach to finding an audience and securing financing as much as Larry Clark. His ambitious feature debut *Passing Through* (1979) plays with form and narrative, dealing explicitly with the plight of a black artist within the white-controlled entertainment industry. The movie centers on jazz saxophonist Warmack (Nathaniel Taylor) as he attempts to cut a record after he is released from prison, balancing aspects of African spirituality with Warmack's self-discovery with a pointed social critique on race and class in America. The film uses experimental formal techniques (for example, fish-eye lenses and abstract superimpositions) and didactic dialogue about art and politics while also retaining a somewhat formulaic storyline, which shows Warmack violently overcoming white gangsters in a plot device not very far removed from blaxploitation tropes. Warmack's attempts to retain personal and artistic integrity as a musician, and break free of the white-dominated record industry, set up the film's central conflict, which is eventually settled in the final reel with black musicians jumping out of a parked van, brandishing shotguns, to murder a group of white record executives.

Using an anticolonial framework to engage black/white relationships in America, Clark's film is an evocative and exaggerated take on racial oppression and revolution. It articulates the rationale of the LA Rebellion and its refusal to work within the confines of Hollywood. As presented in *Passing Through*, Warmack's only choices are to work within the record industry, where he will be financially exploited and forced to make artistically compromised music, or to break free from the structural confines of commercial entertainment by any means necessary.

Clark's decision to work outside of the realm of the commercial film industry lies somewhere between personal choice and political imperative, depending on how his career is interpreted. Either way, the limited access to prints of *Passing Through*—and the decades it took for Clark to finish his second feature, *Cutting Horse* (2002)—make Clark's career emblematic of the LA Rebellion's untenable philosophy. *Passing Through*, like the work of his peers at UCLA, was funded through various grants, including money from the National Endowment for the Arts (NEA) that was being administered by the American Film Institute (AFI). A year before completing the film, Clark had interned at the AFI as part of a program that placed aspiring young directors on the set of a feature film, where they could learn filmmaking firsthand from an established professional. Clark was assigned to one of the few studio productions with a black director, interning with Michael Schultz on *Sgt. Pepper's Lonely Hearts Club Band*.[7] Oddly enough, Clark would transition from working on one of the most commercially inclined projects ever directed by an African American (and one premised on its close ties to the record industry) to making his own film rejecting the arrangement of black artists and white business interests. An even starker irony is that *Passing Through* is cowritten by the actor and poet Ted Lange, who had transitioned from a handful of small roles in film and television to begin a decade-long run playing Isaac the bartender on the television series *The Love Boat*. *Passing Through* was partly created by the uncompromising Clark, while at the same time it was conceived by one of the most visible, mainstream, and nonthreatening black performers of the era.

Since the film's release, Clark has had closely guarded access to prints of *Passing Through*. It shows up on rare occasions in retrospectives, but has never been made available on VHS or DVD; it has also remained largely absent from the bootleg network of fans and scholars. Instead of searching for a wider audience, like most filmmakers, Clark has consciously taken *Passing Through* out of circulation. As early as 1984 he expressed his intention to have the film recede into memory, stating, "When I make my next film, *Passing Through* will go into the closet and you'll never see it again."[8] If Clark wished to enhance the film's reputation by making it scarce, taking a reproducible medium and treating it like more traditional art objects, he has most certainly succeeded. The separation between the scholars who have mentioned Clark's work in writing and the people who have actually seen *Passing Through* is precariously close. Like Gerima, Burnett, and Woodberry, Clark has rejected popular genre tropes and commercial exhibition strategies, making his work appeal to scholars and cinephiles, but failed to reach a wide audience, as *Passing Through* is otherwise unknown and unavailable.

JAMAA FANAKA

Jamaa Fanaka's work as a director shows an alternative route for independent filmmaking. Unlike his classmates at UCLA, Fanaka has unapologetically expressed his love for Hollywood films. Rather than willfully opposing the stylistic and economic construct of Hollywood and remaining a perpetual outsider, he has been intent on creating opportunities within the industry. Fanaka was known to have prolonged arguments and debates with Gerima about everything from film form to how a black artist should engage the business side of filmmaking.[9] Nevertheless, Fanaka remained an integral part of UCLA's growing collective of black film students, working alongside his peers as both a friend and an equal. As Fanaka remembers, "We didn't always agree, but we always supported each other."[10] His career is both a counterpoint to the LA Rebellion and an extension of their revolutionary project, expressing an uncompromising vision of blackness on screen while also remaining mindful of audience and box-office dollars. Rather than reflecting the outside-looking-in approach that makes so many films about black urban subjects read like anthropological surveys, Fanaka's films are infused with a first-person perspective rooted in what he calls "'hood life."[11]

Fanaka was born Walter Gordon on September 6, 1942, in Jackson, Mississippi, the only child of Robert and Beatrice Gordon. The family moved to Los Angeles in the 1950s, and Walter was given a Super 8 camera when he was eleven, which he used to document family life, weddings, birthdays, and trips to Disneyland. Part of the second Great Migration that saw blacks move from the American South to urban areas in the North and West, the Gordons arrived in Southern California looking for new opportunities. As Walter entered adulthood, however, South Central Los Angeles was becoming emblematic of the growing divide between white opportunity and unemployment for African Americans. The mood of despair and tension that arose in the era would culminate with the Watts rebellion in the summer of 1965.[12] Lacking opportunities, Walter joined the US Air Force, fulfilling his enlistment only to return to Los Angeles and run afoul of the law, serving a bid in the county jail for just under a year.[13] Back on the streets of South Central, Walter was again faced with limited opportunities and was tempted by friends to make ends meet outside of the law.

Fanaka talks of a life-changing experience he had that came through something resembling divine intervention. On his way to join his friends for a robbery, he saw a sign in a store window advertising opportunities for black students to attend UCLA. Instead of joining his friends, Walter traveled across town to the Westwood campus, met with an admissions officer, and charted a plan for attending college. Utilizing the benefits of the GI Bill that he had earned from his service in the Air Force, Walter attended Compton College for two years to become eligible for UCLA, eventually transferring as a junior. Having a lifelong interest in moviemaking, Walter sought out film courses in the theater and arts program once he arrived at the university. His story is a remarkable one, predicated on expanded opportunities through affirmative-action legislation and the transformation of American universities in the late 1960s and 1970s. Not simply a Horatio Alger myth, Fanaka's success was more than hard work and a can-do attitude. It was dependent on federally mandated and subsidized opportunities.

Walter's ambition set him apart from other undergraduates at UCLA. In a film production course, he was assigned to make a "project two," which usually consisted of a five- to ten-minute short subject, with the option to use synchronous sound. Either through naïveté or supreme self-confidence, Walter decided to shoot a full-length narrative feature instead. Financed with his parents' life savings, which was spent mostly on 16 mm stock, the finished product was *Welcome Home Brother Charles* (1975), one of the most comically audacious films of the era. Eventually it would make the unlikely transition from being an undergraduate class project to earning theatrical distribution. With a bare-bones budget, Walter had enlisted the help of friends, family, and classmates to make the film. His mother handled craft services, his father scouted filming locations around Los Angeles, and upperclassmen at UCLA lent their technical know-how to the project. Ben Caldwell provided still photography for a key montage sequence, while Charles Burnett operated the camera and helped with the cinematography.

The film tells the story of Charles Murray, a low-level street hustler castrated by a dementedly racist white police officer during an arrest. In prison, Charles receives surgery to reattach his severed penis, and he returns from his three years behind bars intent on turning his life around. However, he is still haunted by the violence he experienced at the hands of the police officer and the failure of the justice system to recognize his suffering. Charles vows to get back at the police officer, the prosecutor, and the judge who were responsible for his arrest and conviction, laying out a plan to systematically exact vengeance. While this revenge fantasy may not have been far removed from other blaxploitation films, Charles's method for killing is wholly unique. Though the mechanism is never fully explained, somehow in the process of the medical procedures that Charles underwent to reattach his sexual organ, his penis has gained mystical powers, so that it is able to grow to enormous lengths at will. He uses his sexual prowess to romance his enemies' wives, who are in turn hypnotized by Charles's powers in bed and help him corner their husbands. With a wife watching excitedly, Charles removes his pants, concentrates with an intense rage, and expands his penis over twenty feet in length to strangle his white male adversary. Ultimately, Charles's killing spree comes to an end, and he jumps to his death when cornered on a rooftop rather than return to prison. The ending is accompanied by a curious postscript, reading, "Let them indulge in their pride if thinking I am destroyed is a comfort to them; let it be."

The specifics of the plot are sometimes hard to follow, but the pacing of the film is vibrant and its over-the-top humor is blended with points of sincerity. Fanaka touches on a wide range of topics and themes. Focusing on the mythology of black male sexuality, he takes the phallus-obsessed poster art from the blaxploitation era to new levels by literally placing the hypersexualized black character's power in his penis. He also tackles the problem of police brutality, articulating an ongoing tension between the black community and the Los Angeles Police Department in an otherwise forgotten era situated midway between the Watts rebellion and the Rodney King uprising. At the same time, the psycho-sexual nature of Charles's surgery and his being used as a medical case study for the state evokes the Tuskegee syphilis experiments, which had come to public attention in 1972. These layers of meaning show Fanaka to be a politically concerned filmmaker, even if his mode of expression is comedic and exaggerated.

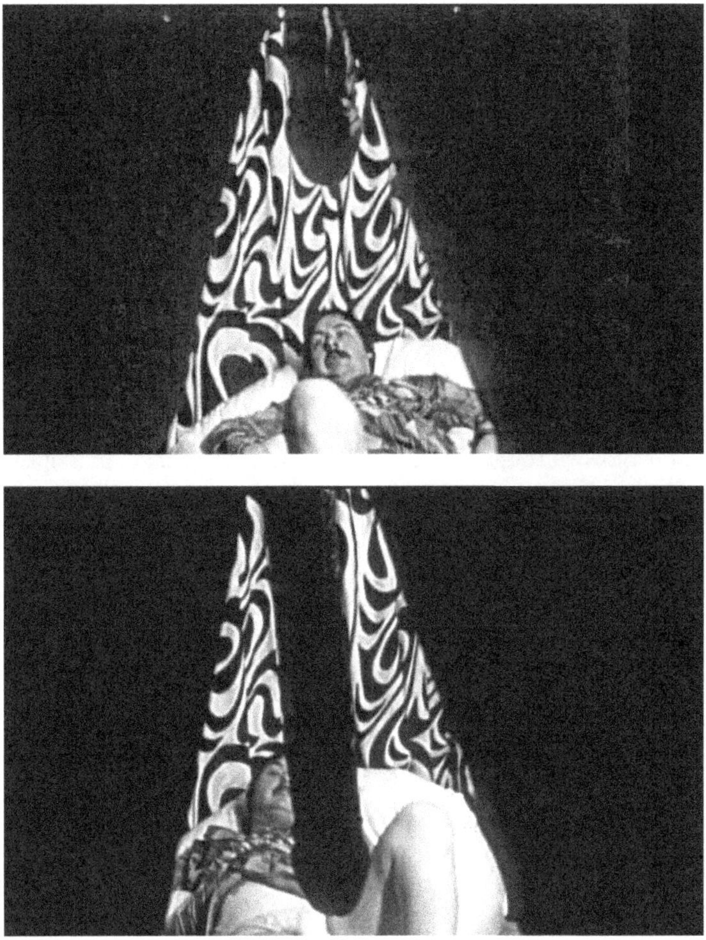

The expanding phallus as weapon in Welcome Home Brother Charles.

With a full-length feature complete, Walter decided to hit the streets of Hollywood to look for a company to distribute *Welcome Home Brother Charles*. It was also around this time that he decided to change his name to Jamaa Fanaka. In Swahili, *jamaa* means community and togetherness, while *fanaka* means success and progress. With this change he signaled his intention to take on virtues that he hoped to embody both personally and professionally: it was as much about self-actualization as it was about avoiding the kind of racial ambiguity he found in Michael Schultz's *Cooley High*. As Jamaa Fanaka, he found addresses for distribution companies in trade papers and phone books and showed up unannounced at the companies with film cans in hand. When he arrived at the Beverly Hills offices of

Crown International Pictures, a low-budget distribution house that dealt in exploitation and grindhouse features (as well as an importer for Asian martial arts films), the secretary called back to the president's office, telling him, "There's a black guy here with a film."[14]

Intrigued by Fanaka's audacity and outgoing personality, Crown's president, Mark Tenser, had a formal meeting and screened *Welcome Home Brother Charles* that day.[15] Tenser was looking for a black-focused feature, having been late to the trend. He had recently missed out on the chance to distribute the Rudy Ray Moore action-comedy *Dolemite* (1975, D'Urville Martin), which was instead picked up by Dimension Pictures, a rival low-budget drive-in-oriented outfit that had shifted to black-focused features in 1975.[16] Although *Welcome Home Brother Charles* was a student film, and an undergraduate effort at that, Fanaka's brief tenure in film school gave him a formal foundation that was more than equal to that of the directors who were working on the majority of independent blaxploitation-era productions. With tax credits and risk-free investments often opening doors to novice filmmakers, Fanaka's utilization of tracking shots and expressive editing made *Welcome Home Brother Charles* stand out from other low-budget features.

The film was far from a runaway hit, but its small budget was easily recouped at the box office. The audacity of the project helped Fanaka get accepted into the master of fine arts production program at UCLA. With bolstered confidence, he wasted no time in beginning work on his thesis film. Completed less than a year after *Welcome Home Brother Charles* hit theaters, his second feature, *Emma Mae*, shows Fanaka's improvement as a writer, director, and editor, as well as the benefits of an expanded budget, which totaled $272,000.[17] Using their profits from *Welcome Home Brother Charles*, his parents once again helped finance the film, receiving credit on the film as Bob-Bea Productions. Additional financing came from an AFI grant. During the application process Fanaka thought his chances were limited, because the AFI's selection committee was all white, but surprisingly, he was awarded a production grant and invited to serve on the selection panel the following year, where he helped push through the grant proposal that financed Larry Clark's *Passing Through*.

The story of *Emma Mae* revolves around the titular character, a young black woman from "down South" who comes to Los Angeles to live with her aunt and uncle. Drawing from his own fish-out-of-water experience moving from Mississippi as a child, Fanaka conceptualizes urban migration from a female perspective. The depiction is informed by aspects of second-wave feminism as well as by contemporary black female screen heroines such as Pam Grier and Tamara Dobson. Emma wears fashions rooted in the 1950s, with a yellow Sunday dress and her hair in a perm. Her cultural differences shine through when her cousins are forced to take her along for a night out with friends. But her time as social outcast is short lived, as she wins over her cousins and their friends with her toughness and down-home wisdom.

Emma then begins to date a low-level street hustler named Jesse, but he runs afoul of the law, gets roughed up by the police, and gets thrown in jail. Angry over Jesse's arrest, Emma takes up his cause and becomes a community activist, raising money for his legal defense and proselytizing to her peers with vaguely revolutionary rhetoric. Along the way, she sheds the outer trappings of her southern identity. A key scene with her hairdresser aunt shows Emma ditching her perm in favor of an African head wrap. When Emma's attempts at legally raising money operating a car wash are shut down by local authorities, she gathers a group of friends to rob a bank to raise the rest of the legal fees, only to have Jesse cheat on her and become physically threatening once he is released. No longer willing to be passive, Emma attacks Jesse, exacting her revenge by repeatedly punching him in the crotch. She then delivers a speech about missed opportunities and the need for black communities to cut themselves free of gang members.

Contrasting the rural South with the urban West Coast, *Emma Mae* forms a cultural exchange where ideas of a broader black community are explored and a united political awakening is proposed. Emma's mantra, "Back home we got one rule. Family gotta stick together," is meant to bridge divides within black America, be they geographic, generational, or cultural. Like *Welcome Home Brother Charles*, *Emma Mae* has a plot that is sometimes difficult to follow. Like Fred Williamson's films, Fanaka's films contain hollow, meandering moments that defy screenwriting rules insisting that each scene should forward the narrative. These flaws are complicated by Fanaka's sense of moral ambiguity, as there is no clear sense of right and wrong, or good and bad. Jesse's criminality is alternately excused and demonized, leaving the final speech about community somewhat shapeless and confused. *Emma Mae* nevertheless provides a unique insight into the black urban experience, showing the "other LA" that Burnett's *Killer of Sheep* is often lauded for capturing. Fanaka again found a small distributor to release his film theatrically, this time PRO International Pictures. *Emma Mae* had a modest run in theaters, as had *Welcome Home Brother Charles*, but the low budget helped the film turn a profit.

LOCK UP

Emma Mae fulfilled the program requirements for Fanaka's master's degree, and he was eligible to receive his MFA, but instead of graduating, he chose to hold on to his student status, despite the fact that he was no longer taking courses. Although he had directed two theatrically distributed features as a student, the end of the blaxploitation cycle had dried up financing options in Hollywood for his next film, *Penitentiary* (1979). By technically remaining a student, he was able to use the facilities at UCLA on his next project, which he would have to fully finance personally. But as he was able to use cameras, tracking gear, and lighting equipment from UCLA, all Fanaka had to pay for were the actors, the crew, and the film stock. Fanaka cut corners on locations by turning the back of UCLA's Melnitz Hall into a makeshift prison yard, and he recycled musical elements from *Welcome Home Brother Charles*. The rest of the score was composed without any upfront costs by Frankie Gaye, the brother of superstar singer Marvin Gaye. Again, Robert and Beatrice Gordon financed the film, dipping further into their savings and using the little money they had earned from *Welcome Home Brother Charles* and *Emma Mae*.

Fanaka's goal for his third film was to step up the level of distribution by targeting major studios. His approach, as he saw it in 1978, was to "make low budget, high quality films." As he explained to *Jet* magazine, "the major studios don't want to put up any front money. But if you can get enough money to make a first print, you can then take it to a major studio for possible financing."[18] Fanaka was able to secure a line of credit that ultimately pushed the budget to around $100,000 and allowed him to use postproduction facilities at MGM, but he was unable to convince a studio to distribute his film.[19] He shopped his film to minor distributors next, finally reaching a deal with Jerry Gross, a renowned promoter and distributor of exploitation and drive-in films who had released *Sweet Sweetback's Baadasssss Song* in 1971 while at Cinemation. Now he had his own company, and the first release for the Jerry Gross Organization would be *Penitentiary*.

Surprisingly, perhaps to everyone except for Jamaa Fanaka, *Penitentiary* was a breakout hit at the box office, picking up momentum through word of mouth after its limited release in December 1979. Making its way to new cities throughout 1980, the film ended up earning $7.4 million at the box office, becoming the highest-grossing independent feature of the year.[20] The success of *Penitentiary* outpaced Jerry Gross's previous success in the realm of black-focused features—Melvin Van Peebles's *Sweetback*—

Too Sweet (Leon Isaac Kennedy) fights Half Dead (Badja Djola) in Penitentiary.

in terms of cost-to-profit ratio. *Sweetback* grossed a remarkable twenty dollars for every single dollar spent on production, while Fanaka's film earned money at a clip of seventy-four to one. Like *Sweetback*, *Penitentiary* arrived at a historic low point in black representation in American cinema: Richard Pryor's costarring role in *Stir Crazy* was the only feature film released in 1980 to have an African American in a leading role. *Stir Crazy* and *Penitentiary* have interesting parallels, since both depict prison life and athletic competition among inmates, but they are vastly different in tone and audience. *Stir Crazy* consciously courted a crossover crowd, while *Penitentiary* aimed to meet the needs of underserved black male spectators. While the void in black representation may help explain *Penitentiary*'s success at the box office, the film's grim depiction of prison life and bizarre tone hardly made it a natural fit for a wide audience.

The basic premise of *Penitentiary* is standard enough, with a wrongfully convicted man forced to serve hard time, but the contours of the film quickly deviate from the standard prison picture. The film opens on a desert highway, with Vietnam veteran Martel "Too Sweet" Gordon (Leon Isaac Kennedy) hitchhiking to Los Angeles. After a brief romance with a truck-driving prostitute, Too Sweet gets into a fight with two white bikers while trying to defend her honor. Getting knocked unconscious in the melee, Too Sweet wakes up to find that one of the bikers is dead and he is charged and convicted of the murder. He's sent to a maximum-security prison and lands on a cellblock controlled by a gang of violent sexual predators, led by the cunning Big Jess (Donovan Womack) and muscle-bound Half Dead (Badja Djola). When Too Sweet arrives, he is placed in a cell with Half Dead, who tries to "break in" Too Sweet by attempting rape. In a long and brutal fight sequence, Too Sweet fights back, eventually knocking out Half Dead and retaining his dignity. After the jail cell battle with Half Dead, the film takes a detour as Too Sweet is recruited to participate in a prison boxing tournament. He gains his freedom after winning against Big Jess in the climactic bout and is released into the care of the warden's brother, a boxing promoter.

What separates *Penitentiary* from other prison films from the era, such as *Brothers* (1977, Arthur Barron) and *Short Eyes* (1977, Robert M. Young), is that it makes no effort to convey a didactic message about the prison system. Departing from any attempt at strict cinematic realism, Fanaka's style as a director is expressive, with stark lighting setups, attention-grabbing tracking shots, and fast-paced editing that defy the seamless, invisible style of most Hollywood films. Fanaka also uses expressive double-dolly shots with characters in close-up, creating the impression of floating through time and space with a technique that would later become a stylistic calling card of Spike Lee. Nevertheless, *Penitentiary* captures the idea of "the real" by locating a primary fear of incarceration, coupling violence and sex to create a space where heterosexuality is under attack both literally and metaphorically.

The film's preoccupation with male rape, as well as the textures and levels of homosexual activity in prison, provide a far from simplistic view of masculinity and sexuality behind bars. Fanaka finds a way to bypass judgment while at the same time allowing for contrasting points of view from openly flamboyant homosexuals, defiantly homophobic straight men, victimized straight men, and characters who think of themselves as straight but use sex with other men both as a tool of power and as a substitute for denied heterosexual outlets. This last point is best exemplified in the moments before Half Dead attacks Too Sweet, as he psyches himself up for the moment by looking at nude pictorials in *Players* magazine. Fanaka's preoccupation with sexuality is central to the entire film: the promise of conjugal visits motivates the boxers, and sexual liaisons with visiting female prisoners are intercut with each boxing match. Sex and violence are thus portrayed as being inherently connected within prison walls. Of course, sexuality is not the only component of the film. *Penitentiary* is nominally a boxing film, with the prerequisite training montage and climactic showdown in the ring. The film also attempts to articulate the personal and spiritual struggles of life behind bars. Too Sweet's elderly mentor, Seldom Seen (Floyd Chatman), is a wise lifer who delivers a heartfelt speech about becoming institutionalized; his years in prison have stripped him of any desire to rejoin the outside world.

Much of the film's success at the box office rested on the performance of Leon Isaac Kennedy as Too Sweet. Kennedy conveys an easy charisma and has an impressive physique. He moved from his native Cleveland to Los Angeles in the early 1970s with his wife, Jayne, a former Miss Ohio and aspiring actress, and both of them were intent on breaking into the movie business.[21] He started working as a disc jockey and nightclub promoter, rubbing elbows and making connections before landing a small role in Fred Williamson's *Mean Johnny Barrows*, which allowed Kennedy to get a Screen Actors Guild card.[22] He then landed a small role as a villain in the *Fighting Mad* (1978, Cirio H. Santiago), a Philippines-US coproduction starring blaxploitation action star James Iglehart that also features Kennedy's wife as the primary love interest. Kennedy accepted his first leading role in *Penitentiary* as a springboard for future projects—he wanted to become a mainstream star. After the film's success, Fanaka began developing a follow-up project and enjoyed his newfound celebrity. He went to parties with the likes of Stevie Wonder, Marvin Gaye, and Robert DeNiro. Kennedy, meanwhile, acted fast to capitalize on his sudden stardom.[23]

While Leon Isaac Kennedy's star was rising, Jayne's modeling career began to take off. She appeared on a number of magazine covers before becoming a sportscaster on CBS's *The NFL Today*, starred in her own aerobics video, and appeared as a spokesperson for the diet soft drink Tab. After only a few years in Los Angeles, the fortunes of the Kennedys were expanding. Leon, continuing his attempt to transition from his independent success in *Penitentiary* into more mainstream films, wrote the screenplay for the remake of *Body and Soul* (1981, George Bowers), hoping for an opportunity to play the role made famous by John Garfield in Robert Rossen's 1947 original. Kennedy ended up co-producing the film, which was released by the Cannon Group, along with Cannon's owners Menahem Golan and Yoram Globus.

The Israeli cousins had purchased the company in 1979 and were still developing a strategy for the studio's releases. In 1980, the studio showed a brief interest in developing black-focused features, announcing two projects in October, beginning with *The Dorothy Dandridge Story*, which was to be produced by Leon Isaac Kennedy and would star Jayne in the title role. Veteran director John Berry, who had made *Claudine* (1974), was attached to the project as well. The second black-focused feature announced by Cannon was based on Oscar Williams's screenplay *Harvest of Fear*, with Michael Schultz slated to direct.[24] Neither project came to fruition, leaving Cannon still attempting to conceive a project that could tap into Kennedy's previous success and broader industry trends. In *Body and Soul*, Kennedy turns the hard-nosed boxer protagonist—who did not stray far from Too Sweet, Kennedy's role in *Penitentiary*—into a smooth and confident ladies' man, imaging himself as an ideal of black upward mobility.

The budget on *Body and Soul* far outpaced that of *Penitentiary*, and the tone and filmic style were aligned with mainstream genre pictures. It pulled heavily from renewed interest in boxing films after the success of *Rocky* (1976, John G. Avildsen).[25] The film strives to be uplifting and even features a small role for Muhammad Ali, who plays himself as he helps Kennedy's character train for the big fight. *Body and Soul* gives the impression of Kennedy shifting the benefits of *Penitentiary*'s success onto himself, building his own career and leaving Fanaka behind, but the two would reconvene the following year and make another film together.

Kennedy reprised his role as Too Sweet in *Penitentiary II* (1982), but the similarities between *Body and Soul* and Fanaka's sequel deflated most of the anticipation. Making matters more frustrating for Fanaka, he was still unable to gain traction within the film industry in terms of financing, despite the incredible success of *Penitentiary*, although he had received a number of offers from talent agents who promised to get him deals with the studios. Perhaps drawing from a shared ideology with the LA Rebellion, Fanaka refused offers from talent agencies and chose to remain independent and continue representing himself instead. Whether or not an agent could have secured a deal in the early 1980s for a black director with such an offbeat body of work is debatable, but Fanaka proved unable to sell himself to major studios. With exploitation studios and distributors increasingly going out of business, he was lucky enough to secure a distribution deal with United Artists for *Penitentiary II*, but Fanaka failed to get any money up front to cover the production costs.

Unlike his peers in the LA Rebellion, Fanaka openly admired Hollywood filmmakers and wanted to carve out a niche for himself within the film industry. He desired the financing and distribution machinery of the studios as well as the prestige of being a mainstream director. He eventually gained access to the distribution reach of a major, but he had to self-finance his film. Fanaka therefore again directed a Bob-Bea Production that was dependent on his parents' money. The earnings from *Penitentiary* afforded Fanaka a much larger budget for the sequel, but the infrastructure of a studio was not at his disposal. *Penitentiary II* was a better-funded independent effort than *Penitentiary*, but it still lacked the polish of a mainstream film.

Penitentiary II may not look like a Hollywood film, but the thematic arc of the story certainly speaks to a shared desire on the part of Jamaa Fanaka and Leon Isaac Kennedy to embody a more dominant ideology of financial aspiration and middle-class bliss. Rather than being set exclusively on the cellblock, *Penitentiary II* mostly places its action outside of the prison, only returning briefly for a contrived climax. Beginning two years after Too Sweet's release from prison (explained with a scrolling prologue in a style lifted from *Star Wars*), the film follows his quick rise in the boxing world to a championship contender. With the help of his lawyer sister and her husband, Too Sweet begins training hard and developing his celebrity persona outside of the ring. The goal, as stated by his brother-in-law (Glynn Turman), is to "make Too Sweet too rich."

Half Dead (now played by Ernie Hudson) escapes from prison and begins to hunt Too Sweet and his family, swearing vengeance after being defeated in the first film. More preposterously, Too Sweet also has to return to prison to fight Big Jess in a pair of televised championship bouts. Here the film departs from any sense of reality, imagining a boxing world where prison bouts are televised: holders of the title belt are serving life sentences, but still competing professionally. Too Sweet wins the climactic fight, against all odds, while the members of his entourage (led by Mr. T) take out Half Dead and his henchmen.

The dramatic thrust of the first film is largely absent from *Penitentiary II*. Financial accumulation and domestic bliss take the place of survival, pride, and vengeance as key themes. The sexual tension is also absent, with Too Sweet's cultivation of a ladies' man persona moving the film toward more traditional heteronormative concepts. The two boxing matches are again intercut with the sexual pursuits of prisoners, but this time they are comic relief: a dwarf (Tony Cox), for example, negotiates with a prostitute at ringside.

The most compelling aspects of *Penitentiary II* are often fleeting or contextual. By incorporating brief cameos from former light heavyweight champion Archie Moore and comedian Rudy Ray Moore, Fanaka advances a more standard boxing formula while keeping a blaxploitation-era star in the spotlight. *Penitentiary II* also marks the film debut of Mr. T, who would become a pop culture sensation following his appearance in *Rocky III* a month later.[26] Fanaka's use of music in the film is also notable: a performance from the R&B group Klique and scenes of Too Sweet roller skating and dancing at Venice Beach underscore a tension between the demise of disco in the early 1980s and the efforts of some African Americans to keep the genre alive. These scenes bring out the largely racist and homophobic undercurrents of the disco backlash among white tastemakers. In a more direct use of music to articulate a black cultural and political perspective, two women sing "Lift Every Voice and Sing" during the pre-fight ceremonies of the climactic bout, with the ring announcer introducing the song simply as "the national anthem." Instead of using "The Star-Spangled Banner," Fanaka inserted James Weldon Johnson's composition as an unapologetic assertion of black identity and collective pride. "Lift Every Voice" had become the official song of the NAACP in the 1920s, and it has often been referred to as the "Black National Anthem."[27]

Fanaka's second pairing with Leon Isaac Kennedy failed to equal the success of its predecessor, but thanks to a small budget, its box-office gross of over $3 million kept the film profitable.[28] Hoping to move past the *Penitentiary* films, Fanaka announced in early 1984 that he was starting work on a new film called *Street Wars*, based on his original screenplay. *Street Wars* was slated to be financed by the small studio and distributor Arista Films, which was modeled on 1970s exploitation-era companies, but nothing ever materialized.[29]

As Fanaka struggled to get his next project made, Kennedy saw his once-promising career take a downturn. He and Jayne Kennedy divorced in 1982. Considering Jayne's popularity and wholesome image, the divorce certainly hurt the public's perception of the less famous Leon. He exacerbated the controversy by releasing a sex tape of the couple after their split, supposedly to cause his ex embarrassment.[30] Kennedy landed supporting roles in the Chuck Norris action film *Lone Wolf McQuade* (1983, Steve Carver) and the slasher flick *Too Scared to Scream* (1985, Tony Lo Bianco), but these jobs were a step backward for him. Hoping to take control of his career, he co-produced and wrote the original screenplay for his first starring role since working with Fanaka, *Knights of the City* (1986, Dominic Orlando). A low-budget action film and musical about street gangs, it rehashes some of the cleaned-up hip-hop sensibilities of the *Breakin'* films a few years earlier, featuring cameos from the Fat Boys and Kurtis Blow, but is otherwise out of step with youth culture. The film failed to revive its star's lagging career. It was beset by problems during production, and Kennedy is almost laughable as the slick gang leader in the film.[31]

Fanaka's inability to locate financing for *Street Wars*, coupled with Kennedy's fading fortunes as an actor, made their reunion for *Penitentiary III* (1987) inevitable. This time around, Fanaka and Kennedy produced the film together, with the credits saying the film was a "Jamaa-Leon Production." The film received additional financing and distribution from Cannon.[32] The budget for *Penitentiary III*, while never disclosed, was likely equal to or greater than all four of Fanaka's previous films combined. It has a bright, professional, glossy look that starkly contrasts with the gritty, sometimes cobbled together aesthetic of his other films. Cannon not only helped Fanaka secure his most sizable budget to date, but also provided professional crew members to work alongside holdovers from the first two *Penitentiary* films. But even with Cannon overseeing shooting and Kennedy playing a greater role as a co-producer, *Penitentiary III* remained Fanaka's film.

Despite a few compromises in casting and Cannon's slicker production values, the third film in the series is as unique and bizarre as anything else in Fanaka's filmography, pushing boundaries and defying expectations about what an audience could expect from a Cannon film. Although the company had been searching for an identity when it produced *Body and Soul* with Kennedy in 1981, by the mid-1980s the Cannon Group had found its niche. It was specializing in a brand of action films that clearly reflected the Reagan era's conservatism. Cannon's two biggest stars were Charles Bronson and Chuck Norris, who became cinematic extensions of Republican domestic and foreign policies in films like Bronson's *Death Wish* series and Norris's *Missing in Action* (1984, Joseph Zito), *Invasion U.S.A.* (1985, Joseph Zito), and *The Delta Force* (1986, Menahem Golan). Cannon also released a number of white ninja films, like *Enter the Ninja* (1981, Menahem Golan) and *American Ninja* (1985, Sam Firstenberg); put out two blatant knockoffs of *Raiders of the Lost Ark* (1981, Steven Spielberg) by reimagining H. Rider Howard's novels, including *King Solomon's Mines* (1985, J. Lee Thompson) and *Allen Quartermain and the Lost City of Gold* (1986, Gary Nelson); and found time to make low-budget comedies and musicals.

Cannon's rise under Golan and Globus was swift, and by 1987 they were looking to expand the scope of the company's productions and compete with the major studios. Hoping to make Cannon the seventh major in Hollywood, they began to diversify the types of films they produced, making art-house films like *King Lear* (1987, Jean-Luc Godard) and *Barfly* (1987, Barbet Schroeder), and bringing in top-flight Hollywood stars, such as Sylvester Stallone for *Cobra* (1986, George P. Cosmatos) and *Over the Top* (1987, Menahem Golan). They also pushed far beyond the financial boundaries of previous efforts at the studio with (unsuccessful) big-budget attempts like *Superman IV: The Quest for Peace* (1987, Sidney J. Furie) and *The Masters of the Universe* (1987, Gary Goddard). *Penitentiary III* was an outgrowth of Cannon's expanded production strategy, but it was also an anomaly, becoming the first film the company released with a black director.

Penitentiary III is not a typical Cannon release, but even as Fanaka indulges in excesses that would suggest complete autonomy, the studio's style and sensibilities can be seen in the final product. The first two *Penitentiary* films were highly stylized, moving away from the strict real-

The Midnight Thud (Raymond Kessler, aka "The Haiti Kid") in Penitentiary III.

ism typically associated with prison and boxing genre films, but *Penitentiary III* is almost devoid of real-world markers. The plot and setting are wholly unbelievable, the characters are cartoonish, and the laws of physics no longer apply. Five years later, Too Sweet, now a successful boxing champion, lands back in prison through complicated and confusing circumstances involving an incarcerated master criminal named Serengeti (Anthony Geary) and a rage-inducing serum. Too Sweet finds himself in the middle of a power struggle as he is courted for the prison boxing tournament by Serengeti and the warden. He refuses to fight, and Serengeti sets out to break Too Sweet's will, unleashing the prison's most violent inmate, the Midnight Thud (Raymond Kessler), against him. The Midnight Thud, a muscular dwarf wearing a dog collar who foams at the mouth, is invoked to beat Too Sweet into submission in a jail-cell replay of the fight with Half Dead in the first film.[33] In one of the strangest fight scenes in cinema history, Too Sweet defeats the Midnight Thud. But the Midnight Thud has the strength of ten men, and he literally flies around the cell.

The Midnight Thud character follows Fanaka's interest in the grotesque and monstrous that began with *Welcome Home Brother Charles.* Breaking from anything remotely realistic, Thud lives in a torch-lit dungeon beneath the prison, where he stays in his cell smoking crack cocaine while pornography is projected onto the walls to whip him into a violent, sexualized frenzy. Like Half Dead, Thud is released to break in new pris-

Anthony Geary's over-the-top performance as Serengeti in Penitentiary III.

oners, raping and emasculating them so that they can be used by other inmates. His entrance is backlit, with smoke machines providing a nightmarish ambience. Thud eventually transforms from an animalistic warrior into a wise trainer in the mode of Yoda in *The Empire Strikes Back*, teaching Too Sweet to harness his energy and "feel" his opponent without having to rely on sight. Like Half Dead, the Midnight Thud serves as an embodiment of the most overblown fears associated with prison, but this time there is redemption, with Too Sweet teaching his nemesis about the value of self-respect and goodwill.

Aside from Too Sweet and Thud, the cast of the film is mostly white—a distortion of the racial balance of the real-world prison population. The decision to cast white actors came from Cannon, who, rather than changing Fanaka's script, simply placed white actors in roles written for African Americans. In addition to extras and marginal characters, two lead roles in the film stand out as Cannon casting choices. Too Sweet's cellmate and close friend, a jazz saxophonist named Roscoe Lee Johnson, is played by Steve Antin, a young white actor best known at the time for playing the preppy foil in *The Goonies* (1985, Richard Donner). More glaring, the prison's most powerful criminal, Serengeti, is played by Anthony Geary, a veteran television actor best known for his role as Luke Spencer on *General Hospital*. Geary's bleached hair does not exactly match the evocation of Africa in the name "Serengeti."

The casting shifts Fanaka's conception of a predominantly black world in order to mirror the "diverse" casting trends of the 1980s, in which minorities were nominally represented in mostly white ensembles. Instead of undercutting Fanaka's authorial voice, the performances of his white actors create an even more affected world than he had imagined in his first four films, with Geary standing out as the most over-the-top and consciously campy. Inside his secluded cell, which is adorned with red velvet curtains, Oriental rugs, and oil paintings, Serengeti holds court along with his own transvestite plaything, Cleopatra (Jim Bailey). Sporting red silk pajamas, kimonos, long manicured nails, and a decorative cane, Serengeti speaks of himself in the third person and demands that all prisoners look away when in his presence, refusing to let any common prisoners "cast their eyes" on him. It is a comically overdrawn character and is one example among many that *Penitentiary III* is a reflexive blend of satire and camp, showing Fanaka to be one of the most original and offbeat filmmakers working in the 1980s.

There are other compelling elements to the film outside of its comic excess. The plot is focused on boxing and features small roles for Bundini Brown, one of Muhammad Ali's corner men, and Danny Trejo, the venerable character actor, who was making one of his first film appearances after being a real-life prison boxing champion while serving time in San Quentin.[34] But at the same time the film moves away from boxing. Too Sweet's final bout takes a hybrid form that mixes boxing, karate, and wrestling. This decision marks a broader trend in the United States: the sport's declining popularity dating from the 1980s. The final fight reflects the growing popularity of kickboxing and professional wrestling at the time and foreshadows the growth of mixed martial arts (MMA), which would overtake boxing in popularity by the 2000s.[35]

Most importantly, the *Penitentiary* series provides a much-needed perspective on the prison system. Fanaka's films coincided with the birth of the prison-industrial complex and the growing racial imbalance of incarceration stemming from racially motivated sentencing laws. From 1980 to 1990, the incarcerated population in America more than doubled, with black men disproportionately represented.[36] Moving away from the revolutionary critiques of prison during the Black Power era—including *The Autobiography of Malcolm X*, Eldridge Cleaver's *Soul on Ice*, and George Jackson's *Soledad Brothers*, to name a few—the *Penitentiary* trilogy presents incarceration as an inevitable constant for black men, rather than a system that is capable of being changed. The films articulate a collective anxiety about prison, giving voice to a lingering dread that had become far too real for many young black men. The *Penitentiary* films give voice to a crisis in black masculinity that accompanied the rapid expansion of the prison system.

The wild mixture of sociopolitical allusions, disenfranchised characters, surreal imagery, and camp aesthetics did not serve *Penitentiary III* well at the box office. Despite the film's expanded budget and Cannon's track record in marketing its releases, the film failed to match either of the first two in the series, earning a paltry $1.3 million at the box office.[37] Of course, Cannon had grown into a would-be major by keeping production costs to a minimum and recouping through home video sales, insulating itself from poor box-office performances.[38] *Penitentiary III* certainly made money when all was said and done, but this was a result of Cannon preselling its films to video stores, not Fanaka's drawing power.

Coinciding with Fanaka's bizarre vision and Cannon's lack of experience marketing films to a black audience was the arrival of filmmakers like Spike Lee and Robert Townsend on the national scene, not to mention the growing profile of black stars like Eddie Murphy, Bill Cosby, Denzel Washington, Danny Glover, and Whoopi Goldberg. Fanaka's obsession with violence and dispossessed characters looked crude and out of touch by comparison. Too Sweet no longer filled the same void in terms of black representation that he had in 1980, when prints of *Penitentiary* could travel from city to city for a year without having to compete with any another black-focused feature films on the market.

The lack of audience response to *Penitentiary III* was particularly disappointing for Fanaka. He had finally gotten his foot in the door of a Hollywood studio, but it had not gone well. The film effectively ended the acting career of his friend Leon Isaac Kennedy, and it made the likelihood of Fanaka finally being embraced by the film industry more remote.

STREET WARRIOR

For Fanaka, the silver lining of *Penitentiary III* was that his partnership with Cannon on a more traditional Hollywood production allowed him to finally become a member of the Directors Guild of America. Fanaka became active in the DGA and helped to cofound the African American Steering Committee, which aimed to create more opportunities for young black directors.[39] But over the next few years, he became disenchanted with the DGA, feeling that the organization was not doing enough to help him find opportunities for himself.

Fanaka was still trying to get *Street Wars* made, but had been unable to find investors. He was also trying to land jobs on projects outside of his auteurist mode of production, hoping to earn a living from second-director positions on feature films or by plying his craft on episodic television. Fanaka applied for nearly every job possible (which by his estimate totaled around two thousand applications), but he was turned down for every one.[40] His enthusiasm for the DGA turned to frustration, and he had a number of heated arguments at guild meetings. The guidelines of the DGA stipulated that it would make a good-faith effort to find employment for its members, and Fanaka felt that his inability to secure work—despite the fact that he had directed five theatrically released features—showed that the guild was not making good on its promise. Fanaka decided to file suit against the DGA, charging the guild with discrimination.

Fanaka cited the DGA's 1984 antidiscrimination suit against the studios to accuse them of following the same discriminatory practices they had charged the studios with following less than a decade before.[41] The suit came at a curious time, because the visibility of new African American directors was reaching new heights in the early 1990s. The DGA pointed to directors like John Singleton, the Hughes brothers, Ernest Dickerson, and Reginald Hudlin as examples of the strides that had been made to increase black involvement behind the camera, and it charged that Fanaka's abrasive personality and peculiar body of work were at the root of his terminal unemployment, not race. Ultimately, he resigned from the DGA, but his lawsuit dragged on for a number of years before it was finally thrown out of court.

After fifteen years, Fanaka found himself back where he had started, standing outside of the industry. Rather than walk away from directing, in 1990 he decided to start production on the long-delayed *Street Wars*, using his own money as well as financing from his parents to make another Bob-Bea Production. He shot the film on weekends and cut as many corners as he could to keep costs down.[42] The plot revolves around a bright young military student named Sugarpop (Alan Joseph) who returns home to South Central Los Angeles and takes over for his murdered brother, the top crack dealer in the city. In a borrowing from *The Godfather: Part II* (1974, Francis Ford Coppola), Sugarpop uses his formal education to rethink the possibilities for the existing crime syndicate, planning to transition into legitimate businesses. This scheme instigates a territorial battle among LA's drug dealers, which Sugarpop eventually wins by using a fleet of light recreational aircraft, equipped with machine guns, to control the streets from the sky.

The film explicitly borrows from *Top Gun* (1986, Tony Scott) and *Iron Eagle* (1986, Sidney J. Furie), but the low-budget attempt at matching big-budget Hollywood films makes it read like a parody. As usual, Fanaka breaks from realism through stylized settings, camp performance, and visual gags—one of the best being a crack house with a drive-through window, which is referred to as "crack in the box." Elements of gangsta rap are incorporated into the music and costuming, but *Street Wars* is difficult to read alongside the earnest hood films of the early 1990s. Instead, it is a curious side note to *Boyz n the Hood* (1991, John Singleton) and *Menace II Society* (1993, Albert and Allen Hughes). It is similarly produced in South Central, but it is informed by a generational divide and Fanaka's skewed aesthetic and political sensibilities.

After an initial deal with a foreign distributor fell through, Fanaka was forced to release *Street Wars* directly to home video, with the small and short-lived outfit Triboro putting out a recut version on VHS. Although Fanaka legally owned the film, he never received the negative back from the European company, and the recut version is the only one that has ever been made available. It would be his curtain call as a director.

LEGACIES OF REBELLION

Fanaka's inability to gain acceptance in commercial cinema provides an interesting parallel to the frustrations of the LA Rebellion filmmakers. While he was able to carve out a small space within the film industry, his peers at UCLA largely refused to participate in anything commercially oriented. The principle of nonparticipation is curious when considering that, along with Fanon and Cabral, the LA Rebellion looked to Malcolm X as a figure of inspiration. As South African scholar Ntongela Masilela pointed out, "*The Autobiography of Malcolm X*, like the life of the great leader, proclaimed to us that anything was achievable if there was sufficient political will."[43] For Haile Gerima and Larry Clark (and to a lesser extent Charles Burnett), this political will did not include finding ways to subvert the limitations of the system. Whereas Malcolm had used mainstream media to his own advantage by outsmarting the likes of hostile journalists, such as Mike Wallace and Louis Lomax—not to mention his ideologically opposed collaborator, Alex Haley, on the same *Autobiography* they looked to as a sacred text—the LA Rebellion approached their cinematic revolution in a manner that was neither practical nor realistic, instead finding solace in idealism. The new wave of black independent cinema in the early 1990s helped change some of the rhetoric of the LA Rebellion filmmakers, particularly in terms of how they approached financing and distribution—Burnett's *To Sleep with Anger* (1990) and Julie Dash's *Daughters of the Dust* (1991), for example, both received theatrical distribution.

The separation of Jamaa Fanaka from the LA Rebellion by critics and scholars can be traced to their differing approaches to the economics of film financing, audience, and genre. Clyde Taylor has written of the LA Rebellion with high praise, serving as a collaborative critic in line with Gerima's conception of triangular cinema (a shared aesthetic and revolutionary project among filmmakers, critics, and business interests). In explaining the movement's ideology, Taylor understands the LA Rebellion's films through the concept of anti-aesthetics, or post-aesthetics.[44] By denouncing the film language set forth by the invisible cut style of Hollywood, Taylor argues, independent black filmmakers are able to create their own film language freed from the aesthetic and financial dictates of mainstream cinema.[45] Open framing, nonlinearity, and a "natural" acting style provide formal approaches that actually benefit from financial limitations.

Seemingly taking an anti-aesthetic approach, the LA Rebellion upheld notions of "legitimate" cinema, shooting exclusively on film (mostly 16 mm) rather than embracing video technology or finding nontheatrical sites of exhibition. The Rebellion's films largely reiterated the style and sensibilities of European art cinema, breaking tradition with Hollywood, but the filmmakers never fully committed to developing their own film language. Fanaka therefore stands out as the most unique voice to come out of UCLA. Although *Penitentiary III* came out of a conservative Hollywood studio, it does not feel like a mainstream film. Fanaka's body of work seems to have been sent from another dimension entirely, with its own unique logic and style.

Two decades removed from his last turn sitting in the director's chair, Jamaa Fanaka passed away on April 1, 2012, from complications related to diabetes. Alternately upbeat and disappointed, he had a modest lifestyle in his final years but still harbored a desire for recognition. After his disastrous membership in the DGA and the botched release of *Street Wars*, his career had been placed on hold as his health deteriorated. In the last two decades of his life he could be found promoting his six films, often appearing at screenings for cult movie buffs and selling DVDs out of his backpack. Instantly recognizable, Fanaka rarely left home without donning a *Penitentiary* baseball hat and T-shirt. His pride in his accomplishments was unmistakable, and he was delighted when celebrities like Snoop Dogg or Quentin Tarantino praised his work.

But his greatest sense of fulfillment came a year before his passing when he was included in the LA Rebellion collection at UCLA's Film

& Television Archive. Thanks to the efforts of film scholars and archivists Jacqueline Stewart, Allyson Field, and Jan-Christopher Horak, Fanaka was finally considered a full-fledged member of the LA Rebellion, and prints of his features, student shorts, and home movies were housed and preserved alongside those of his UCLA classmates. The collection of these long-separated records helps to break down the bifurcation between Fanaka and the rest of the LA Rebellion, with the understanding that he shared in the broader intellectual project, even though his films took a different financial and aesthetic approach than those of Gerima, Burnett, and Clark.

Summing up the connections and differences between his career and those of his peers at UCLA, Fanaka once explained, "I didn't want to be Hollywood. I just wanted to make films people saw."[46] Everyone in the LA Rebellion made strides in conceiving a black cinematic departure from the mainstream. Unquestionably a member of the group, Jamaa Fanaka pushed boundaries as much as anyone else who ever stepped foot on the Westwood campus.

CHAPTER SIX

Dreams Deferred

UNTAPPED POTENTIAL, THE TRANSFORMATION OF BLACK POPULAR CULTURE, AND THE CINEMATIC LEGACIES OF GILBERT MOSES AND STAN LATHAN

THE YEAR 1984 WITNESSED TWO DEBUTS THAT WOULD come to shape popular representations of African Americans in the following decades. In March, Run-DMC released its first album on Profile Records, a little-known label. The eponymously titled *Run-DMC* became the first rap album to be certified gold by the Recording Industry Association of American and placed the group at the center of hip-hop's worldwide rise to popularity. In October, Michael Jordan made his professional debut for the Chicago Bulls, scoring 16 points against the Washington Bullets at Chicago Stadium. Over the next few seasons he would become the National Basketball Association's signature superstar and redefine sports marketing, helping the league attain global recognition while becoming a successful brand in his own right. Run-DMC and Michael Jordan filled arenas, set fashion trends, sold sneakers (Adidas and Nike, respectively), pitched Coca-Cola, and thoroughly changed the media landscape for African Americans. Their success—like that of *The Cosby Show*, which also debuted that year—was notably of the crossover variety.

But unlike the venerable Dr. Cliff Huxtable, Run-DMC and Michael Jordan had an appeal that was rooted in their difference rather than their universality, as their chosen fields were linked to cultural expressions born on the blacktops of inner-city playgrounds, not in the living rooms of comfortable middle-class homes. Using Jordan and Run-DMC as symbols of urban black youth is clearly problematic, as their middle-class backgrounds challenge the myth of hip-hop and basketball being used as ways out of the ghetto. Nevertheless, their shared popularity gave birth to a certain typology imposed on young black men in the 1990s and 2000s. Hip-hop and basketball have now served as cultural cornerstones of masculine definitions for a quarter-century, gaining a global reach that has provided the world with prepackaged commodities (clothing, mass media, etc.) emphasizing black expressivity and the urban experience. The arrival of Run-DMC and Michael Jordan transformed global perceptions of blackness, and their images were amplified and distorted to turn black masculine ideals into marketable commodities.

Of course, neither Jordan nor Run-DMC were created in a vacuum—both had clear and specific antecedents. Run-DMC's music was a continuation of the New York City hip-hop scene that had been around for a decade prior to their debut, and that had formed around the combined expressions of breaking, graffiti, and turntablism—and later, rapping. Jordan's style of play and his dynamic aerial maneuvers were largely a reinterpretation of the high-flying playground approach of Julius "Dr. J" Erving, who had been a star since the early 1970s and was playing out his career as respected elder statesman with the Philadelphia 76ers when Jordan entered the league. Both antecedents had been the subjects of Hollywood movies—made by African American directors—during the ebb in black-focused features that followed the blaxploitation cycle. The basketball comedy *The Fish That Saved Pittsburgh* (1979, Gilbert Moses) and the musical drama *Beat Street* (1984, Stan Lathan) provide invaluable documentation of the genesis of two closely linked cultural enterprises, marking rare opportunities for two black directors whose talents were underutilized by Hollywood and who otherwise had no traction in the industry at that time.

The careers of Gilbert Moses and Stan Lathan share a number of striking parallels. Both came from humble beginnings in the inner city, excelled academically, and achieved success in their twenties directing outside of the medium of feature films, working for stage and television, respectively. Moses and Lathan were both courted by major studios to make their first narrative feature films at the height of the blaxploitation cycle in 1974 only to return to stage and television for the majority of their careers. Unlike Michael Schultz and Sidney Poitier, neither Moses nor Lathan was able to capitalize fully on his initial Hollywood films and become a regular feature director, but both avoided the fate that met other black directors from the blaxploitation cycle, such as Oscar Williams and Ivan Dixon, who never made another feature after the end of the cycle in 1976. When looked at together, their careers stand out as clear examples of Hollywood's inability and unwillingness to cultivate talented black directors.

Their professional survival away from movies, however, highlights the differences in their artistic and political sensibilities. Moses was frustrated during the 1970s and 1980s, unable to find a place that was an equal match to his talents and his perspective in the conservative media industry. Lathan, in contrast, was wildly successful, navigating the television industry to become a major power broker by the 1990s. Their two features in the post-blaxploitation era help explain the growing cultural significance of hip-hop and basketball, but their careers at large provide separate, unique windows into the creative and political landscape and the viewpoints that were missing from Hollywood between 1977 and 1986.

GILBERT MOSES

Gilbert Moses III was born in Cleveland, Ohio, on August 20, 1942, the first of two children to Gilbert Jr. and Bertha Moses, and raised alongside five older half siblings.[1] Although neither of his parents had completed high school, both were exceptionally intelligent and cultivated an interest in literature and music in their children. Gilbert III played piano and violin as a child and began studying French in third grade as part of an enrichment program. Because of his performance on achievement tests, he attended an accelerated program in Cleveland and took public transportation to a more affluent section of the city to attend school starting in seventh grade. He proved to be an exceptionally bright and creative child and at the age of nine began taking part in theater workshops and productions at Cleveland's Karamu House.[2]

Karamu House had been established in 1915 by white social workers Russell and Rowena Jelliffe as an integrated settlement theater. Like the Hull House Theater in Chicago, Cleveland's Karamu House was part of a turn-of-the-century reformist movement that hoped to generate a more interdependent society by having upper and lower classes live, work, and create together in close proximity. By the time Moses began participating in workshops there in 1951, the center mostly served the surrounding black community and had become a training ground for black artists.[3] Langston Hughes had learned art there as a child, and Karamu House also helped develop black actors Ivan Dixon, Robert Guillaume, and Ron O'Neal.[4] Moses took part in Karamu House productions for nearly a decade, playing the lead in *A Certain Joy*, studying photography and music, and developing himself as a writer.[5] He was an outstanding student and earned praise for his work, and after high school he was awarded a scholarship to attend Oberlin College.[6] Moses had a broad range of interests at Oberlin but concentrated in French literature; during his junior year he traveled abroad to study at the Sorbonne.[7] While in France, he attended the Théâtre National Populaire, and he was influenced by its director, Jean Vilar, to pursue socially relevant theater. Once he returned from his year in France, he began to immerse himself in the black freedom struggle.[8]

Rather than return to Oberlin to finish his degree, Moses spent time in New York before moving to Jackson, Mississippi, to work for the *Mississippi Free Press* as a photographer and editor.[9] The *Free Press*, a weekly, had been founded by NAACP field secretary Medgar Evers; Moses joined the paper around the time of the civil rights leader's assassination.[10] He worked there only briefly, however, before turning his attention to theater, founding the Free Southern Theater (FST) in 1964 with John O'Neal, Tom Dent, and Richard Schechner. Although Moses's subsequent work directing for the stage in New York for television and film would span twenty-five years, his two years at the FST would come to define his career. Following his death in 1995, the breadth of his career was largely overlooked, as his work with the FST conveyed a more accessible narrative about the role of art in the civil rights movement.

Foregrounding his time at the FST, however, is not necessarily limiting, as Moses's artistic approach and ideological struggles were indeed shaped in these heady days of youth. "The idea of the Free Southern was a natural outgrowth of my experience at Karamu and Oberlin rather than any political sledge hammer effect," Moses recalled in 1972. "It was essential that we provide Black people with true images of themselves. And because most of the media was controlled by whites, the theater was the freest media in which we could do this."[11] In later years he would attempt to "free" other mediums with mixed results.

Merging politics and art in the mode of Jean Vilar, the FST embodied the goals and perspective of the civil rights movement by performing largely for rural black audiences throughout Mississippi, Alabama, Louisiana, Georgia, and Tennessee. The plays ranged from *Waiting for Godot* to socially relevant works like Martin Duberman's *In White America* and, eventually, Moses's own original play *Roots*, which was written explicitly for FST audiences and was based on his observations of southern life during his time touring with the company.[12] The FST was an idealistic artistic and economic collective, with Moses serving alternately as director, actor, writer, producer, composer, executive, secretary, driver, and ticket taker, although most of the decision making and administrative responsibilities also fell to him.[13] While he abhorred fundraising and the necessary trips to New York that distracted him from the theater's stated purpose in the South, his role as pitchman for the company allowed him to make connections.[14]

Balancing an experimental concept for a touring company with the rigors of economic sustainability were not the only tensions for Moses. He and John O'Neal had contrasting philosophies and tastes, with Moses favoring comedy and satire over tragic drama.[15] More importantly, Moses became disillusioned with the FST's multiethnic makeup and frustrated by its lack of politically radical material. As he would write shortly after leaving the FST, there was a faction within the company that "wanted a theater to deal with black artists and the black audience," but didn't go far enough for him because "its political aims reflected the political aims of the Movement at that time: integration."[16] This faction included his first wife, Denise Nicholas, and actor Roscoe Orman. Moses wanted the FST to adopt a new business model that eschewed white institutional money and urged the black community to be financially responsible for supporting black art and culture, making the same call for self-sufficiency that would later be articulated in dramatically different forms by everyone from the proponents of the LA Rebellion to Tyler Perry.[17]

Moses left the company abruptly in 1966 without fully explaining his reasons, but the struggle to reconceive the FST as a black radical venture and the dissolution of his marriage to Nicholas were certainly factors in his leaving. Moses briefly enrolled at Tisch School of the Arts at New York University before moving to Chicago, where he spent a year pursuing music, playing guitar in a number of different groups.[18] When he returned to New York in 1968, he committed himself exclusively to theater, finding himself at the epicenter of the Black Arts movement. Moses, who had given up in his efforts to guide the FST toward becoming a troupe concerned primarily with black cultural expression just a few years earlier, now suddenly found himself at the center of a scene populated by black-focused companies. They included the New Lafayette Theatre, the Negro Ensemble Company, the New Federal Theatre, the New Heritage Theatre, the Afro-American School for Acting and Speech, and the National Black Theatre.

Moses directed Amiri Baraka's *Slave Ship* in 1969, winning an Obie for his work, and he would go on to direct close to a dozen stage productions over the next decade, winning a second Obie for Ed Bullins's *The Taking of Miss Janie* in 1977 and a Drama Desk Award for Most Promising Director with Melvin Van Peebles's 1973 play *Ain't Supposed to Die a Natural Death*. Moses also directed Giusseppe Verdi's *Rigoletto* for the San Francisco Opera and oversaw productions of plays in Boston and Washington, DC, as well as New York.[19]

Hollywood Calling

Moses's success directing for the stage placed him at the center of a growing tension within the black theater community. Flourishing black theater troupes in the late 1960s reached a point of crisis in the 1970s as their most talented actors, playwrights, and directors were raided by Hollywood. Yet Moses did not share the disdain for film as a medium that was common among stage artists. Moses stated in 1972 that "television is totally controlled by economics which suggests that no serious or realistic portrayal of a Black person will be forthcoming."[20] "Theater and film," however, "happen to be the most viable media through which Black people can rapidly effect a self-consciousness which will eventually influence them economically, politically, and culturally."[21] This coupling of film and theater, as well as their separation from television, speaks not only to Moses's enthusiasm about cinema but also to the changing landscape of the film industry in the early 1970s, as its economic imperative had been obscured by its relative openness to black artists and radical politics.

Moses was first approached by film industry representatives in 1972, the first year of the blaxploitation cycle, when Universal flew him out to Los Angeles to gauge his interest in writing or directing for the big screen. Despite his lack of training in filmmaking, Universal hired him to direct a feature titled *Eli's Game*. Moses spent a few months in Los Angeles working on the screenplay and doing preproduction for the film, but Universal ultimately canceled the project.[22] Little is known about the nature of the project, but Al Green wrote and recorded a song called "Eli's Game" in 1972 that went unreleased; it was most likely the title track to the abandoned project.[23] Green's song suggests an earnest drama rather than the brand of comedy and satire that marked much of Moses's work.[24] The film was abandoned before shooting began, and Moses returned to New York with the promise of directing a feature film left unrealized.

Months later, Universal offered Moses another chance to direct with *Willie Dynamite*, a tale of a New York pimp's fall from grace from a screenplay by Ron Cutler.[25] The film was being produced for the studio by two of its chief executives, David Brown and Richard D. Zanuck, making it one of the rare blaxploitation films both fully financed and distributed by a major studio. With a budget of $1 million, *Willie Dynamite* was nowhere near a big-budget picture by Hollywood standards, but among the black-focused films of the era its budget was sizable.[26] There were plenty of cheaply made black-focused features; Universal invested heavily in *Willie Dynamite*, hoping it would stand out from the crowd and replicate the box-office success of studio-financed releases like *Shaft*, *Super Fly*, and *Cleopatra Jones*. And while the financial ambitions for the project outpaced those for most blaxploitation features, the artistic ambitions for the project—thanks to Gilbert Moses—also surpassed what was typically expected of black-focused films at the time. Although the film is set in a familiar urban criminal milieu, *Willie Dynamite* is less a straightforward tale of the hustler's life than it is a nuanced satire of Hollywood's conception of black life.

Willie Dynamite is a morality play: its criminal protagonist not only receives his comeuppance but also commits to a new way of life by the final reel. The transformation is reflected in Willie's appearance, with the outer trappings of his pimp persona being literally stripped away when he is left half naked and beaten in the same streets that he previously rolled through in his tricked-out car, sporting preposterous fur coats and hats. Moses uses elements of satirical commentary through *mise-en-scène*. In the opening scene, for example, Willie drives through Manhattan in his Cadillac Eldorado, passing by a Times Square marquee reading "Pornography in Hollywood." It's a self-aware nod that recognizes that *Willie Dynamite* is a part of the blaxploitation cycle and signifies that the film's stereotyped black masculinity is intentional.[27] In the final shot of the film, as Willie walks away from his past life and into a new beginning, there is a sign for a bookstore placed prominently in the frame. This over-literal connection to dialogue earlier in the film suggests that Willie's intelligence, had it been properly cultivated, could have produced an exceptional citizen instead of a successful criminal. Framed between a theater marquee and a bookstore sign, Willie's experiences follow a broader commentary on the debilitating fantasies of blaxploitation and the need to invest in education.

While the commentary is literal, the most authorial elements of the film can be found in the excesses and affectations of key scenes and performances bordering on camp sensibilities and melodrama. Moses does not employ satire in a transparent fashion, but instead codes his sense of irony for the knowing spectator. The best example of this technique comes in a board meeting between the top pimps in the city. The over-the-top performance by Roger Robinson as Willie's chief rival, Bell, is an outright send-up of the caricatures populating other blaxploitation films, undercutting any romantic notion of the player lifestyle by making it appear wholly ridiculous. Moses pushes credibility to the edge, seeing how far he can take the humor without it crossing over into transparent parody. At the same time that he employs his most audacious comic elements, however, he uses dialogue among the pimps to provide the primary social critique of the film. Willie rejects a plan to collectivize with his peers,

Bell (Roger Robinson) holds court in Willie Dynamite.

instead embracing an American capitalistic ideal where every man takes what he can for himself. In locating the crux of the film in his funniest scene, Moses employs the same philosophy of truth in comedy that he had articulated to John O'Neal at the FST.

Much of the responsibility for articulating Moses's unique sensibility fell to the cast. Moses noted that he wanted "to try to achieve honesty in the film," and his decision to cast Roscoe Orman in the title role reflected his desire to embody the New York locale in his leading actor and bypass the affectations of an established screen star.[28] Orman and Moses had developed a close relationship during their time together at the FST, but they had not worked together since Moses's departure in 1966.[29] Orman had been raised in the Bronx, and he imbues the Willie Dynamite character with a sense of menace that was diametrically opposed to the role that would later come to define him as an actor—he played the affable Gordon on *Sesame Street* for over four decades. His character in the film is often placed opposite Diana Sands's Cora, a former prostitute who now counsels women on the street, threatening Willie's "stable." Cora provides a poignant counterbalance to Willie, giving a credible female perspective that is absent from other blaxploitation pimp films, such as *The Mack* (1973, Michael Campus).[30]

Despite strong performances and Moses's layering of satire and social commentary, the film failed to make much of a wave at the box office or connect with critics. Its failure to recoup its investment, much less turn a profit, provided further evidence for the major studios that investing in black-focused features was no longer profitable. Universal had already lost money on the features *That Man Bolt* (1973, Henry Levin and David Lowell Rich) and *Trick Baby* (1972, Larry Yust), other black-focused films that the studio had fully financed and distributed. Nevertheless, Universal's view that *Willie Dynamite*'s failure at the box office was indicative of the limited financial prospects of black-focused film was largely a self-fulfilling prophecy. Rather than dedicating itself to promoting the film, the studio put the majority of its energy into promoting *The Sting* (1973, George Roy Hill) as an Oscar contender.[31] Also produced by Zanuck and Brown, *The Sting* ended up winning Best Picture at the Academy Awards, and the long campaign and subsequent spotlight for that blockbuster left *Willie Dynamite* as an afterthought. Without the studio or its producers behind the film, *Willie Dynamite* fell victim to poor reviews from a white critical establishment that failed to make sense of the satire or locate the levels of social commentary. Needing promotion to contextualize the tone, the film was instead lumped together with the most derisive connotations of blaxploitation.

Willie Dynamite became emblematic of the fall of the blaxploitation cycle at the major studios. The decline in studio-produced black features followed immediately after a disappointing 1974 release season, with opportunities for black directors drying up along the way. Nevertheless, Moses remained optimistic about moviemaking following his first experience in Hollywood. Speaking in 1975, Moses said, "At the moment, I'm very interested in cinema. More black people are involved in the movie industry, so there is a greater choice. The Grade B potboilers like 'Super Fly' will always be there, but I now think we're ready to move on to a different kind of black film."[32]

This optimism proved to be unwarranted, as his next few years would be filled with stalled projects. Moses was attached to the unrealized film *Mimi*, which was set to begin production in July 1974 for Columbia Pictures but was canceled at the last moment.[33] The film was going to star Curtis Mayfield in a reworking of Puccini's *La Bohème*, with Paris being replaced by New Orleans, and contemporary soul music taking the place of opera.[34] Moses had also started work on a vehicle for Redd Foxx titled *The Snatch*. The comedy about a stolen dog was slated to begin shooting in September 1975, but was abandoned in the months leading up to its production.[35]

Over the next few years Moses would work in dual capacities, directing for the stage and television. He was the original director for the first production of *The Wiz*, but was replaced when the show went to Broadway. Because of a conflict with the producers, he was fired a week before the Broadway debut; the play's costume designer, Geoffrey Holder, became director in his stead.[36] Although Moses's contribution went unnoticed as the play became a hit on Broadway, he did meet his future wife—the actress-singer Dee Dee Bridgewater, who played Glenda the Good Witch—during the production.[37]

Moses pulled from his musical background to compose tracks for Bridgewater's 1977 album *Just Family*, on which she appeared on the cover in silhouette, pregnant with their daughter China. His songs included "Maybe Today" and "Thank the Day (You Walked into My Life)"; he was also a cowriter on the tracks "Just Family" and "Children Are the Spirit (of the World)." Moses had performed as a musician before and had written the title song for *Willie Dynamite*, but for all of his work on film, stage, and television, his four songs on *Just Family* remain his most personal and autobiographical work. They express his love for Bridgewater, their shared excitement for the birth of their child, and his amazement with his first daughter, Tsia.

Moses remained active in the theater, but he also used his experience on *Willie Dynamite* to follow the path of a number of black directors, including Ivan Dixon and Mark Warren, by working for television. Moses was one of four directors on the ABC miniseries adaptation of Alex Haley's *Roots* (1977), becoming one of the only black artists behind the camera on a project that was criticized for primarily employing white writers and directors.[38] Moses also directed the television movie *The Greatest Thing That Almost Happened* for CBS in 1977, starring Jimmie Walker in a rare dramatic role as a high school basketball player stricken with leukemia. These television outings were a form of economic survival, but they also allowed Moses creative input. With the fall of blaxploitation, theatrically released feature films were rarely an option for black directors, and Moses had no particular reason to expect a project to come his way. To his surprise, however, he came to the attention of a couple of young producers looking to make a basketball comedy.

Shooting Fish

The Fish That Saved Pittsburgh, released in 1979, would become Moses's lone theatrical feature in the post-blaxploitation years. The film was critically panned and a box-office flop, and Moses was unhappy with the finished product and expressed regret over his participation. In the years to follow he made a habit of omitting the film from his résumé, an unusual move for a director with only one other feature film to his name.[39] Despite his misgivings about the film and the lingering perception of its low quality, *The Fish That Saved Pittsburgh* is a unique look at a watershed moment in professional basketball when the sport was redefining itself racially, stylistically, and economically. The film's financial failures can largely be traced to the sport's marginalization at the time. But its central aesthetic aim—combining music and athletic movement to see basketball as a creative expression—was prophetic of the global success of the NBA in the years to come.

The Fish That Saved Pittsburgh was born out of the friendship between two white men working in the realm of black music in the 1970s, Gary Stromberg and David Dashev.[40] Stromberg had produced *Car Wash*, and its success at the box office (as well as with soundtrack sales) gave him relative freedom to produce a new project of his choosing.[41] Riffing on ideas one night, Stromberg and Dashev came up with a story concept about a down-on-its-luck professional basketball team that finds success with the help of astrology.[42] Following a team walkout, the players are replaced by a group of cast-offs who share the zodiac sign of Pisces. They proceed to play beyond their talents thanks to the alignment of the stars and the ability of Pisces-born people to work together.

The concept was consciously ridiculous, but the humor was well received when Stromberg and Dashev pitched the concept to Merv Adelson at Lorimar Pictures. Stromberg sold *The Fish* to Lorimar using the same strategy he had employed on *Car Wash*, banking on soundtrack sales to offset any risk at the box office. Whereas *Car Wash* had used producer Norman Whitfield as point man, *The Fish* used producer-arranger Thom Bell to provide the soundtrack. Bell, who along with Kenny Gamble and Leon Huff helped develop the "Philadelphia Sound" at Philadelphia International Records in the 1970s, had an impressive track record that looked to guarantee album sales. With a modest budget, a unique story concept, and the promise of ancillary revenues, Lorimar agreed to fully finance the film and negotiated a distribution deal with United Artists, leaving Stromberg and Dashev to produce the film on their own.

With a green light on the project, Stromberg and Dashev approached NBA star Julius "Dr. J" Erving to star in the film. According to Dashev, the project had been envisioned from the very beginning with Erving in mind. Had he said no, the entire project would have been abandoned.[43] Erving was sold on the promise that the film would pay homage to the sport's playground tradition and that his character would provide a positive black role model, which had all but disappeared in feature films by 1979.[44] Having landed Erving as the lead, Dashev and Stromberg then assembled a wide array of NBA stars to appear in non-acting roles, adding an air of authenticity to the basketball scenes that was wholly absent from most basketball sequences on film and scripted television.[45] With Erving,

The Fish had a lead actor who not only was believable as a basketball player, but also embodied a sense of style and creativity on the court that challenged the sport's tradition, embodying black expressivity through his improvisational moves and prominent afro.

Without cable and Internet, Erving's talents in the 1970s were shrouded in mystery, unseen by most Americans but conveyed through word of mouth and breathtaking accounts of his exploits by sportswriters. The American Basketball Association (ABA), the upstart rival to the NBA founded in 1967, lacked a national television contract during his first six seasons with the Virginia Squires and the New York Nets, and Erving played to mostly empty arenas. Nevertheless, he became a sensation. His high-flying style electrified the lucky few who saw him play, and he became the face of the league (alongside star players like David Thompson and Artis Gilmore). The quality of play in the ABA began to rival that in the NBA, and serious debates grew over which league's champion was better.[46] When Erving led the Nets to a game seven victory against the Denver Nuggets in the 1976 ABA Finals, *Sports Illustrated* dutifully informed the public unable to watch on television: "Too bad, America, but you missed one of the greatest basketball shows on Earth."[47]

By the time Erving arrived on the national scene, with the NBA and ABA merging before the 1976–1977 season, the myth of Dr. J was fully formed. Although he had succeeded within the bureaucratized confines of professional team sports, he had come to embody a defiantly individual approach to the sport that particularly resonated with young black fans. Not only had he played in the renegade ABA and proudly donned a large afro and goatee, but his acrobatic dunking was an unapologetic extension of the playground game.

By the time Erving was cast in *The Fish That Saved Pittsburgh*, he had been in the NBA for two seasons, now as a member of the Philadelphia 76ers.[48] The film may not have shown Dr. J to a national audience for the first time, but the story traded in on the mythology of Erving in the ABA and reflected the barnstorming legacy of the defunct league.[49] The film's goal was to capture basketball as a form of creative urban expression in a manner that television coverage of the NBA could not, focusing in on the rhythm and spontaneity of the sport. As film scholar Todd Boyd has pointed out, basketball conceptually mirrors jazz, with a loose structure leading to improvisation that gives individuals the freedom to shine (or solo) within the ensemble.[50] The producers wanted a director attuned to black musical traditions who could convey this connection. Although Gilbert Moses was not on Stromberg's or Dashev's radar, they agreed that they wanted to have a black director on the project.[51] Moses was likely suggested by Lorimar, who would have been aware of his recent work in television. The producers were also looking for someone who handled movement well, as they envisioned the film as an R&B ballet of sorts, using Thom Bell's music to dictate the action on the court.[52] Moses's experience both as a musician and as a director for the stage made him a good fit for the project.

In preparation for the film, Moses spent a season going to Los Angeles Lakers games with Dashev and Stromberg and learning the sport firsthand.[53] By the time he entered shooting on *The Fish* in the summer of 1978, he had been contemplating the film for a number of months and had formed particular ideas about what he wanted to accomplish with the project. Never shy to express his thoughts, he was soon at odds with Stromberg and Dashev, wanting to abandon the astrology angle and tell a more realistic story.[54] These basic creative differences, along with Moses's strong-willed personality, were exacerbated by Stromberg and Dashev's lack of experience as producers. Trouble away from the set for everyone involved also intruded.[55] Stromberg had one film under his belt after co-producing *Car Wash*, and Dashev was working on his first. With shooting on location in Pittsburgh, far from the watchful eye of the studio, the production quickly lost focus. Stromberg was kicked off the set for his erratic behavior, leaving Dashev, a novice producer, in charge.[56] Shooting continued, but the eventual shortcomings of the project soon became apparent to almost everyone involved. Unable to turn the project into his own vision, Moses dispassionately finished working on the film. Having completed shooting at all may have been an accomplishment. Stromberg, looking back on the project, later said, "We were lucky that the film was finished."[57]

The end product is a curious mix of ensemble comedy, sports drama, and an earnest examination of the black working class's struggle to get out of the ghetto. The satiric intellectual underpinnings of *Willie Dynamite* and Moses's 1966 play *Roots* are wholly absent in *The Fish*, replaced by simple gags and one-dimensional characters. For all the effort put forth in staging realistic basketball sequences, from casting professional players, to shooting with Steadicam, to using glass floors to provide a unique vantage point and emphasize height, the sloppy final cut of the picture is rife with mismatched edits that make the game segments look cheap and cobbled together.

Nevertheless, the film provides a number of compelling moments of commentary, much of it focused on a teenage ball boy (James Bond III) who is being raised in poverty by his older sister (Margaret Avery). More importantly, the comedic structure gives way to a more critical framing

Moses Guthrie (Julius Erving) returns to the playground in The Fish That Saved Pittsburgh.

of basketball as a site for creative expression, articulating a crucial break from the vantage point of the mainstream sports media. The film's casting of real-life basketball players, and its incorporation of the sport's legacy within black communities, makes *The Fish* stand apart from the majority of sports movies. Harlem Globetrotters legend Meadowlark Lemmon appears in a supporting role, providing a link to the barnstorming tradition of Abe Saperstein's teams that were part sport and part vaudeville, and the inclusion of Connie Hawkins, who plays for the "LA Team" in the climactic championship game, provides a redress of the star player's banishment from the sport in the 1960s, working to properly credit him as a stylistic forebear of Dr. J.

One sequence that especially stands out involves Erving's lead character Moses Guthrie making a late-night visit to the outdoor basketball court where he learned to play the game as a child. In a montage sequence of Erving performing his aerial maneuvers in street clothes, he speaks in voiceover to explain his own investment in the game, and, through extension, the growing hold of basketball for inner-city youth looking for a way out of the ghetto. He explains, "I had to learn how to squeeze through that hole, as you call it, for my future. It was serious business, not play," expressing the same all-encompassing investment in the sport that would be portrayed in more sobering terms through the documentary *Hoop Dreams* (1994, Steve James) fifteen years later. The sequence captures Erving in his prime with a stylized rendering that could never be matched by televised coverage of a game. With slow motion and double exposure of his dunks synchronized to the Spinners song "(Do It Do It) No One Does It Better,"

Dr. J dunking as an artistic expression.

the playground sequence not only represents the best-composed expression of Erving's artistry, but also foreshadows the highly stylized marketing of Michael Jordan via Nike commercials and home videos produced by NBA Entertainment a decade later.[58]

Despite the playground sequence and the opportunity to see Dr. J on the big screen, *The Fish* failed to make money at the box office. Stromberg had envisioned the soundtrack as a financial safety net, but Thom Bell's music failed to generate much interest. Bell's lyrics are overly invested in the specifics of the film's plot, and the Philadelphia Sound that he had helped to cultivate was on the wane by 1979.[59] The poor reception from film critics may have been expected, but the backlash within sports circles became particularly frustrating for everyone involved. Sportswriter Frank Deford took the odd turn as a film critic and used the pages of *Sports Illustrated* to rail against the film, taking the opportunity to present a strangely old-fashioned and racially tinged diatribe against dunking.[60] If Deford painted *The Fish* as symptomatic of a low point for the sport, his proclamation that the dunk was a mere "fad" illustrates the ineptitude of his analysis and shows just how prophetic the film was. The NBA's transition from a marginal league whose championship series were televised on tape delay in the late 1970s into a multibillion-dollar global venture by 1990 was realized largely through marketing the very same aerial expression that *The Fish* helped place in filmic terms.

Moses left the project with a bitter taste in his mouth, seeing the film as the only project he had worked on that was not "his."[61] He remained in Los Angeles working on television; meanwhile, the success of August Wilson and Broadway hits like *Dreamgirls* obscured the marginalization of black perspectives elsewhere on New York stages. Moses reconnected with Alex Haley, directing an episode of the race relations series *Palmerstown, USA* (1980) that Haley was co-producing with Norman Lear. He also worked alongside Stan Lathan on the PBS series *You Were There* (1981), making a short-subject biography of blues musician Willie Dixon. But as the 1980s progressed, the prospects that had presented themselves to Moses a decade earlier began to vanish.

Lauded as a child prodigy in Cleveland, and ascending quickly in the theater world by dazzling his contemporaries with his intelligence and creativity, Moses was relegated to being a craftsman for the networks, directing the occasional sitcom and television movie with little room to put forth his creative vision. He worked with Robert Guillaume, an old friend from their days together at Karamu House, on the sitcom *Benson*, and directed episodes of *The Paper Chase*. He also directed the NBC television movie *A Fight for Jenny* (1986), starring *Miami Vice*'s Philip Michael Thomas in a drama about an interracial couple struggling to retain custody of their daughter.

Moses's career took an even more curious turn in the late 1980s as he moved his family to Virginia Beach and began working on episodes of the *700 Club* for the Christian Broadcast Network (CBN), owned by televangelist turned Republican presidential candidate Pat Robertson. Moses was part of a group of black celebrities courted by Robertson, and for a brief period Moses sincerely committed himself to Christianity and CBN's evangelical message before returning to the spiritual wandering and religious skepticism that defined most of his adult life.[62]

Shortly thereafter, Moses also found work directing installments of *ABC Afterschool Special* and *CBS Schoolbreak Special*. While these assignments may not have been as artistically or intellectually demanding as Moses would have liked, he still found a way to make them meaningful. When he directed the after-school special *The Day They Came to Arrest the Book* for CBS, an adaptation of the young adult novel by Nat Hentoff, he took the opportunity to open the door for a fellow black artist who had long been ostracized by Hollywood, hiring Melvin Van Peebles to write the screenplay. Since being fired from *Greased Lightning*, Van Peebles had been placed on the extreme margins of the culture industry. With Van Peebles on board, Moses used *The Day They Came to Arrest the Book*, a fable about the evils of censorship, to offer a meta-textual commentary on the censoring of black artistic and political expression, repurposing the didactic nature of the after-school special to make a more personal statement.

The success of Spike Lee and Robert Townsend and the growing cultural capital of hip-hop increased opportunities for black directors heading into the 1990s, and Moses looked to redouble his efforts to produce fulfilling work. He made the television movie *Runaway* (1989) for PBS, returning to the realm of black-focused material with a film about a homeless teenage boy living in the subway stations of New York City. Moses also directed music videos and continued to work in episodic television, directing, for example, *Law & Order* for NBC. Unfortunately, his career came to an end all too soon when he died from multiple myeloma, an incurable form of cancer affecting bone marrow, on April 15, 1995, in New York City.

In the final years before his death, Moses began working on a passion project, a documentary feature about the life and times of black comedian Jackie "Moms" Mabley, which he hoped Whoopi Goldberg would narrate. He spent two years researching Mabley's career, accumulating boxes upon boxes of press clippings, videotapes, and interviews relating to the comedian. Moses received financing for the film, but his health deteriorated during preproduction, and his passing left the documentary as an interesting idea rather than a realized project.[63]

STAN LATHAN

There is a fascinating intersection between Moses's would-be final project and Stan Lathan, whose first narrative feature, *Amazing Grace* (1974), starred Moms Mabley. Paying homage to a tradition of black entertainers too easily dismissed as retrograde in the 1970s and beyond, Moses and Lathan melded their own generational perspective with open-minded appreciation of youth culture, celebrating the present without dismissing the past.

Stan Lathan was born July 8, 1945, in Philadelphia, the youngest of three children.[64] Raised by his single mother, Julia, after his father, Stanley, left the family, he lived in the city's Richard Allen Homes and James Weldon Johnson housing projects.[65] The young Stan attended a racially mixed elementary school and a predominantly Jewish junior high school after his mother found a way to bypass the jurisdictional rules that would have otherwise sent him to the struggling neighborhood schools. While his aesthetic world was shaped by his appetite for literature, television, and movies, he also had a passion for music, regularly attending live shows at the Uptown Theatre on North Broad Street and performing in a doo-wop group called the Veltones during high school.[66] The group was part of a vibrant and upcoming scene in Philadelphia that included the likes of Kenny Gamble, Thom Bell, and Patti LaBelle. Lathan left the Veltones at the end of high school, choosing to follow in his brother Bill's footsteps and attend Penn State University rather than pursue music. The promise of education was also a missed opportunity, however, as the Veltones changed their name to the Delfonics and enjoyed a string of hit records that helped define the Philadelphia Sound.

Lathan studied journalism and drama as an undergraduate and began learning how to work with the moving image. He made a short film and interned at KDKA in Pittsburgh and KYW in Philadelphia, both Westinghouse-owned television stations.[67] He then worked toward a master's of fine arts in broadcasting at Boston University in 1967 and interned at WGBH, then a National Educational Television (NET) station, before dropping out of grad school to join Boston's Ohm Theater Workshop, where he worked his way up to director in a troupe dedicated to protest theater.[68] Lathan directed the play *Riot* at Ohm before being called back to work at WGBH on the new series *Say Brother* in June 1968.[69]

Say Brother was conceived after the assassination of Martin Luther King Jr. as a proactive effort to reach out through a topical public affairs program that dealt exclusively with issues relating to the black community. Lathan's success on the project led to a host of opportunities in New York, beginning with Bill Greaves at *Black Journal*, a TV news and commentary show. As media historian Devorah Heitner has pointed out, these were just two examples of a brief and unique climate in which public broadcasting found the political impetus and financial backing to support dozens of radical black television programs.[70]

Lathan was a central figure in this movement, becoming a sought-after television director. For a span in 1972 he worked on three series at PBS simultaneously, directing episodes of *Sesame Street* and the music series *Soul!* in addition to *Black Journal*. Lathan also developed a reputation for directing dance with the special *Alvin Ailey: Memories and Visions* (1974) and eight episodes of the series *In Performance at the Wolf Trap*, featuring performances by Martha Graham, Mikhail Baryshnikov, and Moshe Paranov. His success at PBS and his growing reputation for directing live performance brought him to the attention of film producers who approached him to make a feature-length documentary rooted in live music.

Saving Grace

Lathan was working with writer-producer Matt Robinson, a childhood friend from Philadelphia, on a narrative film concept when the two were approached by Jesse Jackson and Clarence Avant to make a documentary film capturing the 1972 PUSH Expo in Chicago.[71] The Expo was born out of Jackson's civil rights organization Operation PUSH (People United to Save Humanity), which focused on economic issues such as job programs, corporate accountability, and the creation and cultivation of black-owned businesses. The event featured a host of performers, who, as Jackson remarked in his opening speech at the Expo, were all "black people who felt morally responsible to perform." Jackson arranged a grant from the Ford Foundation to provide the $750,000 production budget for the documentary and put together a distribution deal with Paramount.[72]

Pulling from his experience at PBS capturing music and dance on film, Lathan's *Save the Children* (1973) captures Expo performances from Isaac Hayes, the Jackson 5, Marvin Gaye, Al Green, Nancy Wilson, Bill Withers, Sammy Davis Jr., Cannonball Adderley, Roberta Flack, Curtis Mayfield, Gladys Knights and the Pips, and Wilson Pickett. Filming over three days at the Chicago Amphitheatre, Lathan oversaw eleven cameramen and along with Robinson helped to orchestrate a shooting philosophy that would convey the Expo experience for viewers. At the urging of Lathan and Robinson (and with the support of Jesse Jackson), nine of the eleven cameramen were black, leading to a battle with the local union that was eventually worked out with a deal struck behind closed doors.[73] The documentary takes its name from the Expo's theme, which balanced corporate advertising and its musical showcase with unifying social issues, namely education and child poverty. The film mirrors the agenda of the Expo by intercutting second-unit footage alongside each live performance, turning each song into a topical montage.

The song sequences in *Save the Children* function as rudimentary precursors to music video a decade later, providing a visual component that expands from simple filmed performance. Lathan matches songs to social issues, with Bill Withers's "Lean on Me" addressing homelessness, shots of poor children on Chicago's South Side set to Marvin Gaye's "Save the Babies," and footage of the Vietnam War, famine, and Soviet military displays accompanying "What's Going On." The sometimes plodding editorial treatments, however, lack the potency and excitement of the live footage. The most compelling moment in the film comes with Sammy Davis Jr.'s introduction, which was given a hostile reception stemming from his public support for Nixon's reelection campaign and the perception that he had sold out the black community.[74] Davis accepts the jeers, telling the crowd, "Good. Be angry," before telling them, "You can disagree with my politics . . . but I will not allow anyone to take away the fact that I am black." Winning over the crowd with an impassioned rendition of "I've Gotta Be Me," Davis leaves the stage giving a Black Power salute, his fist triumphantly raised as cheers wash over the arena.

Save the Children's combination of concert footage, social critique, and agenda promotion did not have the intended impact upon the film's release in September 1973. Earlier in the year, Columbia had released *Wattstax* (1973, Mel Stuart), which not only shared the structure and mood of Lathan's film, but also opened with Jesse Jackson leading the crowd in his trademark "I Am Somebody" call-and-response routine. The key point of departure between the two films comes from the economic and historical rationale of the projects. Wattstax was organized to commemorate the seventh anniversary of the Watts rebellion, with $1 tickets cultivating an open event for the community and deflecting any concerns over opportunism. *Save the Children*, on the other hand, reflects the PUSH Expo's complicated and often contradictory aim of promoting black-owned business while providing inroads for multinational corporations with black consumers.

The charitable healing and political earnestness of *Wattstax* appears as a counterpoint to the crass consumerism that sometimes dominates *Save the Children*. With *Wattstax* as a recent precedent, Paramount struggled to market *Save the Children*, and it never was able to devise an approach to properly capitalize on the unequaled footage in Lathan's film. The studio did later hire an editor to recut the original film for release in the South, excising all of the film's political material and retaining only the musical performances. It was an attempt to solve the problem of the precarious balance between the film's politics and its economic boosterism, but the message was gone: Lathan would later dramatically refer to the recut version, titled *Brothers and Sisters in Concert*, as a "raped film."[75]

Before the disappointing release of *Save the Children*, Lathan and Robinson returned to their initial narrative collaboration and began shooting the feature *Amazing Grace*, which was produced for United Artists. The project stemmed from Robinson's love and respect for an older generation of black entertainers who had performed on the so-called Chitlin' Circuit and made inroads in Hollywood during the 1930s and 1940s. Robinson wrote the film explicitly for comedian Jackie "Moms" Mabley, casting Slappy White, Butterfly McQueen, and Lincoln "Stepin Fetchit" Perry in supporting roles. As Lathan remembers, Robinson was an authority on black entertainers, writing the film partially from the vantage point of a historian.[76] Robinson, a writer and producer by trade, became a performer himself. Before Roscoe Orman assumed his iconic role as Gordon in 1974, it was Robinson who had originally portrayed the character on *Sesame Street*.[77] *Amazing Grace*, in many ways, was Robinson's attempt to create a platform to pay homage to the long list of black performers who had come before him.

In a number of ways, *Amazing Grace* is a meditation on the legacy of black entertainers. It strives to bridge a generational divide between politicized youth coming of age in the Black Power era and a set of performers now looked at derisively as reminders of an oppressive past. The idea of stereotypes in black performance as a point of embarrassment can be seen, for example, in the 1968 television documentary *Black History: Lost, Stolen, or Strayed?*, which looked back at film history and placed black representation in a simple positive/negative binary rubric. *Amazing Grace* follows earlier efforts by African American directors to bring black entertainers from the 1930s and 1940s into the fold of the 1970s film explosion. Comic actor Mantan Moreland was invited by Melvin Van Peebles to make an appearance in *Watermelon Man*, while Clarence Muse was a cast member in Poitier's *Buck and the Preacher*. *Amazing Grace* goes beyond mere inclusion, creating a narrative about generational division that places black entertainers within a broader history of black labor and political enfranchisement.

Mabley plays Grace Teasdale Grimes, a widowed grandmother returning to her home in Baltimore by train. She befriends Forthwith Wilson (Slappy White), a Pullman porter on his last route before retiring. Once in Baltimore, the new friends stumble across a plot to use the campaign of a black mayoral candidate, Welton J. Waters (Moses Gunn), to divert black votes from the white opposition candidate to the incumbent mayor. Accepting a bribe, Waters agrees to run a halfhearted campaign and help maintain the status quo. Rather than expose the corruption, Grace confronts Waters and forces him to reconsider his betrayal of the community. With a spiritual and political reawakening, Waters campaigns in earnest with the help of Grace and Forthwith, who enlist a group of students at Morgan State College, a historically black institution, to hit the streets of Baltimore and mobilize the black vote.

By opening the film with train travel and having Slappy White appear as a Pullman porter, the filmmakers establish from the outset that the film will involve a reconsideration of stereotyped screen representations. The scene adds context to problematize simplistic notions of a positive/negative binary understanding. Pullman porters were largely viewed as remnants of the past by the early 1970s; they were increasingly being phased out as a result of the increasing popularity of air travel and the installation of vending machines on trains. For a younger generation of African Americans, porters were symbols of a subservient labor dynamic that was seen as demeaning and outdated, despite the fact that Pullman porters made the first major strides in black labor representation, with the founding of the Brotherhood of Sleeping Car Porters in 1935, and the additional fact that they were instrumental in building the black middle class in the twentieth century, providing sustained economic and educational opportunities for the following generations.[78] *Amazing Grace* uses the train porter as an analogy for black entertainers, recognizing a previous generation that paid its dues in navigating an exclusionary culture industry and helping to pave the way for the next generation of performers.

Lathan shared Matt Robinson's personal interest in black performers as far as comedians were concerned, as both had grown up going to the Uptown in Philadelphia, where Lathan recalls seeing Redd Foxx, Slappy White, and Nipsey Russell.[79] Lathan was not as enthusiastic as Robinson about black film performers, however, seeing Stepin Fetchit as an embodiment of the negative stereotypes. As he would recall years later, "I began to realize the kind of career that Step had had and I gained a great respect for him. . . . The 1960's created symbols, many of them negative. And those of us who bought into them were missing the big picture."[80] Although Lincoln "Stepin Fetchit" Perry's appearance is brief, the dialogue that Robinson wrote for him has the actor taking a step outside of the narrative to explain his legacy. Playing himself, Perry announces that he is "from the artistic archives of Hollywood," and that he was "its first universal, unique movie star." Two decades later, in 1993, Robinson would draw from the time he spent on set with Perry to write the one-man play *The Confessions of Stepin Fetchit*, starring Roscoe Orman and directed by Stan's older brother, Bill Lathan.[81]

While the film provides a compelling moment for Perry, and features Butterfly McQueen and Slappy White, the real impetus for the film rested with Jackie "Moms" Mabley. A star in vaudeville dating back to the 1930s, Mabley was a mainstay on the Chitlin' Circuit while also making inroads with white audiences. Unfortunately, by the time she was set to appear in *Amazing Grace*, the seventy-nine-year-old Mabley was in poor health. She was forced to leave the film midway through shooting to have a pacemaker installed.[82] Mabley insisted on returning to the production, but much of the film is shot using a double, with Mabley appearing only in necessary close-ups. The end result is an often stiff film that features Mabley as a mere shell of her former self. Her starring role in *Amazing Grace* can be read as a grand gesture on the part of Lathan and Robinson—they helped her fulfill her lifelong dream to star in a Hollywood film.[83] Mabley appeared in two late-era race films, but did not headline a feature film until *Amazing Grace*.[84] Mabley took great pride in the film and enjoyed her brief turn as a Hollywood star, passing away in 1975 with a sense of fulfillment.

More than wish fulfillment for an aging star or an ode to black performers, *Amazing Grace* reflects the changing climate of city-based poli-

Grace (Jackie "Moms" Mabley) on the campaign trail in Amazing Grace.

tics in the post–civil rights years. Black communities had begun to exercise their voting power to elect candidates that better represented their interests and experiences. In 1967, Cleveland became the first major American city to elect a black mayor — Carl Stokes — followed the same year by Richard Hatcher in Gary, Indiana, and Walter Washington in Washington, DC.[85] In 1970, Detroit's Coleman Young and Newark's Kenneth Gibson joined the list, followed by Tom Bradley in Los Angeles and Maynard Jackson in Atlanta in 1973. With white flight to the suburbs in the preceding decades, the changing demographics of American cities increased the political clout of black communities. For example, Maynard Jackson's victory in Atlanta found him winning 95 percent of the black vote and only 17.5 percent from whites, showing that a unified and active black voting bloc could dictate its own terms regardless of white consent.[86] *Amazing Grace*, particularly in its second half, becomes a didactic call for black communities to assert themselves politically, with a montage sequence covering Waters's campaign that goes so far as to have Mabley imploring the audience via direct address, "Make him the mayor! . . . We can do it, children. You all can do it! Do it!"[87]

The political earnestness of the film, combined with a brand of humor rooted in the past, made *Amazing Grace* an unlikely entry in the blaxploitation cycle. Although the film was successful at the box office, Lathan recalled the struggles and compromises in making the film with a fragile leading lady and modest budget, saying years later that *Amazing Grace* is "really not a good film."[88] As the studios moved away from black-focused features in 1975, and independent black productions all but disappeared after 1976, Lathan returned to television as a more reliable and prosperous medium. After working with an older generation of comedians on

Amazing Grace, he signed on to become a director on *Sanford and Son* at the behest of Redd Foxx, who had requested a black director for his hit sitcom.[89] Lathan's success on the show led to a wealth of opportunities directing episodic network television, and he earned a reputation for making quality shows that came in under budget and ahead of schedule. Lathan directed episodes of *That's My Mama* before transitioning away from programs with explicitly black themes or casts, directing shows like *The Waltons*, *Barney Miller*, *Eight Is Enough*, and *Cagney & Lacey*.

At the same time that he was busy working on commercially oriented network shows, Lathan was also making a number of projects through PBS that allowed him creative freedom to explore racial themes. He made a few films in the *American Short Stories* series, directing a filmed version of Richard Wright's *Almos' a Man* (1976) followed by Ernest J. Gaines's *The Sky Is Gray* (1980), both of which traveled the film festival circuit in addition to airing on television. Through PBS Lathan also filmed Daniel A. Stein's stage play *The Trial of the Moke* (1978); *A House Divided: Denmark Vessey's Rebellion* (1982), about a failed South Carolina slave revolt in 1822; and a dramatic exploration of Booker T. Washington's childhood in *Booker* (1984). He then reconnected with Matt Robinson to make the documentary *A Celebration of Life: A Tribute to Martin Luther King, Jr.* (1984).

Among a host of projects for PBS, Lathan also directed episodes for the dramatic series *Up and Coming*, a well-received show that consciously looked to move past the slapstick nature of network fare like *Sanford and Son*, *Good Times*, and *The Jeffersons* by using realism to explore the struggles of a black family in San Francisco.[90] He was briefly attached to a feature project in 1978 for Barry Hankerson, the record-producer husband of Gladys Knight, who had costarred in and produced her failed star vehicle *Pipe Dreams* (1976, Stephen Venora), but the film never materialized.[91] Ultimately, the promise of a theatrically released feature did not matter all that much to Lathan. Television had provided ample work and creative opportunities. A return to box-office-oriented filmmaking was not important to him.

Beat Street Breakdown

A decade had passed since the release of *Amazing Grace* before Lathan found himself directing his next theatrical feature, *Beat Street*. Produced by Harry Belafonte and David V. Picker for Orion Pictures, the film is based on a series of *Village Voice* articles about the burgeoning hip-hop scene in the Bronx by journalist Steven Hager. Three screenwriters shaped Hager's research into a narrative, and initially, white director Andrew Davis was hired to direct. However, Davis was fired early in the production, and the producers set out to replace him with a black director who could handle movement and add an air of authenticity to the project.[92]

Aside from Belafonte, all of the above-the-line talent was white, but producers feared having a white director would create an awkward sense of outsiders commenting on black culture. Lathan was an obvious choice, not only because he was one of a handful of working black directors at the time, but also because of his long track record with music and dance. He was hired quickly, but he was not rushed into shooting; Belafonte gave him time to reconceptualize the project on his own terms. While his success on the television side of Hollywood in the 1980s was increasingly tied to his ability to work on projects that had little to no articulation of issues pertaining to race, his work on *Beat Street* hinged on him bringing a much-needed black perspective to the project.

Beat Street was not the first feature film to focus on hip-hop culture: the previous year's *Wild Style* (1983, Charlie Ahearn) had received a small-scale release by the art-house distributor First Run Features. Made on a shoestring budget and featuring a cast of non-actors, *Wild Style* was shot in a *cinéma vérité* mode, functioning as documentation of a culture that was beginning to gain national attention. The Sugarhill Gang's 1979 single "Rappers Delight" had brought rap out of the Bronx and its surrounding boroughs, becoming a staple at discos and garnering radio play across the nation and overseas. Over the next five years, hip-hop had gained traction through releases from small labels like Sugar Hill and Enjoy Records; mainstream tributes, such as Blondie's "Rapture"; and breaking's visible presence in Hollywood films such as Paramount's *Flashdance* (1983, Adrian Lyne), in which Jennifer Beals dances on a street corner with the Rock Steady Crew, incorporating their moves into her climactic dance audition.

By 1984, hip-hop had sparked the interest of a number of minor studios. The Cannon Group rushed out the inept *Breakin'* (1984, Joel Silberg), its sequel *Breakin' 2: Electric Boogaloo* (1984, Sam Firstenberg), and its ill-conceived spin-off *Rappin'* (1985, Joel Silberg), while New World released the hilariously bad *Body Rock* (1984, Marcelo Epstein), starring Lorenzo Lamas. Thanks in large part to Stan Lathan, the level of incompetence and lack of authenticity that ran through *Breakin'*, *Rappin'*, and *Body Rock* did not transfer over to *Beat Street*. With contributions from artists at the center of hip-hop's origins, *Beat Street* was far from a hollow exploitation of the then-red-hot break-dancing fad.

Like *Wild Style*, *Beat Street* was an attempt to document the hip-hop movement, but it departed from Ahearn's film by placing the narrative at its forefront in order to make itself commercially viable. *Beat Street* nevertheless struggles to balance commercial aspirations with its desire to capture the authentic origins of hip-hop culture. Complicating matters further, the culture that *Beat Street* was attempting to document was quickly disappearing, as it was in the process of being transformed by the record industry into something wholly separate from the scene's origins in the Bronx during the 1970s. Recalling the impetus for turning his *Village Voice* articles into a feature film project, Steven Hager recalled, years later, "I wanted to get the story told as accurately as possible, and I knew the influx of money was rapidly changing the scene."[93] By attempting to re-create a moment that had passed, *Beat Street* presented a conflated space simultaneously representing noncommercial origins and a commodified present.

The structure and focus of the film is heavily influenced by the PBS documentary *Style Wars* (1983, Henry Chalifant and Tony Silver), which explored definitions of art and criminality through conflict between New York City's graffiti writers and the anti-graffiti campaign of Mayor Ed Koch and the Metropolitan Transit Authority (MTA).[94] *Beat Street* expands from *Style Wars*' focus on graffiti and incorporates music and dancing to tell a stand-in narrative for the origins of hip-hop culture through the friendship between Kenny (Guy Davis), an aspiring DJ; Lee (Robert Taylor), his break-dancing brother; and Ramo (Jon Chardiet), their graffiti-writing friend. Graffiti and break dancing are each provided with a social rationale and justified as legitimate art throughout the film. Ramo's "bombing" of subway trains is seen as a form of urban beautification and emotional survival rather than mere vandalism, while Lee's break dancing becomes a group activity that replaces street gangs. Battles on the dance floor serve as a nonviolent substitution for the turf wars of the 1970s. Both art forms are placed in conflict with the authorities, with Ramo being chased by MTA security and Lee getting arrested for dancing in a subway station. Interestingly, Kenny's turntablism is also explained as an art form, but never placed in legal limbo. Rather than raising concerns over sampling and intellectual property, which were not widespread until the late 1980s, the film represents DJs in a strictly 1970s context, with Kenny spinning exclusively at parties and clubs, but not aspiring to become a recording artist.

Beat Street's focus on retelling hip-hop's origin story at times resembles early rock-and-roll feature films like *Rock Around the Clock* (1956, Fred F. Sears) in that it incorporates detailed explanations of the music and art geared toward uninitiated audience members. Just as early rock-and-roll films used brief appearances by Chuck Berry, Little Richard, and Frankie Lymon & the Teenagers, *Beat Street* uses performances and cameos from

Afrika Bambaataa & the Soulsonic Force, Kool Herc, Jazzy Jay, Sha Rock, the Treacherous Three, Doug E. Fresh, Melle Mel, the Rock Steady Crew, and the New York City Breakers to convey a sense of the new music. In effect, the film is a crash course in hip-hop's first decade, explaining the basic concepts behind the movement and introducing the key figures in its development.

What separates *Beat Street* from early rock-and-roll films (and from other hip-hop films in the mid-1980s) is that the story is told from the perspective of characters that are cultural producers, not consumers or entrepreneurs. Although it often conflates and simplifies hip-hop's history, *Beat Street* attempts to remain faithful to the social, political, and economic factors that helped shape the movement. Hip-hop repurposed bleak cityscapes and ordinary items, turning concrete walls and subway trains into canvases, cardboard boxes and discarded tiles into dance floors, sneakers and sweatsuits into high fashion, and record players into instruments. As Kimberley Monteyne pointed out in her book on hip-hop in film, *Beat Street* shows a topography of urban ruin, conveying the bleak realities of life in the South Bronx that informed hip-hop's sense of cultural resistance.[95]

For all of its ambition to present an authentic portrait of hip-hop culture in the Bronx, *Beat Street* was initially held in contempt by a number of the people closest to the project. Compared to the low-budget and independently produced *Wild Style*, which has an almost amateurish aesthetic that matches the makeshift nature of hip-hop, the Hollywood polish of *Beat Street* often seems in conflict with the film's subject. Steven Hager expressed his disappointment by saying, "Not a single word of anything I actually wrote made it into that unfortunate film"; he felt that the conflation of facts and events into a Hollywood narrative obscured his original intent of documenting the culture.[96]

The most glaring Hollywood convention comes with the saccharine-sweet love story between Kenny and Tracy (Rae Dawn Chong), a composer and choreographer at City College. The romance between opposites is underscored by the preposterously literal song "Strangers in a Strange World," which not only paints the characters as the blandest of clichés, but uproots the tone of the rest of the film's music.[97] More exacting criticism was leveled at the film's graffiti, which was painted by the film's theatrical union crew and not actual graffiti artists. The majority of the murals and tags are completely out of step with the aesthetics of tagging and bombing.[98]

The film's central selling point, its portrayal of breaking, also came under fire for being inauthentic. While the battle scene at the Roxy cap-

The choreographed subway battle in Beat Street.

tures the natural alignment of breaking, the second dance battle on the subway platform was choreographed by Lester Wilson to resemble the movements and geometry of dance in a traditional musical; he seems to have completely abandoned true breaking, misrepresenting its form, structure, and purpose.[99] However, even though the film's choreography was denounced by many, including the Rock Steady Crew, for occasionally straying from original breaking forms, *Beat Street* stands out from other contemporary films in terms of its presentation of breaking to audiences as a legitimate art form.[100]

Cannon's *Breakin'*, on the other hand, engages in the crassest form of cultural appropriation, creating a version of "break dancing" that is largely divorced from the style developed in New York. Instead, *Breakin'* presents West Coast funk dances like locking, popping, and electric boogaloo as if they were interchangeable with breaking, borrowing the New York form's name for marketing purposes and confusing popular understandings of the lineage and aesthetics of hip-hop culture. The subsequent visibility of this sanitized California version of break dancing reached its peak in 1984, spawning countless how-to manuals aimed at children, showing up in commercials for McDonald's, and even being featured in the closing ceremonies of the Summer Olympics in Los Angeles.[101]

Beat Street, by contrast, at least maintains most of the formal qualities of breaking. Lathan makes a number of concessions to fit breaking into the framework of a mainstream narrative film, but it is never bastardized or exploited in the manner of *Breakin'* or *Body Rock*. Unfortunately, the box-office success of *Beat Street* ($16.5 million), alongside both *Breakin'* films ($53.7 million combined), solidified their connection in the summer of 1984 and in the years to follow.[102] Twenty years later, MGM packaged the films together for DVD release, despite the fact that the films could not be more different in tone, purpose, cultural understanding, and artistry.

Beat Street is by no means a straightforward documentation of hip-hop culture, at least in the manner Hager envisioned. However, it does capture the movement at a crossroads between local subculture and the global commercial force it would become. Although the film is set in the Bronx and mirrors the noncommercial expression of hip-hop in the 1970s, it also hints at the possibilities of the phenomenon as a financial refuge. Kenny's friend Chollie (Leon W. Grant), a would-be manager and entrepreneur, is a prime example of the film's conflated setting. Hager's articles explored hip-hop in terms of a pre-commercial culture, but Chollie sees it as economic salvation, something that might provide a pathway out of the ghetto and toward fame and fortune. Chollie points toward figures like Russell Simmons, and the focus on hip-hop as a record industry product, a theme that Michael Schultz would touch upon with *Krush Groove*. Throughout *Beat Street*, there is a sense of opportunity outside of the Bronx that defies the insulated culture of Hager's essays. No longer art for art's sake, hip-hop was quickly being defined by the allure of money and celebrity.

While a recurring theme in early hip-hop films is the move toward "legitimate" outlets of expression, namely the incorporation of breaking into formal modern dance and the stage, the characters in *Beat Street* remain skeptical of outsiders and, unlike the characters in *Breakin'* and *Body Rock*, eschew assimilation into the larger popular culture. At the same time, there is the acknowledgment that hip-hop will not remain static, and that it will ultimately move from the Bronx and take on new forms, meanings, and possibilities. The optimism of the title song in the film's finale points to hip-hop's transition, with Kenny rapping (through the disembodied voice of the great Melle Mel), "So after this there'll be no more hard times / No more bad times and no more pain / No more chump change, none of that bull / Just movies, museums, and the hall of fame."

Two decades later, the final lyric proved prophetic. Hip-hop's incorporation into film, of course, was not limited to the first rush of movies in the mid-1980s, but also provided big-screen stars like Will Smith and Ice Cube. Graffiti's move from subway cars and brick walls to easel painting and the art gallery was started by Dondi in the early 1980s and furthered with the rising celebrity of Jean-Michel Basquiat and Keith Haring. As for the final line of "Beat Street," Melle Mel would join the Rock and Roll Hall of Fame in 2007 as a member of Grandmaster Flash and the Furi-

Melle Mel raps the title song in Beat Street.

ous Five, the first rap group to be inducted. As implausible as it may have seemed in the early 1980s, hip-hop has long since transitioned from subculture to mainstream popular culture.

Lathan made the most of his return to Hollywood filmmaking, creating a critically acclaimed picture that looked to place him alongside Michael Schultz and Sidney Poitier as another black director able to find consistent work on theatrical features. Instead, Lathan returned to television full-time, and *Beat Street* is his final theatrical feature to date. Lathan's creative autonomy on the *Beat Street* project—not to mention the film's box-office success—was the polar opposite of Gil Moses's experience on *The Fish That Saved Pittsburgh*. Nevertheless, both men found themselves working in television after directing their sole theatrical features in the decade following blaxploitation. But while Moses retreated to television almost by necessity, sacrificing much of his creative voice in order to earn a living and provide for his family, Lathan's talents were in high demand, and he looked to television as a medium with far more creative and financial possibility than feature filmmaking. After *Beat Street*, Lathan once again split his time between PBS and the networks, directing the American Playhouse series adaptation of James Baldwin's *Go Tell It on the Mountain* (1985) and working on episodic shows like *Miami Vice*, *Falcon Crest*, *Remington Steele*, and *Hill Street Blues*. Entering the 1990s, he was situated to continue along the same path. Instead, he sought to gain greater creative and financial control of his work by becoming a producer as well as a director.

Lathan developed a working relationship with Russell Simmons in the early 1990s, and together they formed Russell Simmons Visual Productions (later renamed as the Simmons-Lathan Media Group) to produce film and television projects.[103] While their partnership initially mirrored Motown's Hollywood ambitions in the 1970s, focusing on feature films, Lathan and Simmons hit their stride with the development of projects for the small screen. Their breakthrough success came with HBO's *Def Comedy Jam*, which provided a venue for black stand-up comics free from the censorship of broadcast networks and basic cable. Lathan worked on a number of black-focused sitcoms in the 1990s, directing seventeen episodes of *Roc* with Charles S. Dutton and the pilot episode of *Martin*, both of which aired on Fox.[104] Increasingly, however, the projects that came out of the Simmons-Lathan partnership were geared toward cable channels and upstart broadcast networks like WB and UPN, where black-focused sitcoms were a staple of the programming. They produced a wide array of shows, including *Def Poetry Jam* for HBO and six seasons of the WB sitcom *The Steve Harvey Show*, with Lathan serving as executive producer and directing the majority of its 122 episodes.

Lathan's decidedly commercial approach to working in the media industry has placed him in a rare position of power; he is able to create his own opportunities and foster young black talent. However, some of the programs Lathan has worked on have drawn criticism (most notably from Spike Lee and Bill Cosby) for perpetuating stereotypes and underestimating the intellectual capacity of black audiences. Lathan deflects these criticisms with the simple statement, "I give people what they want."[105] This economically focused response is both curious and telling. On the one hand, Lathan's seeming lack of concern for the broader implications of the shows he produces contradicts his initial investment in the medium in the 1960s and 1970s, when he aspired to carve out a space for black expression within an otherwise all-white television landscape. On the other, his primary concern with audience and profitability reflects his experiences in the industry, which have led him to replace his youthful idealism with a more pragmatic approach.

Despite their varying degrees of success and satisfaction working as directors, Stan Lathan and Gil Moses are linked in more ways than one. Capturing key points in the development of basketball and hip-hop as expressions of black identity, both directors took advantage of rare post-blaxploitation opportunities to make films that use narrative to document cultural transformation. Directing for stage, television, and film, Lathan and Moses also had musical backgrounds that informed their directorial styles and choice of content. They helped pay homage to Moms Mabley and had close friendships with Gordon from *Sesame Street*. They came from humble backgrounds, excelled academically, and were put on by major Hollywood studios at the height of the blaxploitation cycle.

Beyond their credits as directors, their legacies continue to be shaped by the work of their daughters. Gil Moses's daughter China is a respected jazz singer living in Paris, while his eldest daughter, Tsia, is an accomplished television producer. Stan Lathan's daughter Sanaa has been one of the busiest and most visible black actresses in Hollywood over the past twenty years. These are intelligent, talented, and strong women whose lives have been shaped by the creative force of their fathers. Their careers may point to missed opportunities on the part of Hollywood to foster the growth of two unquestionably talented artists; nevertheless, they are also a reminder that the importance of Gil Moses and Stan Lathan is not limited to the handful of films they were allowed to direct.

CHAPTER SEVEN

Dirty Minds Reformed

CELEBRITY, POWER, AND THE DIRECTORIAL TURNS OF RICHARD PRYOR AND PRINCE

FILM HISTORY IS LITTERED WITH ACTORS USING THEIR celebrity status to gain access to the director's chair, ranging from Charles Laughton and his one-off *Night of the Hunter* (1955) to a string of actors with long and fruitful careers behind the camera, including Charlie Chaplin, Gene Kelly, Jerry Lewis, Clint Eastwood, Robert Redford, and Sidney Poitier. Learning the trade firsthand on set, film stars benefit from the impression that they have earned their chance to direct and can often leverage their power to convince studios to support new endeavors. Richard Pryor's ascension in Hollywood followed an established path: his transition to director built on the decade he spent observing people like Poitier, Michael Schultz, Paul Schrader, and Sidney Lumet plying their craft. Prince lacked Pryor's credentials and became a director with only one acting credit to his name. Both Pryor and Prince would make their directorial debuts in 1986, on the cusp of Spike Lee's arrival with *She's Gotta Have It*. Each of them now has an expansive body of work. But the move to becoming a filmmaker for both Pryor and Prince shows just how difficult it had become for African Americans to gain access to the director's chair in the film industry—it took exceptional cases of celebrity to make Hollywood amenable to hiring a first-time black director.

Pryor's *Jo Jo Dancer, Your Life Is Calling* (1986) promised to be a watershed moment for a movie star who had yet to find a balance between his emotionally penetrating comedic style and narrative cinema. When the film was released, there was a hope that being his own director would allow Pryor the creative freedom to bypass the awkward genre formulas that had sanitized his comedic edge in so many of his star vehicles. This same hopefulness did not extend to Prince, whose decision to take over directing *Under the Cherry Moon* (1986) mid-production became a point of contempt, further fueling the growing consensus that his unchecked ego needed to be reined in. Critics and the general public seemed to be asking the same question: What made a pop star think he could direct a film?

Pryor and Prince may have had different backgrounds, but neither of them made sense as a director in any traditional way. Neither of them had formal director training; they both broke from the "movie brat" model of university-trained directors prevalent in the 1970s and 1980s. Yet both also managed to convince major studios to invest in their films and grant them the sort of artistic autonomy that was usually reserved for established auteurs, using their celebrity as leverage to gain access to financing and a level of creative control that was being denied to other black filmmakers. If Prince lacked cinematic experience, Pryor surely lacked the focus and work ethic to succeed behind the camera. What the two shared, above all, was the reputation for being geniuses.

Boundlessly creative and artistically daring, both Pryor and Prince retain a sense of black identity at the core of their personas even while their appeal moves past racial designations. They also share a reputation for being temperamental and eccentric, simultaneously frustrating and endearing themselves to even their most ardent admirers. They have complex and multifaceted personalities that are the subject of ongoing public fascination, spawning endless speculation into the contours of their private lives and how it shapes their art. Most importantly, their chosen fields (comedy and music) place them in the realm of commercial entertainment, where their work is filtered through audience expectation and the financial demands of the culture industry. The eventual calling of Hollywood and the economic promise of translating their success on record and stage to the screen brought with it new opportunities for expression and a financial windfall for the studios.

Pryor and Prince both found new creative outlets through cinema, but their time as directors also brought with it both compromise and frustration. The very idea of a genius directing a film falls in line with the most romantic notions of authorial expression. As literary scholar Marjorie Garber has pointed out, "the further our society gets from individual agency—the less the individual seems to have real power to change things—the more we idealize the genius, who is by this definition the opposite of committee or collaborative enterprise."[1] Prince and Pryor found it impossible to live up to this ideal as directors. Hollywood filmmaking, of course, is collaborative by nature, and it could never give them the same kind of opportunity for unfiltered expression that they found on stage and in music. Their directorial debuts, however, nevertheless provide unique insight into their personal, political, and artistic perspectives.

Jo Jo Dancer, Your Life Is Calling was the culmination of Pryor's long flirtation with the idea of taking control of his career. The semiautobiographical story reframes his life, making amends for past sins and crafting a redemptive tale of personal triumph that was more fiction than fact. The film also shows that a great artist, left to his own devices, does not necessarily create great art. *Under the Cherry Moon*, by contrast, resulted from Prince's swift ascendancy in Hollywood and masks introspection by placing it within an allusive (and some would argue elusive) fictional narrative. For an artist so steeped in mystery, the film strips away constructed layers of his rock god persona to show a relaxed, funny, and surprisingly normal man. *Under the Cherry Moon* also is evidence that corporate synergy and ample promotion do not always lead to commercial success, even when structured around a global superstar.

In *Jo Jo Dancer, Your Life Is Calling* and *Under the Cherry Moon*, one can see some of the most ambitious work of two unique artists. But the films also demonstrate just how hesitant Hollywood still could be about hiring black directors. Before Pryor and Prince made their first films in 1986, not a single black director had been given the opportunity to make a theatrically released debut since the end of the blaxploitation cycle in 1977. The other six directors working during this era (Schultz, Poitier, Williamson, Fanaka, Moses, and Lathan) had all made their first features during the blaxploitation cycle, and they used their experience navigating the film industry to continue working. Pryor and Prince, in contrast, had to make up their approach on the fly, and they used the only tool they had at their disposal—their celebrity—to get over as directors.

RICHARD PRYOR

Pryor is a cultural icon rife with contradictions and curiosities. His value as an artist is closely associated with stand-up routines and comedy albums, and yet the majority of his professional life was spent working in film and television. He is often called a genius, though his most visible projects have largely failed to capture his brilliance. Pryor expressed a desire to take an active role in controlling his film career, but he squandered a number of opportunities given him that were never presented to other black screen artists.

Pryor signed unprecedented contracts with Hollywood studios that not only made him one of the highest-paid actors in the movie business but also handed him creative autonomy. At a time when African Americans were being pushed to the extreme margins of the film industry, Pryor was granted control over his own career and presented with the opportunity to cultivate projects for other black screen artists who otherwise lacked access in Hollywood. Unfortunately, Pryor was the wrong man for the job. Personal demons, poor health, and growing indifference to his own creative output led to disappointing turns as a producer and advocate for black artists. He only attempted to make a few films as a director and producer, choosing instead to chase lucrative paychecks acting in hackneyed studio comedies.

Pryor's career as a film actor and producer simultaneously complicates and reinforces some of the prevailing notions of Hollywood's relationship with black artists and audiences in the decade following blaxploitation. On the one hand, Hollywood's willingness to grant creative control to a black actor defies the logic of the closed system that largely excluded African Americans. On the other, his embrace by the film industry echoed the Hollywood of the 1960s. Pryor served as a highly visible re-articulation of Sidney Poitier—like Poitier, he was a lone black star whose success obscured the erasure of blackness elsewhere from the Hollywood frame. He was an unlikely successor to Poitier, trading in well-mannered compassion for raw comedy rooted in pathos, but both actors were given responsibilities as symbols of African Americans at large, and both were charged with using their celebrity to create opportunities for other black artists. Poitier took these responsibilities seriously, while Pryor's personal and professional life suggest his reluctance to assume the role, or even resentment of his power in the film industry.

Pryor did not arrive in Hollywood as a readymade star. Instead, he spent a decade trying to prove himself as a viable screen performer and writer. Playing supporting roles in blaxploitation and mainstream fare, Pryor pursued a movie career that coincided with his rise to fame as a stand-up comedian and recording artist.[2] Overhauling his stage persona in the early 1970s, he ditched his Bill Cosby–inspired delivery for a more outspoken—and at times obscene—brand of comedy that translated easily to albums and nightclubs. Adapting his comic sensibilities for narrative films proved to be more difficult. Rather than waiting for someone else to figure out how to use his talents onscreen, he decided to create his own projects. If the blaxploitation cycle brought new opportunities for black screen artists, Pryor must have found the climate in Hollywood stifling. When he began writing scripts, working briefly with author Ishmael Reed, he was unable to find either an interested studio or an independent producer to finance his projects.[3]

Pryor struck up a friendship with Michael Schultz around 1973, and the two began developing a film together. With a screenplay from Matt

Robinson, Schultz and Pryor began talks with David Picker at United Artists to make *Simmons from Chicago*, a farcical comedy in which a pimp becomes president of the United States.[4] When *Simmons from Chicago* fell through, Schultz and Pryor began shopping a new project to the studios, a film called *The Black Stranger*, written by Pryor. A far cry from his stand-up routines, *The Black Stranger* was a serious-minded western with a supernatural twist involving voodoo.[5] *The Black Stranger* was never produced, as financiers were scared off by its idiosyncrasies and bending of genre norms. Elements of the script were likely incorporated into the final script for *Blazing Saddles* (1974, Mel Brooks) when Pryor was hired to improve the screenplay and add more nuanced elements to the black cowboy character.[6]

As Pryor struggled to develop his own projects, the climate changed for him thanks to his growing album sales and a string of well-received television appearances. All of this led to high-profile opportunities for him as an actor in film.[7] He took a brief supporting role opposite Gene Wilder in *Silver Streak* (1976, Arthur Hiller), and his scenes garnered the majority of attention from both audiences and critics, prompting Hollywood to reconsider him as a box-office commodity. His supporting appearance in *Silver Streak*, as well as his growing clout as a recording artist and concert draw, solidified his reputation as a bankable star across mediums. In 1977 he reportedly became a "20-Million-Dollar Man" owing to his new film deal with Universal, his album sales, and his television contract with NBC for the ill-fated *Richard Pryor Show*.[8] The six-picture deal at Universal allowed him to develop his own projects, option material with studio funding, and receive a percentage of the profits.[9] Positioned to become a breakthrough star at the very moment that Hollywood was shifting away from black-focused pictures, Pryor saw his earlier struggles to find his bearings in the film industry seemingly disappear overnight. The projects he had hoped to start a few years earlier, *Simmons from Chicago* and *The Black Stranger*, were now real possibilities, but he chose not to revisit them.

Despite his swift ascendancy as a major player in Hollywood, Pryor was full of contradictions and setbacks as a rising star, never fully capitalizing on the opportunity and promise of the late 1970s. In 1977 he made the leap from supporting roles to being the top-billed draw in *Greased Lightning* and *Which Way Is Up?*, taking advantage of the sudden demand for his talents by signing a four-picture deal with Warner Bros. that would run concurrent with his deal at Universal. Warner Bros. promised him $1 million per film, 50 percent ownership of the material, full creative control (along with his lawyer, David Franklin), and the opportunity to direct.[10] As luck would have it, the creative autonomy and financial backing that had been so elusive just a few years earlier were now being provided by two major studios. All Pryor had to do was choose a project and see it through, having already bypassed the biggest stumbling blocks by securing financing and studio approval.

Unfortunately, Pryor's deal with Warner Bros. was voided when he failed to deliver any scripts to the studio or show much interest in pursuing projects.[11] The failure to take advantage of his contract at Warner Bros. marked just one in a number of unrealized opportunities for Pryor in the late 1970s. He was slated to star in an all-black adaptation of *Cyrano de Bergerac* in 1977—the film was to be shot in Haiti as part of a concerted effort by President Jean-Claude Duvalier to make his country the movie center of the Caribbean and a prime tourist destination for African Americans—but for myriad reasons, the project never came to fruition.[12] As early as 1977, Pryor also began pursuing a biopic about jazz legend Charlie Parker, in which he was going to star.[13] He began training for the role, enlisting Sonny Rollins to teach him to play the saxophone and signing Miles Davis to be a technical adviser on the film.[14] The Parker biopic would be discussed for the next decade, but it never became a reality for Pryor. In addition to these unrealized efforts, his film *Family Dreams* (later titled *Bustin' Loose*) was shelved midway through production; he also left the cast of the Mel Brooks film *History of the World Part I*, being replaced by Gregory Hines.[15]

The Warner Bros. agreement now voided, Pryor still had a contract with Universal and continued acting in mainstream releases. But he had not become the box-office draw the studio had envisioned, and the projects that did come to fruition in 1978 and 1979 were a mixed bag in terms of quality and box-office success. Pryor revisited the terrain of *Which Way Is Up?* with *Blue Collar* (1978, Paul Schrader), again focusing on class and labor politics, but this time with a more serious tone, suggesting that he might turn toward self-consciously dramatic roles in years to come. After his straightforward comedic role in *California Suite* (1978, Herbert Ross), however, he and costar Bill Cosby were scolded in the press. Pauline Kael's review of the film in the *New Yorker* singled out the slapstick scenes with Cosby and Pryor for being racially stereotyped, causing Cosby to take out a full-page ad in *Variety* to respond to the criticism.[16] To round out 1978, Pryor made a brief appearance as the titular character in *The Wiz*. Though he certainly was not the cause of the film's lack of success at the box office, being associated with the project did Pryor no favors. It did not help him position himself as a bankable star with crossover appeal. His next three appearances in narrative films were notably lacking in ambition: he had walk-on cameos in *The Muppet Movie* (1979, James Frawley), *Wholly Moses!* (1980, Gary Weis), and *In God We Tru$t* (1980, Marty Feldman).

As the 1970s drew to a close, Pryor's movie career seemed to be tapering off. Just a few years into the 1980s, however, he would become the biggest movie star in Hollywood, appearing in a string of box-office hits and earning an unprecedented amount of money. His transition into a full-fledged movie star rested on two separate events, one of which showed him breaking from the studio model of production, and the other premised on the cult of celebrity. The success of *Richard Pryor: Live in Concert* (1979, Jeff Margolis) provides a clear example of his genius as a stand-up comic, capturing an unfiltered performance freed from the constraints of narrative filmmaking. Produced and distributed outside of Hollywood's major studios after Universal passed on the concert film (a genre that was an anomaly at the time), *Live in Concert* became a surprise hit. Pryor's stand-up routine is sharp and incisive, and in it he sheds much of the outward nervousness that defined his earlier work on stage. The film also shows that for all of Hollywood's intentions and its efforts to cultivate stardom through narrative vehicles, Pryor's creative instincts were more attuned to locating the balance between medium and audience.

Unfortunately, the second event that helped raise his profile and make him such an indispensable property in Hollywood had nothing to do with his creative independence. Pryor nearly died after lighting himself on fire inside of his Northridge home in 1980, and the media feeding frenzy that ensued catapulted him into the upper crust of celebrity fame. News reports on the incident fueled speculation and myth, and progress reports on his recovery drew the story out for months. The Northridge fire and the media attention that accompanied it solidified the public's fascination with the intersection between his art and personal demons, generating an appetite for new Pryor films even as he lay prone and bandaged in the intensive care unit. Buoyed by notoriety, Pryor's first two releases after the Northridge fire, *Stir Crazy* and *Bustin' Loose*, marked breakthroughs at the box office despite their artistic shortcomings. Directed by Sidney Poitier and Michael Schultz, respectively, *Stir Crazy* and *Bustin' Loose* are anomalies in the post-blaxploitation years as studio-financed hits employing black directors.

Pryor suddenly found himself to be one of the most sought-after talents in Hollywood. Realizing his artistic ambitions and transitioning into a more serious-minded film career, however, were complicated by his troubled finances and by his highly publicized fallout with manager David Franklin.[17] Although he had physically recovered from his massive burns, Pryor came out of his personal crisis financially strapped, emotionally spent, and lacking creative focus. He was also still very much under the grip of drug addiction, even as he made claims to being clean and sober.[18] At best, Pryor's subsequent efforts were flawed but ambitious. Examples include his role as a Vietnam veteran in *Some Kind of Hero* (1982, Michael Pressman), and his return to stand-up comedy in *Richard Pryor: Live on Sunset Strip* (1982, Joe Layton). At worst, his newfound stardom brought about lucrative paydays but disimpassioned performances. There were troublesome projects like the offensive neo-slavery comedy *The Toy* (1982, Richard Donner), for example, and an ill-conceived *Superman III* (1983, Richard Lester). Pryor earned $3 million and $4 million for these films, respectively.[19] It was another in a long line of contradictions that the height of Pryor's stardom coincided with his most critically reviled performances.

Mood Indigo

Although 1983 may not have seen Pryor at his artistic best, he had proved to be a major box-office attraction and a boon to Columbia Studios, which had produced both *Stir Crazy* and *Live on Sunset Strip*. Through box-office precedent and the desire to meet audience demand, Columbia entered into a $40 million four-picture agreement with Pryor to start his own production company, Indigo Films. Moving beyond the freedoms granted in his previous contracts with Warner Bros. and Universal, Columbia's contract for Indigo granted him complete autonomy. He could use the $40 million as he saw fit, and was only required to serve as producer, with no obligation to act in, write, or direct any of the projects made under the Indigo banner.

For Columbia, the goal was to further capitalize on Pryor's celebrity, using the Indigo brand as an extension of Pryor's reputation at the box office. Pryor's stated goal, while not necessarily antithetical to those of the studio, was to "provide opportunities for people who haven't had opportunities to do films in the past."[20] Hiring friend and former blaxploitation star Jim Brown as the president of Indigo, Pryor approached the company as a means of providing African American filmmakers an entry into the guarded gates of Hollywood. With Indigo, he not only had the opportunity to assist black-focused projects, but also had a chance to take an active role in reclaiming his screen persona.

Indigo was meant to serve as a venue for black film artists and a primary provider for features targeted toward an otherwise underserved black audience, giving writers and directors the chance to put forth nuanced meditations on identity. The end result, however, fell short of these goals. Indigo made a quick first feature, with Pryor returning to the stand-up concert format with *Richard Pryor: Here and Now* (1983, Richard Pryor). It was a more confident but less compelling performance than *Live on Sunset Strip*. The first two narrative projects that Indigo developed were *The Charlie Parker Story* and *Double Whoopee*, the latter a proposed reteaming of Pryor and Gene Wilder. Neither went into production, as Indigo became mired in disagreements between Pryor and Brown over the company's direction.

As it turned out, Pryor's initial statements suggesting that Indigo would cultivate black-focused features were largely hollow, as his primary focus at the company was to create star vehicles for himself. Brown, on the other hand, regularly brought ideas to Indigo and argued for their cultural importance as well as their potential profitability. Pryor disregarded every one of Brown's proposals and ended up firing him as president of the company after only seven months on the job.[21] Columbia stated that Brown's firing was Pryor's decision alone, based on the prerequisite "creative differences."[22] The Hollywood branch of the NAACP, however, protested the firing and suggested that it was due to pressure from Columbia and its parent company, Coca-Cola, speculating that the company saw Brown's penchant for activism as a threat to its corporate image.[23]

Regardless of the reasons for Jim Brown's departure from Indigo, his absence changed the tone of the company. A fleeting, unrealized vision of a flourishing African American cinema in Hollywood seemed to go with him. Brown's artistic vision for Indigo, as well as his business sense, would be vindicated in the coming years, however, as a number of the projects that he first brought to the table became major successes for other companies. Brown had pushed hard for Indigo to produce Alice Walker's novel *The Color Purple* as the company's first non-Pryor film, and had encouraged the company to finally realize the long-rumored Charlie Parker biopic.[24] He had also disagreed with Indigo's decision to pass on *Purple Rain*. Publicly, Pryor had expressed interest in realizing the long-dormant adaptation of *The Autobiography of Malcolm X*: in the late 1970s he had been suggested as a possible star for such a film, but he had never actively pursued the project.[25] The script for *The Charlie Parker Story* became *Bird* (1988, Clint Eastwood), while adapting *The Color Purple* for the big screen eventually fell into the hands of Steven Spielberg. In addition to pushing these projects, Brown attempted to carve out a space in Hollywood for established black talent. He tried to bring Robert Hooks back into the fold of feature film, and he unsuccessfully sought financing for a joint venture between Glynn Turman, Whitman Mayo, and Paul Winfield to make a black-focused science-fiction film.[26]

Indigo went into freefall after Brown left. Pryor hired Charles Smiley, a black entertainment manager, as the company's new president, but Smiley lasted only a few months before he stepped down from the position.[27] Indigo failed to complete any films under Smiley or even announce any intended projects, although the company claimed to be working on a number of scripts. Pryor decided to leave the company's role of president permanently vacant after Smiley's departure, allowing Indigo to drift along without leadership or infrastructure. Meanwhile, Pryor dedicated himself to projects outside of the company. He earned the most lucrative payday of his acting career while on leave from Indigo, receiving $6 million to star in the comedy *Brewster's Millions* (1985, Walter Hill) at Universal. He also looked to emulate one of his major comedic influences, Bill Cosby, by developing the Saturday-morning children's television show *Pryor's Place*, which aired for one season (1984–1985) on CBS. Although the show failed to find an audience, *Pryor's Place* helped further sanitize his image, following the trend in 1980s children's programming of actively promoting a pro-social agenda.[28]

Outside projects played a role in Indigo's stagnancy, but Pryor's health became a major concern as well. Following an appearance on *The Tonight Show* with Johnny Carson in April 1984, where Pryor appeared frail, rumors began to spread that he was suffering from AIDS and was close to death.[29] Pryor made a public response, stating that he had undergone eye surgery and had lost weight after a bout of pneumonia, but expected to make a full recovery. The truth of the matter was that he was suffering from multiple sclerosis (MS), which would eventually be diagnosed in 1986.[30] Pryor only revealed his condition to a select number of friends and associates, keeping it a secret from everyone else so as not to jeopardize his career. Between Pryor's deteriorating health, outside projects, lack of business acumen, and continued struggles with drug abuse, it is no wonder that he failed to become an effective executive at Indigo. Perhaps sensing that it would be his final opportunity to throw himself into a film project before becoming unable to withstand the physical demands of a long shoot, Pryor used Indigo to direct his first narrative film and provide a creative coda to his professional life.

Is That You, Jo Jo?

Out of all of Pryor's narrative films, *Jo Jo Dancer, Your Life Is Calling* is the one that has the closest connection to his stand-up routines and albums. With Pryor wearing multiple hats—as star, director, writer, and producer—the film achieves the same sense of authorial control that he

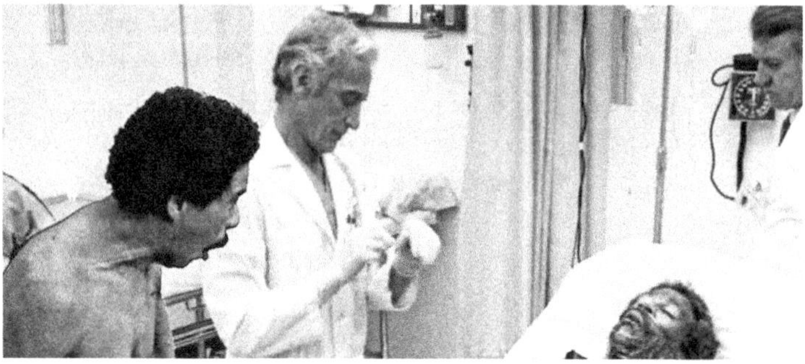

Richard Pryor steps out of his charred body to reassess his life in Jo Jo Dancer, Your Life Is Calling.

enjoyed on stage and in the recording studio. This notion of Pryor as a lone auteur is complicated, particularly when taking into account the role of collaborator that Paul Mooney played in writing portions of Pryor's routines. Nevertheless, Pryor (along with Mooney and Rocco Urbisci as cowriters) in *Jo Jo Dancer* shapes a story that helps provide a personal perspective on his experiences in and out of the public eye.

Like the majority of Pryor's material on stage, the film is built around the details of his private life and past trauma. At times *Jo Jo Dancer* underscores a tendency toward self-mythologizing, while elsewhere it counters popular notions of Pryor and debunks notions of the "crazy nigger" persona that he had cultivated and performed in the previous decades. The lines between fact and fiction are blurred throughout, as public and private are interwoven to comment on the deep contradictions in Pryor's life and art. The film is equal parts a confessional, detailing personal demons and misdeeds; a reiteration of his public persona and mythology; and a calculated effort to conform to the cultural and political climate of 1986 by spinning a triumphant tale of redemption.

Jo Jo Dancer is not a strict autobiography, but a fictionalized representation of Pryor's life relying on composite characters and scenarios. The story closely mirrors actual events, and the end credits list Pryor's character as "Jo Jo Dancer Alter Ego," making the connection to reality clear. Beginning with the Northridge fire, the story is framed around Jo Jo fighting for his life in an emergency room. The film borrows elements from *It's a Wonderful Life* (1946, Frank Capra), *8½* (1963, Federico Fellini), and *All That Jazz* (1979, Bob Fosse), in that it imagines Jo Jo seeing his life from outside of his body as he travels to key moments from his past and back to his present struggles in the hospital burn unit. Using an awkward green screen, a healthy Jo Jo steps out of his charred body and travels through

The adult Jo Jo returns to the brothel and talks with his child self.

his past as a spectator, reflecting on personal relationships and the emotional trauma that led him to the brink of death. Revisiting scenes from his childhood in a brothel, his early struggles as an aspiring stand-up comic, and his eventual rise to fame, numerous troubled marriages, and times of crippling drug addiction, Jo Jo is left to contemplate his past and find a reason to make it out of the hospital alive. Speaking in third person, he repeatedly insists that "he's not a bad guy." He serves as both counselor and patient with his other selves, telling himself to "straighten up" at one point. His younger self asks, "Why can't you change things?"

Introspection, however, awkwardly merges with self-interest. By revisiting major events from his life through the fictitious Jo Jo Dancer character, Pryor could simultaneously set the record straight, by adding his own perspective, and keep in place a number of the myths and half-truths that he had used to cultivate his public image. He seems to be attempting to clarify and correct inaccuracies, and yet the details of his childhood as presented in the film may consciously diverge from the facts. Biographers John A. Williams and Dennis A. Williams noted that, by most accounts, Pryor's lurid tales of growing up in a brothel with his parents and grandmother in Peoria, Illinois, are highly exaggerated fantasies.[31] Pryor's childhood, while far from idyllic, did not consist of the Dickensian despair and moral confusion that he describes in his stand-up routines. In some respects, the film manages to convey the possibility that a childhood spent inside a house of ill repute may have been a construction, as Pryor's hometown of Peoria is changed to the fictitious "Marion, Ohio." But instead of choosing just any postindustrial town for location shooting, Pryor insisted on using Peoria, pushing for a sense of verisimilitude that only further confuses the boundaries between fact and fiction.

The film's portrayal of the Northridge fire is far more straightforward, visually reaffirming Pryor's later accounts of the incident, in which he said he doused himself in rum and intentionally lit himself on fire in a failed suicide attempt.[32] It therefore does away with many of the more lurid speculations about the event—which ranged from accounts of a freebase explosion to rumors of a mysterious guest in the room who played a role in the fire. Cutting away at the last moment to show a window-shattering explosion from outside of the house, the film undermines the idea of setting the record straight, however, creating ambiguity through a visually expressive flourish. The intent and function of the film—ostensibly to show Pryor commenting on his life—are complicated by the film's fictitious nature.

Jo Jo Dancer draws from real-life events, but it never claims to provide a true account. Instead, it gives an impression of a life while commenting on the inability to ever truly understand that life, or the real Pryor, at least on a factual level. Jo Jo's split self helps to flesh out the divisions between public persona and private life that had become conflated through Pryor's first-person storytelling as a stand-up comedian. The film offers a nod to the difference between how he presents himself to an audience and how he actually lives off stage, showing a routine from the perspective of his white wife as he expounds on the reasons he refuses to hang out with white people. The revelation that the stories he tells on stage do not necessarily match his lived experience—or his personal beliefs—also brings the film's broader message into question.

Jo Jo Dancer's optimistic and reflective tone mirror Pryor's transformation in the mid-1980s, a time when he attempted to distance himself from the persona he had constructed for himself in the 1970s. The new Pryor, the studio executive with a Saturday-morning children's show, was gentle and restrained, not a madman. The "crazy nigger" now refused to let the N-word pass his lips. He was artistically ambitious, no longer content to simply sell his talents to the highest bidder. And he was clean and sober, no longer controlled by his addictions and despair. The opening of the film clearly articulates this sense of rebirth, with Chaka Khan singing, "I'm the ruler of my destiny / I can determine what becomes of me," repeatedly over the Columbia logo and credits. The film pivots on the concepts of free will and self-actualization, using Jo Jo's cocaine addiction and the Northridge fire as the point of hitting "rock bottom" that is needed to initiate recovery. Slipping into imagery that had become omnipresent through public service announcements during Reagan's "War on Drugs," Pryor uses the film to fit himself neatly into the rehabilitation rhetoric of the era.[33] Alas, the way Pryor wanted to be perceived clashed with his continued drug abuse in the years after the Northridge fire.

The film follows the press narrative of Pryor in the 1980s, looking at the

Northridge fire as a point of rebirth both spiritually and professionally. In taking creative control of the project and shaping a dramatic narrative that borrows stylistic cues from art cinema, Pryor also tries to assert that the rebirth was artistic. The new self that emerges after the fire is therefore complete. The final scene evokes his acclaimed comeback concert (and accompanying film and album) *Live on Sunset Strip*, which was received by audiences and critics alike as evidence of his full recovery and a harbinger of great things to come. Beyond the fact that he was professing sobriety while still using cocaine, his two concerts at the Hollywood Palladium were far from triumphant: much of the final cut of *Live on Sunset Strip* uses footage of Pryor delivering his routines months later on a Columbia soundstage, but it is passed off as a seamless live performance.[34] The commercial and critical response to the film was more a case of people wanting him to succeed than a true indicator of Pryor's return to form. He may have lacked the reflexive ability to understand that his art severely suffered after the fire—or perhaps he was willfully deceiving himself by buying into his own recovery narrative—but the moral proselytizing of the film only tells part of the story.

Like his career as a whole, *Jo Jo Dancer* is unevenly split between genuine moments of brilliance, tapping into a deep well of emotions, and contrived elements sliding into cliché. At its worst, the film is a sanitized biopic crusading against drug abuse. Pryor lacks command of the visual style and pacing, and his egregiously fake wig and mustache are evidence of a basic lack of organization and knowledge of film production.[35] At its best, the film is intimate and contemplative, providing space for the type of dramatic performance that was too rarely seen from him on the big screen. Its faults and contradictions aside, *Jo Jo Dancer* is the most artistically ambitious effort of Pryor's long sojourn in Hollywood. The film may not show the mark of a great filmmaker in terms of its pacing, narrative construction, or shot selection, but Pryor's direction points to someone with an understanding of mood and performance. With the exception of Michael Schultz, no other director had been able to capture such a multidimensional performance by Pryor in a narrative film. *Jo Jo Dancer* shows his pain, anger, and manic humor. Pryor gives a nuanced performance that manages to blend all of his contradictions into a mostly coherent whole. Amid a host of cynical acting jobs that only functioned to bring in paychecks, the Indigo Productions experiment and *Jo Jo Dancer, Your Life Is Calling* show him not only capitalizing on his fame, but also making a concerted effort to transform his film career and reach a new level of artistry.

Pryor wanted the film to be successful for a number of reasons. It was the first narrative project to come to fruition at Indigo, and after three years of the press detailing the company's troubles, Pryor wanted to show that the company was not a complete disaster. In gestation for the entirety of Indigo's existence, the passion project was made at the expense of any other films the company may have also produced.[36] Since the company was not creating opportunities by making other black-focused films, the pressure fell on Pryor's directorial debut to live up to Indigo's promise. Perhaps because of Jim Brown's initial involvement in the studio and their early conversations about the company's philosophy, Pryor used the filming of *Jo Jo Dancer* as a platform for providing African Americans entry into Hollywood, hiring a largely black crew for the production despite pushback from unions.[37]

The $20 million production budget, exactly half of the total investment from Columbia, was far more than Pryor was meant to spend on any single film and brought with it increased expectations at the box office.[38] *Jo Jo Dancer* may have been a passion project, but it was also important to Pryor that it make money at the box office to provide a model for future studio investment in black filmmakers. Rather than having a take-it-or-leave-it attitude, he had the film test-screened, so that focus groups and surveys could help shape the final cut.[39] The film ended up garnering mostly favorable reviews, but despite opening at number one at the box office, it only grossed a total of $18 million domestically in theaters, a take that would have been respectable if not for the film's inflated production costs.[40]

The disappointing box-office return sealed the fate of Indigo Productions. Pryor's deteriorating health, his continued addictions, and the mismatch between his personality and the rigors of running a company all played a role in his underwhelming turn as a producer and director. In the end, only *Richard Pryor: Here and Now* and *Jo Jo Dancer, Your Life Is Calling* were released by Indigo. After *Jo Jo*, Pryor decided to close up shop, returning the remainder of the investment to Columbia. Summing up the endeavor, Pryor would later write, "For my money—which it was—Indigo was a fiasco, something much bigger than I could handle. I didn't know how to run a company, and, come to think of it, I didn't even want a company, you know?"[41] Indigo had the potential of redefining black opportunity and representation during one of the most restrictive moments in cinematic history for African Americans. Instead, it stands as one in a long line of missed opportunities.

Pryor's deteriorating health ended any possibility that he would direct a second film. He attempted to remain active throughout the 1980s, starring in the uninspired comedies *Critical Condition* (1987, Michael Apted), *Moving* (1988, Alan Metter), and *See No Evil, Hear No Evil* (1989, Arthur Hiller), reteaming with Gene Wilder for the box-office hit. Because of the accelerating effects of multiple sclerosis, his frail appearance made him almost unrecognizable in his films made after 1986. During shooting, Pryor would get fatigued. Directors had to find clever ways to shoot around his limited mobility, often blocking scenes to provide an object for him lean against because he could no longer stand on his own.[42] His much-anticipated pairing with Eddie Murphy in *Harlem Nights* (1989, Eddie Murphy) was also a critical and commercial disappointment, marking Murphy's own use of celebrity to get his first (and ultimately only) shot at directing. *Harlem Nights*, like *Jo Jo Dancer, Your Life Is Calling*, is teeming with ambition and points to a novice director who under the right circumstances could have become a serious film artist. Instead, the careers of both Pryor and Murphy are marked by a frustrating squandering of talent. For Pryor, this was largely a matter of the medium, as narrative filmmaking proved incompatible with his genius as a stand-up comic.

PRINCE

On the other side of the spectrum from Pryor, with his fleeting interest in filmmaking and penchant for cynical cash grabs, is Prince, who enthusiastically looked to cinema as an opportunity for natural progression and for the extension of his music. Pryor's experience in Hollywood was marked by squandered opportunities, with studios going out of their way to help him achieve success as a producer and director. Conversely, Prince's sojourn into feature film was defined by discouragement. Prince has never fit easily into the role of a pop star. His music and persona eschew simple categories, and his hands-on approach to every aspect of his career requires levels of creative control rarely granted by media conglomerates.

Although Prince has worked with collaborators on occasion and shares the stage in live performance, the majority of his music has been a solitary endeavor. He writes his own songs, performs most of the instruments in the studio, and produces his own albums. It should come as no surprise that when he began making feature films, he sought to play an active role behind the camera, envisioning cinema as another creative venture where he would be allowed to function independently. He was never destined to follow in the steps of someone like Elvis Presley, who was passively placed into films that exploited his stardom. Instead, Prince's film work is inextricably linked to the rest of his creative output, and, much like his recording career, it has been defined by conflict between his artistic vision and the financial logic that guides the entertainment industry.

Purple Rain (1984, Albert Magnoli), Prince's first foray into feature film, hinted at the possibility of a successful career in movies, but his transition to directing for his next two films, *Under the Cherry Moon* (1986) and *Graffiti Bridge* (1990), put an end to such optimism. Both of the later films were critical and financial disappointments. They were fueled by a growing backlash to his success, but they also suffered from his unwillingness to approach the work with the requisite attention to detail needed to make sense of complex layers of meaning. The prevailing understanding of Prince's film career holds that *Purple Rain* was an isolated success that built on the appeal of his songs and stage presence, and that his subsequent films proved that his artistic gifts did not extend to acting, directing, or expressing ideas via a cinematic narrative. The critical disdain and underwhelming box-office numbers of *Under the Cherry Moon* and *Graffiti Bridge*, however, reflect public discomfort with ambiguous depictions of race and gender more than Prince's capabilities as a filmmaker.

Prince's ability to problematize static notions of race, sexual identity, and genre definitions has paradoxically been both the reason for his appeal as a musician and the cause of controversies and backlash. While Prince's musical talent is unquestionable, public and critical responses to his personality are typically filtered through an unflattering lens. Throughout his career, even the most glowing press coverage has usually been delivered with a tone of condescension. Prince's supposed eccentricities, be they personal, professional, or aesthetic, have helped shape a public imagination making him an almost mythic character defined by egotism, megalomania, paranoia, and erratic behavior. Speculating on Prince's life has become a well-worn journalistic pastime, with amateur psychology employed to analyze his childhood, his sex life, and his emotional well-being.

Conjecture regarding his life is partly the result of Prince's reluctance to grant the media personal access; he has chosen instead to let his music serve as his mode of communication with the public. Since the release of his first album in 1977, Prince has rarely granted interviews, and on the few occasions when he has talked to reporters, his cryptic answers have only further fueled speculation about his enigmatic persona. In an era in which the private lives of celebrities have to a large extent become common public knowledge, Prince has managed to remain a mystery. Clues about his life are scattered in his lyrics, and fans piece together impressions from the secondhand stories and anecdotes told by past associates, but the public has rarely been given the opportunity to see the "real" Prince. His feature films work in unison with his lyrics to comment on his personal life, spiritual growth, political worldview, and relationship to the entertainment industry. More importantly, his films offer a rare glimpse into his personality, with *Under the Cherry Moon* demystifying his stage persona through a performance that is relaxed and conversational.

Prince's eventual development into a feature film director seemed to be a logical progression for him and another realm where he could exercise his need for creative control, but with an increased emphasis on moving images. Touted as a musical prodigy, he had an unprecedented recording contract with Warner Bros. that promised him the ability to write his own songs and to produce his own albums. He made his debut album *For You* (1977) at nineteen, becoming the youngest person ever to produce an album for a major record label. With his fifth album, *1999* (1982), Prince found a mainstream audience, thanks in large part to the videos for the singles "1999" and "Little Red Corvette," which received heavy rotation on MTV. Despite the aesthetic simplicity of his videos (which were simply filmed stage performances of his songs), there was a visual and kinetic nuance coming from Prince himself that set his videos apart from the rest of MTV's offerings. Costuming and subtle choreography blended with smoke and neon to create striking visuals that extended from his live concerts and his album artwork. But for his next album, *Purple Rain* (1984), Prince wanted to do more than produce low-budget music videos.

Purple Rain was not the first time Prince had contemplated film as a venue for self-expression. While his music videos functioned primarily as a marketing tool for the record label, film had a different allure for Prince. His first proposed film project came during the *Controversy* tour in 1981. Tentatively titled *The Second Coming*, the project was conceived as a "drama-documentary" using live concert footage as its foundation, with vignettes interspersed between the songs in a style similar to Led Zeppelin's *The Song Remains the Same* (1976, Peter Clifton and Joe Massot). Prince enlisted Minneapolis-based director Chuck Statler to work on the film and discussed seeking theatrical distribution before abandoning the project.[43] *The Second Coming* would be the first in a long line of filmed projects that either were abandoned or never reached an audience, with Prince's penchant for sudden bursts of creativity filling his famed vault with an unknown number of unreleased songs, videos, and films.[44] If *The Second Coming* provided evidence that Prince had an interest in the possibilities of film, *Purple Rain* showed that cinema could be used to expand his audience and enhance his artistic expression.

Hollywood's lack of interest in black representation made securing financing and distributing *Purple Rain* difficult. Unable to convince executives at Warner Communications about the benefits of corporate synergy, Prince produced the film independently, financing it through a personal loan from Warner Bros. executive Mo Ostin.[45] Prince, collaborating on the story concept with William Blinn, and later hiring Albert Magnoli to flesh out the screenplay and direct, understood that he was a cinematic novice and did not make the same demands for control on the film as he had for his albums.[46] The finished film's blend of music-video aesthetics (fast-paced editing, iconic imagery, etc.) and biopic formula connected with audiences at the box office, part of a symbiotic relationship that helped *Purple Rain* become an industry unto itself. The album sold 15 million copies, and the film grossed $70 million at the domestic box office, with even more money coming in through the endless array of posters, T-shirts, and other related merchandise.[47] The film itself helped mythologize Prince, furthering an air of mystery around him by shaping a story centering on the supposed rivalry between Prince and fellow Minneapolis band the Time that had become a major part of fan discourse.[48] Prince plays "the Kid," a fictionalized version of himself, while the Time's front man, Morris Day, uses his real name despite the fact that his campy performance is clearly a comedic construction. *Purple Rain* is a window into Prince's life, but its veiled approach to biography produces more questions than answers.

The frenzy around *Purple Rain*, which began as an organic response to the quality of the songs and performance, turned into an insatiable public appetite for all things Prince. Eventually, it degenerated into a backlash from a fatigued public. The film's premiere at Graumann's Chinese Theater was broadcast on MTV in the channel's first time covering a live film event.[49] Through the film, Prince went from being a platinum artist to a worldwide superstar whose public profile was only comparable to that of Michael Jackson or Bruce Springsteen in 1984. His political and aesthetic sensibilities, however, would make remaining an entertainer for mass consumption difficult.

Prince made for an unconventional pop superstar and an even more unlikely Hollywood leading man, particularly in the context of the Reagan era. Bad press surrounding his refusal to participate in the benefit song "We Are the World," as well as scrutiny from the Parents Music Research Council, helped shift public opinion. His stylistic departure on the follow-up album *Around the World in a Day* (1985) was more challenging and less commercial than what the public may have been expecting if they thought it would be a reiteration of *Purple Rain*.[50] Prince had capitalized on his fame by using it as leverage to become more independent, releasing *Around the World in a Day* without a single, starting his own label, refusing to tour, and insisting on directing his own music videos.[51] His videos for "Raspberry Beret" and "America" placed Prince in the director's chair for the first time, but they were not consciously planned as a path toward directing feature films. In less than a year, however, he would transition from one-day shoots on soundstages and in concert venues to a full-scale Hollywood studio film shot on location in France and burdened with the pressure of equaling *Purple Rain*'s success.

Dig If You Will a Picture

Warner Bros. had been eager for Prince to make his next movie. This time, the studio was not going to repeat the mistake it had made with *Purple Rain*, when, by passing on financing the film, it had only received a distribution fee instead of having a full stake in its profits. To entice Prince to make another movie (and because of his track record making albums that defied industry trends), Warner Bros. agreed to give Prince creative autonomy, financing the new film without seeing a script beforehand.[52] After reading a trial script for *Under the Cherry Moon* by first-time screenwriter Becky Johnston, Prince hired Johnston and worked closely with her to develop the story concept and major points of action, just as he had done with Albert Magnoli on *Purple Rain*.[53]

Although Prince was interested in directing, he hired a director for the film.[54] It is unclear whether this was his preference or a concession to Warner Bros. But instead of going to a more experienced director, the job went to music-video director Mary Lambert, despite the fact that she had never worked on a feature film. The rationale for hiring Lambert has never been fully explained, but it could have been because Prince saw her work as director on the video for "The Glamorous Life" by his protégé, Sheila E.[55] With the exception of cinematographer Michael Ballhaus and production designer Richard Sylbert, the crew assembled for *Under the Cherry Moon* was not much more experienced than the young pop star at the center of the film. Full of inspiration and ambition, Prince and crew set off for Nice, France, in August 1985 to make his second feature film.[56]

The production ran into trouble from the start. Prince wanted the film shot in black and white to capture a sense of classic Hollywood elegance and romanticism. Warner Bros. argued vehemently for the film to be shot in color, overruling the protests of cinematographer Ballhaus by forcing a compromise: the film would be shot on color stock and later transferred to black and white when the film was processed.[57] This requirement added an extra challenge when lighting scenes, as Ballhaus had to improvise the light/dark contrasts of black-and-white composition without a clear idea of how it would look after the transfer. His camerawork is nevertheless remarkably rich. In addition to placing Ballhaus at a disadvantage, the studio tried to convince Prince to change the film's ending. The lead character's death, said studio executives, would send audiences out of the theater on a down note, and adding an optimistic denouement following the death scene would help mitigate some of the concern.

The compromises with Warner Bros. and the studio's unwillingness to fully honor the creative control they had promised Prince on the film paled in comparison to the frustrations on set. Lambert's work as a director left much to be desired. Extensive retakes put the film behind schedule, and Lambert's reportedly aloof attitude affected the cast and crew.[58] Actor Terence Stamp, the most experienced member of a cast composed largely of non-actors, left the film only a few days into shooting over a "scheduling conflict" that most believed was caused by Lambert's lack of professionalism.[59] Prince took a hands-on approach to shooting and often served as a buffer between Lambert and the rest of the crew, which made his transition to director a natural one.

Lambert left the film after a few weeks of shooting, issuing a statement that read: "I'm leaving under totally amicable circumstances. It's just become quite apparent that Prince has such a strong vision of what this movie should be, a vision that extends to so many areas of the film, that it makes no sense for me to stand between him and the film anymore. So I'm going off to work on my own feature and letting him finish his."[60] While Lambert makes no mention of her relationship with the cast and crew, or the producers' complaints with her work, her positive feelings toward Prince and his ability to make the film himself appear to be sincere. Warner Bros. was not thrilled to have Prince take over as director, but had little control over matters. The studio recognized that finding a replacement would not only be costly and time consuming, but would also threaten to derail the entire production. Outside of Warner Bros., the idea of Prince serving as a director, particularly among film critics, was met with resentment and skepticism.

Starting behind schedule, Prince, now acting as director, shot the rest of the film using mostly single takes. Here he was borrowing a method from his album *Dirty Mind*, which emphasized spontaneity over technical perfection.[61] The film is loose and free formed, allowing for the comic performances of Prince and Jerome Benton to play out organically. His approach to shooting and his unmatched work ethic helped Prince finish *Under the Cherry Moon* ahead of schedule and under budget.[62] Returning from France, he rented a house in Beverly Hills with editing equipment and began postproduction work, playing an active role in shaping the final cut of the film while simultaneously recording the remaining music for the soundtrack.[63]

Under the Cherry Moon revolves around a duo of African American hustlers living on the French Riviera. Prince plays Christopher Tracy, a smooth piano player and gigolo who makes his living by romancing rich women. In this he has the help of his half brother and business manager Tricky (Jerome Benton). Christopher and Tricky woo Mary (Kristin Scott Thomas), the young and beautiful daughter of a ruthless billionaire, with the intent of getting their hands on her $50 million trust fund. But Christopher falls in love with Mary and has a moral and spiritual epiphany that changes his cynical view on life, choosing love over money. He hopes to run away with Mary, leaving her fortune behind, but is killed by bodyguards working for Mary's father.

The classic romance across class lines harks back to the screwball comedy formula, with racial difference adding another layer for interpretation. Screwball tropes are matched to the visual composition, with the black-and-white cinematography, art deco set design, and 1930s-inspired costuming connecting *Under the Cherry Moon* to Hollywood's Golden Age. Modernist touches suggest that the film is a romantic dream more than a depiction of any real space or time. The film violates convention through its lack of a fixed era and through narrative ruptures such as direct address, yet it remains faithful to the style and sentiment of classical Hollywood filmmaking. It functions as homage, recalling *Casablanca* (1942, Michael Curtiz) specifically, but more generally playing with a 1930s model of humor and affluence.

Unlike *Purple Rain*, *Under the Cherry Moon* defies audience expectations by minimizing musical performance. With two exceptions—an impromptu scene at a fancy restaurant, where Christopher takes to the stage and sings "Girls & Boys," and the video of "Mountains" with Prince and the Revolution during the end credits—Prince's music in *Under the Cherry Moon* is either extra-diegetic or embedded in instrumental snippets (either from Christopher's piano or from a stereo). The soundtrack album, *Parade*, becomes a companion piece to the film, fleshing out moments in song that may only be alluded to musically for a few seconds in the film. Prince's acting is at the core of the film, whereas it was his stage presence and musicianship that carried *Purple Rain*.

Although music is not at the forefront of *Under the Cherry Moon*, the film manages to comment on his career, albeit indirectly. Christopher's moral crisis—the choice between love and money—is best understood as a meditation on the role of an artist within the entertainment industry, with the character becoming a stand-in for Prince's desire to make creative decisions freed from the commercial imperatives of the record business. Christopher's death becomes Prince's way of killing off his *Purple Rain* persona—that is, renouncing an existence based around sex and money for a higher pursuit of artistic freedom, love, and spiritual salvation. The film borrows an allegorical tool that Jean-Luc Godard employs in *Vivre Sa Vie* (1962) and *2 or 3 Things I Know About Her* (1967), where Godard uses prostitution to comment on the sacrifices and moral compromises artists are forced to make in order to function in profit-driven mediums. Christopher's side profession is clearly linked to this same idea, with dialogue emphasizing that a gigolo is nothing more than a male whore.

More than making reference to European art cinema, the choice of France as the setting for *Under the Cherry Moon* places Prince within a broader tradition of black artists seeking a refuge from America. Christopher's bejeweled headdress in the film's opening scene evokes the costumes worn by Josephine Baker, and Ballhaus's stylized black-and-white cinematography mirrors iconic photographs of Baker in the 1920s. Although the majority of African American expatriates in France had settled in Paris and not the French Riviera, the film's undefined time and loose structure help to reconcile some of the inexact allusions.

Like Christopher and Tricky, African Americans had gone to France to seek self-definition and escape the racism of the United States. In the 1920s, leftist Parisians embraced black culture as a symbolic form of resistance against the bourgeoisie.[64] Baker's iconic run on Paris stages at the height of the Jazz Age coincided with writers like Langston Hughes, Claude McKay, and Countee Cullen living and working in the city. After World War II, Paris championed bebop and became the home of novelists Richard Wright, James Baldwin, and Chester Himes. The romanticized image of the black expatriate living in France and creating art received the Hollywood treatment in *Paris Blues* (1961, Martin Ritt), with Sidney Poitier removed from his usual problem picture roles as a jazz musician finding love in the City of Light. Not having to perform a race-less identity in order to avoid being strictly defined by racism, Christopher (and by extension Prince) lives in France because it allows him to be more than just a black man. Importantly, the film is a key point of transition in how Prince would present himself in regard to race, in that he largely abandoned the colorblind utopianism of his earlier records and placed himself more explicitly within the tradition of black artists.

Along with missing the film's broader reflexive commentary, which became more evident through the contentious relationship between Prince and Warner Bros. in the following decade, film critics were confused by the layered meanings of *Under the Cherry Moon*. Sexuality and gender are complicated by Christopher and Tricky performing both masculine and feminine roles, alternately playing with homoeroticism and misogyny. They share intimate moments—Christopher takes a bath while Tricky

Christopher (Prince) and Tricky (Jerome Benton) in Under the Cherry Moon.

gently showers him in rose petals—yet they talk about their sexual exploits and plot together to win female affection and gain access to their bank accounts. Shedding some of the race-less idealism that defined Prince's music in the early 1980s, Christopher and Tricky both acknowledge cultural difference and embrace black identity. At dinner with Mary, they tease out the separate nature of black vernacular as Christopher writes down the phrase "Wrecka Stow" on a napkin and asks her what it means. When Mary confesses to not knowing, Christopher answers her with the question, "If you wanted to buy a Sam Cooke album, where would you go?" Pointing out racial and class difference, the scene shows Prince using inside knowledge about black experience that is largely absent in *Purple Rain*, forcing the public to recalculate their understanding of his persona.

His sexual ambiguity and newly sharpened performance of racial identity aside, Prince's supposed ineptitude in handling tone became the major sticking point for critics. The film veers wildly from comedy to melodrama, with a light, breezy exchange one moment giving way to an emotionally overwrought scene the next. What critics failed to consider was that the handling of tone and the utilization of excessive melodrama might have been intentional. Rather than an accidental byproduct of a novice director, this tonal range is evidence of a complicated sensibility. Prince blends comedy, drama, and spirituality in a way that recalls Douglas Sirk and foregrounds the most interesting aspects of Tyler Perry.

The reputation of *Under the Cherry Moon* as a "bad" film rests largely on its initial critical reception and poor showing at the box office. From a business standpoint, there were a number of missteps in promoting the

Prince and the foregrounding of black vernacular.

film. Naming the soundtrack album *Parade* instead of *Under the Cherry Moon* did not help cross promotion, nor did the music video for "Kiss," which had no clear connection to the film and defied the contemporary model of interspersing film clips into soundtrack-based singles. The most public promotional failure came when the film's premiere was awarded to an MTV contest winner and was staged in her hometown of Sheridan, Wyoming, turning the network's free publicity into a bizarre spectacle that painted Prince as being incompatible with mainstream America.

But press coverage and critical responses were most responsible for the film's lackluster showing at the box office.[65] Any curiosity or enthusiasm lingering from *Purple Rain* was washed away by the onslaught of negative reviews printed before the new film's release. The tone of these reviews was succinctly captured by *USA Today*, which warned its readers, "Don't even turn up on the same continent where it is playing."[66] Film critics, fueled by popular backlash against Prince and a sense of displaced hostility toward a person outside of the film community assuming the responsibilities of a director, helped reduce the audience for *Under the Cherry Moon* to little more than the most loyal Prince fans. With a $12 million production budget, the film only earned $10 million at the box office, and sales of the *Parade* album leveled out at just below 2 million copies, despite glowing reviews from rock critics.[67]

The film's status as a flop was solidified when it took center stage at the Golden Raspberry Awards, where Jerome Benton was named Worst Supporting Actor and Prince was given Razzies for Worst Director, Worst Actor, and Worst Song ("Love or Money"). *Under the Cherry Moon* shared the award for Worst Picture with *Howard the Duck* (1986, Willard Huyck).

The Golden Raspberry Foundation's annual tribute to films made in "bad taste" is problematic on a number of levels, beginning with the assumption among the group's members that they possess "good taste" and are qualified to police popular culture.[68] That the guardians of taste are largely older white men is just one of the troublesome aspects of how the film was received and categorized. A film like *Under the Cherry Moon* emphasizes the divide between an artistically idiosyncratic person like Prince and the confines of what passes as high quality for critics. Ultimately, Prince was faulted for having ambition and moving beyond a formulaic pop-star vehicle film by attempting to make great art. It was certainly not the worst film made that year; the piling on from critics was ultimately a warning for Prince to stay in his place. The refusal to treat *Under the Cherry Moon* with the same analytical rigor given to any other art-house release is characteristic of the limitations of black screen artists within the imagination of the critical establishment.

Dawn Breaks

The fallout from *Under the Cherry Moon* was immediate for Prince. Not only were his future film ambitions placed in jeopardy, but the creative autonomy that *Purple Rain* had afforded was scaled back by Warner Bros. The label vetoed his subsequent triple-album concept *The Crystal Ball*, instead releasing an abbreviated double LP, *Sign O' the Times*, (1987) in its place. *Sign O' the Times* would become Prince's signature artistic statement, and is often placed ahead of *Purple Rain* as his essential album by rock critics. Much of it written during the filming of *Under the Cherry Moon*, the album is steeped in the iconography of France, reimagined through a similarly time-displaced black expatriate. Hoping to give the album a dynamic visual counterpart, Prince shot a self-financed concert film in Rotterdam, only to have Warner Bros. refuse to distribute the finished picture. *Sign O' the Times* (1987, Prince) was eventually put out by the distribution arm of the Canadian theater chain Cineplex Odeon, but the film fared poorly at the box office in limited release. The concert film has an interesting parallel to *Richard Pryor: Live on Sunset Strip*, in that much of the supposed "live" performances were actually filmed later on soundstages, with elements shot in Minneapolis edited together with the Rotterdam concerts. However, grainy footage from the English film crew, rather than any shortcomings on the part of Prince as a live performer, was the cause for the reshoots.[69]

While the concert film gave every indication that Warner Bros. wanted to distance itself from his film projects, Prince nevertheless began working on concepts for another feature production. As early as 1986, he started writing an outline for a film called *The Dawn*, which was to be a Broadway-styled musical about rival bands that reinterpreted elements of *West Side Story*.[70] Prince was hoping to write and direct *The Dawn*, but not act in it. Although the project was eventually abandoned, Prince was still discussing making *The Dawn* as late as 1989. Eventually he incorporated elements of the story into *Graffiti Bridge* (1990).[71] Receiving financing for *The Dawn* or *Graffiti Bridge* became less likely as Prince's relationship with Warner Bros. deteriorated. His inability to match the success of *Purple Rain* was compounded by his demands for a last-minute recall of *The Black Album* (1988) and disappointing sales of its replacement, *Lovesexy* (1988).[72] But the run of financial disappointments ended with Prince's contribution of a soundtrack album for the Warner Bros. blockbuster *Batman* (1989, Tim Burton).

While far from a calculated corporate marketing strategy, the *Batman* soundtrack fit perfectly into the media synergy of Warner Communications. Prince's soundtrack album sold 4.4 million copies, his best since *Purple Rain*, and helped promote the film through constant airplay of the single "Batdance" on radio and MTV.[73] *Batman*'s domination of the summer box office (and the role Prince played in its success) helped ease some of the tension with Warner Bros. Although it was never directly articulated as such, being granted funding for his next film project might have been a thank-you from Warner Bros. for *Batman*'s success.

Graffiti Bridge would be Prince's final film as either a director or an actor. Warner Bros. provided a small production budget of $8 million, granting him freedom from studio control in return.[74] To be released in 1990 along with an accompanying soundtrack album, the film, conceived as a sequel to *Purple Rain*, promised to repeat the earlier film's success. It would move away from the nonmusical narrative focus of *Under the Cherry Moon* and again place the emphasis on song performances and the rivalry between Prince's character ("the Kid") and Morris Day. *Graffiti Bridge* lacks the vibrancy of *Purple Rain*, however, and trades in the sweeping visuals of *Under the Cherry Moon* for a claustrophobic set that looks more like a music video than a feature film. Divorced from realism, the soundstage of *Graffiti Bridge* is a conscious invocation of a dream world where Prince's fusion of religious and artistic philosophy could play out. Finding a mass audience interested in exploring Prince's Christian musings was another matter.

Reviews of the film were universally harsh, and the box-office take was even more disappointing. The film earned under $5 million domestically, and the soundtrack album became the first Prince release in over a decade not to be certified platinum. In 1990, Prince looked to be nearing the end of his run as a major pop star; he was being displaced by a new generation of performers and the growing hold of hip-hop. The film is not wholly lacking in artistic merit or points of interest, but these are only decipherable to the most ardent Prince followers. Prince again explores the balance between creative freedom and commercial interests, while also using the film to help re-form the Minneapolis community of musicians with whom he had surrounded himself early in his career.[75] Stylistically, the film borrows heavily from Spike Lee, particularly in regards to camera placement, blocking, and use of color. *Graffiti Bridge* provides fleeting examples of Prince's talent as a director, but it also provides evidence of the incompatibility between filmmaking and his preferred practice of working in isolation.

In the years that followed, Prince moved away from cinematic pursuits; his albums, meanwhile, found varying levels of commercial success. Entering into a protracted and public contract dispute with Warner Bros., he legally changed his name to an unpronounceable symbol and made a habit of scrawling the word "slave" on his face in protest when making contractually obligated appearances to promote his albums. Since his 1996 triple album *Emancipation*, he has produced his albums independently, freeing himself from corporate control as much as possible. He has yet to venture into independent film production, although his inventiveness in promoting and distributing his music outside of the dying model of physical record stores suggests that he may very well be equipped to make films using digital technology and new media, moving past the capital-intensive framework of film production and limited access to multiplex screens.

New media and the opportunities for celebrities to use their fame and resources to create their own platforms for production and distribution were nonexistent when Prince made *Under the Cherry Moon* in 1986. Prince, like Pryor, worked within the framework of the studio system because it was the only available option. Pryor needed the backing of Columbia to realize Indigo, and Prince's status at Warner Bros. as a recording artist was essential to getting the studio to finance a feature film. The fact that Pryor and Prince were the only black directors to make studio features that year speaks volumes about Hollywood's closed system. Spike Lee's arrival on the national scene later that year with his independent hit *She's Gotta Have It*, immediately changed the landscape for black filmmakers.

Shining a spotlight on underserved moviegoers, *She's Gotta Have It*'s art-house success flew in the face of Hollywood's internal logic, bypassing the limitations of genre convention to show a sophistication and multiplicity in black audiences never considered by industry executives. Lee himself was evidence that film schools were producing talented directors across racial lines, foreshadowing the arrival of a new generation of black filmmakers. At the beginning of 1986, any such optimism would have seemed foolish. Hollywood had cracked its door open ever so slightly, allowing only the most famous and powerful African Americans access to the director's chair. *She's Gotta Have It* looked to kick the door wide open.

Conclusion

The box-office success of Spike Lee's *She's Gotta Have It* (1986) and Robert Townsend's *Hollywood Shuffle* (1987) helped open doors for black filmmakers and played a major role in convincing the large studios to reevaluate a business model that had resulted in a decade of struggle and marginalization. Independently produced, both films put Hollywood's shortcomings into stark relief, proving that the blockbuster model had left black audiences unfulfilled and in need of something more than nominal representation. Former Columbia executive David Puttnam said that "the economics of modern studios militated against their handling more specialized pictures aimed at a specific strand of the audience." And yet the independent success of Lee and Townsend challenged this industry logic, forcing studios to change their business model.[1]

Independent companies like Miramax and New Line began to thrive by reaching out to audiences that had been neglected by major studios. This change gave rise to art films, genre pictures, and counterhegemonic movements, such as New Queer Cinema. At the same time, corporate synergy and hip-hop's emergence as a source of commercial success came together to produce a profitable new trend, and studios looked to exploit it until the flow of box-office dollars ran dry. So, on the one hand, the onslaught of black-focused films in the early 1990s can be read as a rearticulation of the blaxploitation cycle. But, on the other, the new wave of black filmmakers was also evidence of political and artistic sensibilities that ran counter to the traditional logic of the culture industry.

Scholars and critics in the early 1990s optimistically viewed the expansion of black-focused releases and the newfound visibility of young African American filmmakers as signals of permanent change. Black directors like Lee, Townsend, John Singleton, Mario Van Peebles, Reginald Hudlin, and the Hughes brothers had found ways to make financially viable films that circumvented the blockbuster mentality of Hollywood, returning to the low-risk / high-reward model of the blaxploitation era. But whether these independent films used Lee's financing approach, detailed in his diaries, of making *She's Gotta Have It* on a shoestring budget, or Robert Townsend's, based on tales of how he maxed out his credit cards to finance *Hollywood Shuffle*, the foregrounding of independent filmmaking and self-made opportunities in assessing the boom in black-focused films in the 1990s obscures the broader issues at play. As had been the case with the blaxploitation cycle, cultural shifts coincided with changes in the film industry to spur the production of black-focused features. Unlike blaxploitation-era films, the majority of the black-focused films made in the early 1990s were produced, or at least distributed, by major studios. And the growing power of media conglomerates has not only tempered the enthusiasm of the early 1990s, but also placed a stranglehold on financing and theatrical distribution. The immediate gains for black screen artists proved to be impermanent, and the continued ebb and flow of Hollywood's interest in black-focused material has deflated the optimism that characterized the early 1990s.

Like Lee and Townsend, members of the new wave of black filmmakers in the 1990s were beneficiaries of the insight, artistry, and toil of the eight directors left standing between 1977 and 1986. But if successes over the past quarter-century can be tied to the groundwork laid by these eight directors, the instability of commercial filmmaking as an open and viable medium for black expression points to the persistence of the same structural racism within the entertainment industry that characterized the years between 1977 and 1986. Access and financing remain stumbling blocks for black screen artists even in a rapidly evolving media landscape.

Rather than being a movement born solely out of the enterprising spirit of Spike Lee and Robert Townsend, the shift in production strategies in the late 1980s was largely due to structural shifts at the major studios. Media conglomerates began to take over, changing the insular logic of the film industry. By the early 1990s, the major studios were mostly part of horizontally integrated corporations with holdings in numerous sectors of the mass media. This shift made Hollywood studios keenly aware of market trends in other facets of popular culture through their parent companies.

Hip-hop's growth in popularity throughout the 1980s was just as important as the independent success of Lee and Townsend in communicating to the studios that black-oriented entertainment could be financially lucrative. The fact that hip-hop's appeal was not limited to black audiences made it even more enticing, since most movie screens were located in suburban multiplexes. Langston Hughes had remembered the Harlem Renaissance as a time "When the Negro was In Vogue"; a similar phenomenon arose in the 1990s as mainstream interest in black culture was fueled by hip-hip—and again, it was intense but transitory.[2]

African American filmmakers initially benefited from the structural breadth of the rising media conglomerates, which fostered films outside of the blockbuster model. But the production model of the 1990s that fostered the "indie" boom was not without its drawbacks. By purchasing independent studios like Miramax and New Line, or founding their own specialty divisions, conglomerates consolidated their control of the film industry. They have been able to control the release of both big and small movies. Diversifying production strategies—while also placing the control of the entire industry with a handful of companies—has been a mixed blessing for African American inclusion in cinema. Assumptions about the inability of black-focused films to make money internationally continue to hold sway, and this limits investment in new productions, especially with Hollywood's growing emphasis on global markets. At the same time, statistics involving the production of black-focused films and the employment of black writers and directors have remained steady since the early 1990s, and they never returned to the low ebb they reached in the years following blaxploitation.

The most prolific African American director since 1986, Spike Lee, exhibits the lasting influence of the eight filmmakers in this study as well as the shared experience of being subject to the constraints of commercial filmmaking. Lee has paid respect to black filmmakers from the 1970s, repeatedly casting Ossie Davis in his films and inviting Melvin Van Peebles to address the cast and crew during the production of *Do the Right Thing.* But the most striking parallels in Lee's career with other filmmakers are the ones found in his similarities to the eight directors who immediately preceded his arrival in Hollywood.

Like Jamaa Fanaka, Lee worked his way through film school before scraping together enough money to make his mark independently. Lee's most famous stylistic flourish, often referred to as the "Spike Lee dolly shot," appeared years earlier in Fanaka's *Penitentiary.*[3] Understanding the power of celebrity, Lee created a star persona by acting in his films, appearing in commercials, giving television interviews, and using whatever other means he had at his disposal to raise his public profile to a level approaching that of Sidney Poitier or Richard Pryor. Lee realized Pryor's abandoned dream of adapting *The Autobiography of Malcolm X*, and, like

Poitier, he moved past the limitations of only directing black-focused films, in his case, with *Summer of Sam* (1999) and *25th Hour* (2002). Lee's 40 Acres and a Mule Filmworks mirrors the self-sufficient Po Boy Productions that Fred Williamson founded, and Lee's business strategy incorporates the Hammer's pursuit of foreign financing and distribution—a borrowing that is best exemplified by Lee's use of Italian financing for *The Miracle at St. Anna* (2008).

Stan Lathan's and Gilbert Moses's work prefigures points of passion for Lee. The use of Public Enemy's music, his Mars Blackmon character, and the critical commentaries of *Clockers* (1995) and *Bamboozled* (2000) all show an engagement with hip-hop that has helped chart the culture's growth beyond the origin story of *Beat Street*. His visible New York Knicks fandom and close professional relationship with Nike and Michael Jordan is only the tip of the iceberg as far as his connection with basketball is concerned. The NBA provides subtext in a number of his films, and the legacy of Dr. J and 1970s playground basketball serves as the explicit subject of *He Got Game* (1998). With Prince, Lee has an even more direct relationship. The musician provided emergency funding when *Malcolm X* (1992) ran into budget shortfalls near the end of production. A few years later, Lee would use Prince's catalog for the soundtrack to *Girl 6* (1996). Not coincidentally, the emotional release at the end of Lee's film is accompanied by Prince's "Sometimes It Snows in April," the same song that mourns the death of Christopher Tracy in the final reel of *Under the Cherry Moon*. Like Michael Schultz, Lee has fostered black inclusion in film unions and mentored young black filmmakers. And his most acclaimed film, *Do the Right Thing*, can only be read as a reimagining of *Car Wash*.

Lee's early string of box-office hits and his rapid ascension in the industry made him famous for balancing artistry and commerce with political perspective. But despite critical praise, his career has been defined by the struggle to truly get over in Hollywood. The tumultuous production of *Malcolm X* was followed by difficulties securing financing as well as by box-office disappointment, compromise, and, many argue, artistic decline. Despite being granted *auteur* status by critics and scholars, Lee has never received the same creative liberties from major studios afforded to Martin Scorsese, Robert Altman, or Clint Eastwood. Lee chooses his own projects, for the most part, but his decisions are filtered through his lack of a corporate benefactor. This disadvantage limits the scope of most of his projects while making other concepts unworkable.

Spike Lee's name alone is not enough to sell a film any longer. Studios have consciously downplayed his involvement when marketing his mainstream features, such as *Inside Man* (2006) and *Oldboy* (2013), turning him into an anonymous craftsman, and idiosyncratic "Spike Lee Joints," like *She Hate Me* (2004) and *Red Hook Summer* (2012), each failed to top $400,000 at the domestic box office.[4] In 2014, Lee came full circle, using Kickstarter to raise funds for his feature *Da Sweet Blood of Jesus*, scraping together money completely outside of the film industry just as he had in 1986.[5] Lee has remained prolific in terms of the number of films he produces, but he has been marginalized in Hollywood. His celebrity has far eclipsed his work as a filmmaker in the public discourse.

Lee is not alone in showing the influence of previous black filmmakers, as the imprint of black directors working before 1986 can be seen in the work of a number of screen artists over the past quarter-century. The legacy of Michael Schultz alone is remarkable. John Singleton's celebrated debut feature *Boyz n the Hood* (1991) clearly reappropriates the plot of Schultz's *Cooley High*, and second-generation director Mario Van Peebles has searched for ways to infuse his films with black political perspectives without completely eschewing the film industry like his father, Melvin, learning lessons from the success of *Sweetback* as well as from the failure of *Greased Lightning*. Ernest Dickerson and Bill Duke both made their Hollywood debuts in Schultz films (Dickerson serving as cinematographer on *Krush Groove*, and Duke receiving his first screen role as Abdullah in *Car Wash*) before starting long careers directing for film and television. Schultz's move toward big-budget mainstream filmmaking with *Sgt. Pepper's Lonely Hearts Club Band* foreshadowed similar attempts to handle high-profile Hollywood properties by black directors like Tim Story, Antoine Fuqua, and F. Gary Gray. The most tangible and direct result of Schultz's career is the role he played in initiating the gospel cinema movement with *Woman Thou Art Loosed*, prefiguring the arrival of Tyler Perry, David E. Talbert, and a new model for black theatrical releases.

The impact of the other seven directors in this study continues to be felt as well. Stan Lathan's use of narrative cinema to document hip-hop culture and explain its key concepts to an uninitiated audience has continued in films like *Juice* (1992, Ernest Dickerson) and *8 Mile* (2002, Curtis Hanson), while Gil Moses's promotion of basketball's biggest star via a slapstick comedy would be revisited with *Space Jam* (1996, Joe Pytka). The theatrically released stand-up concert film, which Richard Pryor essentially invented, has continued to be the primary domain of black comics, with films like *Eddie Murphy Raw* (1987, Robert Townsend), *The Original Kings of Comedy* (2000, Spike Lee), and *Kevin Hart: Let Me Explain* (2013, Leslie Small and Tim Story) turning cinemas into makeshift nightclubs for black audiences, while white comedians stick to DVD releases and cable specials.[6] Actors like Kasi Lemmons and Carl Franklin have followed in the footsteps of Sidney Poitier and Fred Williamson by stepping behind the camera, while Eddie Murphy, Martin Lawrence, and Ice Cube have each used their celebrity as leverage to get studios to allow them to direct.

Quentin Tarantino has openly expressed his love for Jamaa Fanaka's films; cast Sydney Poitier, the daughter of Sidney, in *Death Proof* (2005); and has repeatedly played with Fred Williamson's iconic image, casting him in *From Dusk Till Dawn* (1996, Robert Rodriguez) and using his 1970s westerns as a model for *Django Unchained* (2012). Will Smith has transitioned into the role of international movie star, building from the example of Williamson selling himself to European audiences, albeit on a larger scale. Denzel Washington has openly discussed modeling his acting career after Poitier, but he has also followed Poitier's lead by moving behind the camera to direct *Antwone Fisher* (2002) and *The Great Debaters* (2007).

Poitier's directorial approach to comedic improvisation can also be seen in the work of directors like Judd Apatow and Adam McKay, who have turned what was a novel approach in the 1970s into a dominant model for the genre by the 2010s. Much like Poitier in the late 1960s, Will Smith took control of his career and started his own production company, Overbrook Entertainment, in the late 1990s. Overbrook produces Smith's own films as well as projects for other black artists; it also serves as a contemporary realization of what Indigo Films could have been. Tyler Perry has taken this approach to self-definition a step further by forming his own studio, benefiting from the same kind of branding and self-promotion that Fred Williamson used. Perry has also developed a wholly unique screen presence, celebrating excesses and violating formal and tonal expectations much like Prince. Yet the breadth of African American screen artists since 1986 and the continued impact of the eight post-blaxploitation filmmakers has not obscured the ongoing difficulties in using commercial cinema as a means of black expression. Understanding the accomplishments of the black filmmakers in that era is important, but so is the fact that the problems they faced trying to get over are not distant memories.

This book is not meant to be the final word on the careers of Schultz, Poitier, Williamson, Fanaka, Moses, Lathan, Pryor, and Prince. It is my hope that it will be a starting point for future research and serve as a thoughtful reevaluation of these directors in particular and of commercially oriented African American cinema in general. The easy dismissal and critical neglect of these filmmakers has obscured a broader historical trajectory of black cultural production while also reifying some of the persistent myths about blaxploitation cinema and its aftermath.

It is vitally important that we move past the kneejerk evaluation of genre films as low quality and, therefore, as unworthy of critical analysis or preservation. A number of blaxploitation-era films are currently lost and run the risk of suffering a fate similar to race films, which were only seen as precious and irreplaceable years after their release, as archivists struggled to patch together a handful of surviving prints from a once flourishing movement. By identifying the historical importance of Schultz's debut *Together for Days* or Ossie Davis's *Countdown at Kusini*, we can focus on locating and preserving these films before it is too late. These are just two of a growing number of films that are unavailable to watch and presumed missing. Beyond archival concerns, recognizing the historical importance of these filmmakers is essential to expanding our understanding of African American cinema. We must move away from overreliance on generalizations and a handful of canonized texts.

This book is also meant as a tribute to the achievements and shared struggles of the eight directors. They never were part of a collective, and their sensibilities and experiences vary considerably, and yet there is a common bond in their determination to work against the limitations of Hollywood. This sense of camaraderie has been evidenced through their enduring friendships and mutual respect. A few years before he passed away from cancer, Gil Moses went to Washington, DC, to see his daughter Tsia graduate from Howard University. Graduating alongside Tsia was Michael Schultz's eldest son, Derek. Although they had never worked together, the two proud fathers recognized each other immediately and spent the day reminiscing about past experiences on stage and screen.

One had been embraced by Hollywood, becoming the most prolific black director between Oscar Micheaux and Spike Lee, while the other had been disappointed by the film industry's failure to fully recognize his talents. Yet Schultz and Moses had traveled similar paths. Both self-made men from midwestern cities, they used education as a way out of the inner city and had long careers directing for stage, television, and film. Their fortunes in Hollywood may have differed, but Schultz and Moses were both intellectually curious and socially conscious, and they shared a bond from earning a living making art under prohibitive circumstances and amid the political and cultural energy of the 1960s, 1970s, and 1980s. The fruits of their labor, despite their frustrations and compromises, had allowed them to provide for their families and send their children to college. Sharing the day together, watching their children receive degrees—kids who had been born just before the dawning of the blaxploitation cycle—Schultz and Moses must have shared a sense of pride that was elevated by the realization that they had "gotten over" enough to give their kids a set of opportunities that they never had themselves.

Filmography, 1969–1994

The following list consists of every narrative film that received theatrical distribution in the United States between 1969 and 1994 and had either a clear black focus, a headlining African American star, or a black director. Films have been arranged by year along with the distribution company, beginning with major studio releases and followed by films distributed by minors and independents. The italicized *distribution* signifies that the company did not provide any level of production financing.

* Indicates a black director

1969

100 Rifles (20th Century Fox)
The Learning Tree (Paramount)*
The Lost Man (Universal)
Change of Mind (Cinerama)
Putney Swope (Cinema V *distribution*)

1970

Angel Levine (UA *distribution*)
Cotton Comes to Harlem (UA *distribution*)*
The Great White Hope (20th Century Fox)
Halls of Anger (UA *distribution*)
The Landlord (UA *distribution*)
The Liberation of L. B. Jones (Columbia, *distribution*)
My Sweet Charlie (Universal)
One More Time (UA *distribution*)

Stop (Warner Bros.)*
They Call Me MISTER Tibbs! (MGM, UA)
. . . tick . . . tick . . . tick (MGM)
Watermelon Man (Columbia)*
El Condor (National General *distribution*)
The Grasshopper (National General)
Soul Soldier (Fanfare Films *distribution*)
Walk the Walk (Hallmark Productions *distribution*)

1971

Brother John (Columbia)
The Organization (MGM, UA *distribution*)
Shaft (MGM)*
The Bus Is Coming (William Thompson International *distribution*)*
Honky (Jack H. Harris *distribution*)
Right On! (Leacock-Pennebraker *distribution*)
Soul to Soul (Cinerama *distribution*)
Sweet Sweetback's Baadasssss Song (Cinemation *distribution*)*

1972

Across 110th Street (UA *distribution*)
Black Gunn (Columbia *distribution*)
Buck and the Preacher (Columbia)*
Come Back, Charleston Blue (Warner Bros. *distribution*)
Cool Breeze (MGM *distribution*)
Hammer (UA *distribution*)
Hickey & Boggs (UA *distribution*)
Hit Man (MGM *distribution*)
Lady Sings the Blues (Paramount)
The Legend of Nigger Charley (Paramount)
The Man (Paramount *distribution*)
Melinda (MGM)*
Shaft's Big Score! (MGM)*
Sounder (20th Century Fox *distribution*)
Super Fly (Warner Bros.)*
Trouble Man (20th Century Fox)*
The Big Bird Cage (New World)
Black Girl (Cinerama *distribution*)*
The Black King Pin (AIP *distribution*)
Black Mama, White Mama (AIP)

Blacula (AIP)*
Bone (New World *distribution*)
The Final Comedown (New World *distribution*)*
Georgia, Georgia (Cinerama *distribution*)
The Harder They Come (New World *distribution*)
The Limit (Cannon *distribution*)*
Man and Boy (Levitt-Pickman *distribution*)
Miss Melody Jones (American Films *distribution*)
A Place Called Today (AVCO Embassy)
Slaughter (AIP)
Stigma (Cinerama *distribution*)
The Thing with Two Heads (AIP *distribution*)
Top of the Heap (Fanfare Films *distribution*)*
Wild in the Sky (AIP *distribution*)

1973

Charley One-Eye (Paramount)
Cleopatra Jones (Warner Bros.)
Five on the Black Hand Side (UA *distribution*)*
Gordon's War (20th Century Fox)*
Hit! (Paramount)
I Escaped from Devil's Island (UA *distribution*)
Shaft in Africa (MGM)
The Slams (MGM *distribution*)
The Soul of Nigger Charley (Paramount)
The Spook Who Sat by the Door (UA *distribution*)*
Super Fly T.N.T. (Paramount)*
Sweet Jesus Preacher Man (MGM *distribution*)
That Man Bolt (Universal)*
Trick Baby (Universal)
Black Bunch (Entertainment Pyramid *distribution*)*
Black Caesar (AIP)
Blackenstein (Exclusive International *distribution*)
Book of Numbers (AVCO Embassy)*
Brother on the Run (Rowland-Williams *distribution*)
Coffy (AIP)
Don't Play Us Cheap (Movin' On *distribution*)*
Dynamite Brothers (Independent International *distribution*)
Fox Style (Presidio)
Ganja & Hess (Kelly/Jordan)*
Hell Up in Harlem (AIP)
Kongi's Harvest (Tam Communications *distribution*)*

The Mack (Cinerama *distribution*)
Maurie (National General *distribution*)
Savage! (New World)
Scream Blacula Scream (AIP)
Slaughter's Big Rip-Off (AIP)
A Warm December (National General *distribution*)*

1974

Amazing Grace (UA *distribution*)*
Black Belt Jones (Warner Bros. *distribution*)
Black Eye (Warner Bros.)
Black Samson (Warner Bros. *distribution*)
Claudine (20th Century Fox)
The Education of Sonny Carson (Paramount)
Hangup (Warner Bros.)
The House on Skull Mountain (20th Century Fox)
The Klansman (Paramount)
The Super Cops (MGM)*
The Take (Columbia *distribution*)
Three Tough Guys (Paramount *distribution*)
Thomasine & Bushrod (Columbia)*
Together Brothers (20th Century Fox)
Uptown Saturday Night (Warner Bros. *distribution*)*
Willie Dynamite (Universal)*
Abby (AIP)
The Arena (New World)
Bamboo Gods and Iron Men (AIP)
Black Alley Cats (Entertainment Pyramid *distribution*)
The Black Connection (BIP)
The Black Godfather (Cinemation *distribution*)
The Black Six (Cinemation *distribution*)
Catch My Soul (Cinerama *distribution*)
Dynamite Brothers (Cinemation *distribution*)
Foxy Brown (AIP)
Honeybaby, Honeybaby (Kelly/Jordan)*
Johnny Tough (Dimension *distribution*)*
Mean Mother (Independent International *distribution*)
Savage Sisters (AIP *distribution*)
Shoot It Black, Shoot It Blue (Levitt-Pickman *distribution*)
Street Sisters (Movie Company)*
Sugar Hill (AIP)
Three the Hard Way (Allied Artists)*

Truck Turner (AIP)
The Zebra Killer (General Film *distribution*)

1975

Aaron Loves Angela (Columbia)*
Cleopatra Jones and the Casino of Gold (Warner Bros.)
Let's Do It Again (Warner Bros.)*
Mahogany (Paramount)
Mandingo (Paramount)
Take a Hard Ride (20th Century Fox *distribution*)
That's the Way of the World (UA *distribution*)
The Wilby Conspiracy (UA *distribution*)
Black Fist (Centaur *distribution*)
Black Force (Howard Mahler *distribution*)
The Black Gestapo (Bryanston)
Black Lolita (Cinema Epoch *distribution*)
Boss Nigger (Dimension)
Bucktown (AIP *distribution*)
Candy Tangerine Man (Moonstone)
Cooley High (AIP)*
Coonskin (Bryanston)
Cornbread, Earl and Me (AIP)
Darktown Strutters (New World)
Deliver Us from Evil (Dimension *distribution*)*
Dolemite (Dimension *distribution*)*
Friday Foster (AIP)
Lady Cocoa (Moonstone)
Lord Shango (Bryanston)
Man Friday (AVCO Embassy *distribution*)
Sheba, Baby (AIP)
Super Spook (Levitt-Pickman *distribution*)
TNT Jackson (New World)

1976

The Bingo Long Traveling All-Stars and Motor Kings (Universal)
Car Wash (Universal)*
Countdown at Kusini (Columbia *distribution*)*
Drum (UA *distribution*)
Hot Potato (Warner Bros.)
Leadbelly (Paramount)*

Norman . . . Is That You? (MGM/UA)
Sparkle (Warner Bros.)
Adios Amigo (Atlas *distribution*)*
The Bad Bunch (Dimension *distribution*)
Black Heat (Independent International *distribution*)
Black Shampoo (Dimension *distribution*)
Brotherhood of Death (Downtown *distribution*)
Death Journey (Atlas *distribution*)*
Devil's Express (Howard Mahler)
Dr. Black, Mr. Hyde (Dimension *distribution*)*
Ebony, Ivory and Jade (Dimension *distribution*)
Emma Mae (PRO International *distribution*)*
The Human Tornado (Dimension *distribution*)
J.D.'s Revenge (AIP)
Joshua (Lone Star *distribution*)
The Long Night (Howard Mahler *distribution*)*
Mean Johnny Barrows (Atlas *distribution*)*
The Monkey Hu$tle (AIP *distribution*)
The Muthers (Dimension)
No Way Back (Atlas *distribution*)*
Passion Plantation (Howard Mahler)
Pipe Dreams (AVCO Embassy *distribution*)
The River Niger (Cine Artists *distribution*)
Sounder, Part 2 (Gamma III *distribution*)
Velvet Smooth (Howard Mahler *distribution*)

1977

Brothers (Warner Bros.)
Greased Lightning (Warner Bros.)*
The Greatest (Columbia *distribution*)
A Piece of the Action (Warner Bros. *distribution*)
Scott Joplin (Universal)
Which Way Is Up? (Universal)*
Abar, the First Black Superman (Mirror Releasing *distribution*)
Bare Knuckles (Intercontinental Releasing *distribution*)
Black Samurai (Trans National *distribution*)
The Guy from Harlem (International Cinema)
Kid Vengeance (Cannon *distribution*)
Mr. Mean (Lone Star *distribution*)*
Petey Wheatstraw (General International *distribution*)*

1978

Blue Collar (Universal *distribution*)
Sgt. Pepper's Lonely Hearts Club Band (Universal)
The Wiz (Universal)
Blind Rage (Trans-World *distribution*)
Death Dimension (Movietime *distribution*)
Death of a Snowman (Madison World *distribution*)
Fighting Mad (Caprican 3 *distribution*)
A Hero Ain't Nothin' But a Sandwich (New World *distribution*)
The Tattoo Connection (Pathfinder *distribution*)
Youngblood (AIP *distribution*)

1979

The Fish That Saved Pittsburgh (UA *distribution*)
Scavenger Hunt (20th Century Fox)
Disco Godfather (Transvue *distribution*)
Penitentiary (Jerry Gross Organization)*
The Six Thousand Dollar Nigger (International Cinema *distribution*)

1980

Stir Crazy (Columbia)

1981

Bustin' Loose (Universal)*
Body and Soul (Cannon)
Carbon Copy (AVCO Embassy *distribution*)*
Getting Over (Maverick International *distribution*)
Lunch Wagon (Seymour Brode & Associates *distribution*)

1982

48 Hrs. (Paramount)
Penitentiary II (UA *distribution*)*
Some Kind of Hero (Paramount)
The Toy (Columbia)
One Down, Two to Go (Almi *distribution*)*

1983

Superman III (Warner Bros. *distribution*)
Trading Places (Paramount)
The Big Score (Almi *distribution*)*
The Last Fight (Best Film & Video)*

1984

Beverly Hills Cop (Paramount)
Purple Rain (Warner Bros.)
A Soldier's Story (Columbia)
Beat Street (Orion *distribution*)*
Breakin' (Cannon)
Breakin' 2: Electric Boogaloo (Cannon)
The Brother from Another Planet (Cinecom *distribution*)
Killpoint (Crown International *distribution*)

1985

Brewster's Millions (Universal)
The Color Purple (Warner Bros.)
Krush Groove (Warner Bros. *distribution*)*
The Last Dragon (TriStar *distribution*)*
White Nights (Columbia)
Rappin' (Cannon)

1986

The Golden Child (Paramount)
Jo Jo Dancer, Your Life Is Calling (Columbia)*
Jumpin' Jack Flash (20th Century Fox)
'Round Midnight (Warner Bros. *distribution*)
Running Scared (MGM)
Under the Cherry Moon (Warner Bros.)*
Foxtrap (Snizzlefritz *distribution*)*
Knights of the City (New World *distribution*)
She's Gotta Have It (Island *distribution*)*

1987

Beverly Hills Cop II (Paramount)
Burglar (Warner Bros.)
Critical Condition (Paramount)
Cry Freedom (Universal)
Disorderlies (Warner Bros.)*
Fatal Beauty (MGM)
Leonard Part 6 (Columbia *distribution*)
Lethal Weapon (Warner Bros.)
Deadly Illusion (Cinetel *distribution*)
Hollywood Shuffle (Samuel Goldwyn *distribution*)*
Penitentiary III (Cannon *distribution*)*
The Wild Pair (Trans-World Entertainment *distribution*)

1988

*Bat*21* (TriStar)
Bird (Warner Bros.)
Clara's Heart (Warner Bros.)
Coming to America (Paramount)
I'm Gonna Git You Sucka (MGM/UA *distribution*)*
Moving (Warner Bros.)
School Daze (Columbia)*
The Serpent and the Rainbow (Universal)
Action Jackson (Lorimar)
Colors (Orion)
Mississippi Burning (Orion)
Tougher Than Leather (New Line *distribution*)

1989

Do the Right Thing (Universal *distribution*)*
Driving Miss Daisy (Warner Bros. *distribution*)
A Dry White Season (MGM *distribution*)*
Harlem Nights (Paramount)*
Lean on Me (Warner Bros.)
Lethal Weapon 2 (Warner Bros.)
The Mighty Quinn (MGM)
See No Evil, Hear No Evil (TriStar)
Tap (TriStar)

Chameleon Street (Northern Arts *distribution*)*
Sidewalk Stories (Island *distribution*)*

1990

Another 48 Hrs. (Paramount)
Ghost Dad (Universal)*
Graffiti Bridge (Warner Bros.)*
Mo' Better Blues (Universal)*
Night of the Living Dead (Columbia)
Predator 2 (20th Century Fox)
Def by Temptation (Troma *distribution*)*
Heart Condition (New Line)
House Party (New Line)*
The Return of Superfly (Triton)
To Sleep with Anger (Samuel Goldwyn *distribution*)*

1991

Another You (TriStar)
Boyz n the Hood (Columbia)*
The Five Heartbeats (20th Century Fox)*
Flight of the Intruder (Paramount)
Grand Canyon (20th Century Fox)
Jungle Fever (Universal)*
The Last Boy Scout (Warner Bros.)
New Jack City (Warner Bros.)*
The People Under the Stairs (Universal)
A Rage in Harlem (Miramax)*
Ricochet (Warner Bros. *distribution*)
Strictly Business (Warner Bros. *distribution*)*
True Identity (Buena Vista / Touchstone)*
The Borrower (Cannon)
Daughters of the Dust (Kino International *distribution*)*
Diary of a Hitman (Vision *distribution*)
Driving Me Crazy (MPCA *distribution*)
Hangin' with the Homeboys (New Line)
Heaven Is a Playground (New Line *distribution*)
House Party 2 (New Line)*
Livin' Large! (Samuel Goldwyn *distribution*)*
Mississippi Masala (Samuel Goldwyn *distribution*)

Straight Out of Brooklyn (Samuel Goldwyn *distribution*)*
Talkin' Dirty After Dark (New Line *distribution*)*

1992

Bebe's Kids (Paramount *distribution*)
The Bodyguard (Warner Bros.)
Boomerang (Paramount)*
Candyman (TriStar)
Class Act (Warner Bros.)
The Distinguished Gentleman (Buena Vista / Hollywood)
Juice (Paramount *distribution*)*
Jumpin' at the Boneyard (20th Century Fox)
Lethal Weapon 3 (Warner Bros.)
Malcolm X (Warner Bros.)*
Mo' Money (Columbia)
Passenger 57 (Warner Bros.)*
Sarafina! (Buena Vista / Miramax / Hollywood)
Sister Act (Buena Vista / Touchstone)
South Central (Warner Bros. *distribution*)
Trespass (Universal)
White Men Can't Jump (20th Century Fox)
Aces: Iron Eagle III (New Line *distribution*)
Bank Robber (I.R.S.)
Deep Cover (New Line)*
One False Move (I.R.S.)*
Passion Fish (Miramax *distribution*)

1993

Amos & Andrew (Columbia)
Boiling Point (Warner Bros. *distribution*)
Bopha! (Paramount *distribution*)*
CB4 (Universal)
Cool Runnings (Buena Vista / Disney)
Demolition Man (Warner Bros.)
Just Another Girl on the I.R.T. (Miramax)
Made in America (Warner Bros. *distribution*)
Menace II Society (New Line)*
The Meteor Man (MGM)*
The Pelican Brief (Warner Bros.)

Philadelphia (TriStar)
Poetic Justice (Columbia)*
Rising Sun (20th Century Fox)
Sister Act 2: Back in the Habit (Buena Vista / Touchstone)*
Six Degrees of Separation (MGM)
What's Love Got to Do with It (Buena Vista / Touchstone)
Who's the Man? (New Line)
Posse (Gramercy *distribution*)*

1994

Above the Rim (New Line)
Beverly Hills Cop III (Paramount)
Blankman (Columbia)
Blue Chips (Paramount)
Corrina, Corrina (New Line)
Crooklyn (Paramount *distribution*)*
Drop Zone (Paramount)
Fresh (Miramax)
Gunmen (Miramax/Dimension)
House Party 3 (New Line)
The Inkwell (Buena Vista / Touchstone)*
A Low Down Dirty Shame (Buena Vista / Hollywood)*
Sugar Hill (20th Century Fox *distribution*)
Alma's Rainbow (Xenon *distribution*)*
Drop Squad (Gramercy *distribution*)*
Fear of a Black Hat (Samuel Goldwyn *distribution*)*
Jason's Lyric (Gramercy *distribution*)

Notes

INTRODUCTION

1. African Americans make up 12 to 13 percent of the US population, while the percentage of US-produced films with a black focus reached 16 percent between 1972 and 1976.

2. Micheaux's first film, *The Homesteader*, was completed in 1919.

3. Rollins was a white director with a few television writing credits to his name. He has been a longtime musical collaborator with Daniels.

4. Daniels's work in movies was more of a hobby or an afterthought. He founded the Los Angeles club Maverick's Flat, one of the most important black music venues on the West Coast in the 1960s and 1970s, and was active in the recording industry.

5. Christopher Sieving, *Soul Searching: Black-Themed Cinema from the March on Washington to the Rise of Blaxploitation* (Middletown, CT: Wesleyan University Press, 2011).

CHAPTER 1: BLAXPLOITATION RECONSIDERED

1. *The Landlord* was adapted from Kristin Hunter's 1966 novel of the same name. For a thorough account of the film's production, see Christopher Sieving, *Soul Searching: Black-Themed Cinema from the March on Washington to the Rise of Blaxploitation* (Middletown, CT: Wesleyan University Press, 2011), 161–200.

2. No known prints are available, and the film has never been released on VHS or DVD. However, a personal video copy of the film's star Edward Bell was shown at the Brooklyn Art Museum BAMcinématek on April 4, 2010, the first public screening of *Stop* since its brief Texas release in 1970. The information about

Gunn's disappointment with *The Landlord* comes from a Q&A following the screening with Bell, a longtime friend of Gunn's before they made *Stop* together.

3. Sieving, *Soul Searching*.

4. Ibid.

5. Gunn was not the only African American working on the film to find the mood on the set rife with racial slights and indignities. Actress Lonette McKee quit during production of *The Greatest* after receiving poor treatment from producers, and she received praise from Jim Brown, Richard Pryor, and Cleavon Little for standing up for herself. "Angry McKee Quits *Greatest* and Goes to Pryor Film," *Jet*, November 11, 1976, 119.

6. Bill Gunn, *Rhinestone Sharecropping* (Berkeley, CA: I. Reed, 1981), 17.

7. Frank Kofsky, *Black Nationalism and the Revolution in Music* (New York: Pathfinder, 1970).

8. Clifford Mason, "Why Does White America Love Sidney Poitier So?" *New York Times*, September 10, 1967.

9. Contract, dated December 5, 1963, Gordon Parks Papers, 1946–1991, Manuscript Division, Library of Congress, Washington, DC, Box 24-3.

10. Letter dated October 7, 1964, Alana R. Martin Jr. to Gordon Parks, Gordon Parks Papers, Box 23-4.

11. Ibid.

12. The final budget was $1,963,750. As of September 1970 the film had grossed $3,146,599. Final budget and letter from Robert Lantz to Gordon Parks, January 13, 1971, Gordon Parks Papers, Box 24-8.

13. Generally, rental figures equal approximately half of a film's box-office gross, placing *Cotton Comes to Harlem* in the $10 million range. *Variety*, January 6, 1971, 11.

14. An adaptation of Ernest Tidyman's novel about a black private eye, *Shaft* was produced by the struggling MGM in hopes of matching the isolated success of *Cotton Comes to Harlem*.

15. Contrary to an oft-repeated Van Peebles observation, the title character in *Shaft* was always conceived of as black and was not changed by MGM in a desperate attempt to capitalize on the success of *Sweetback*. Although Van Peebles's film was the first to hit theaters, principle photography on *Shaft* was completed five months before the release of *Sweetback*.

16. Jesse Algernon Rhines, *Black Film / White Money* (New Brunswick, NJ: Rutgers University Press, 1996), 44.

17. These included *Super Fly* (Parks Jr.) and *Come Back, Charleston Blue* (Warren), which were released by Warner Bros.; *Buck and the Preacher* (Poitier) for Columbia; MGM's *Melinda* (Robertson); and *Trouble Man* (Dixon) at Fox.

18. *Blacula* (Crain), *The Final Comedown* (Williams), *The Limit* (Kotto), *Top of the Heap* (St. John), and *Together for Days* (Schultz).

19. *Amazing Grace* (1974, Lathan), *Willie Dynamite* (1974, Moses), *Book of Numbers* (1973, St. Jacques), and *Super Fly T.N.T.* (1973, O'Neal).

20. *Solomon King* (1974, codirected by Watts), *Street Sisters* (1974, Roberson),

Tough (1974, Jackson), *Deliver Us from Evil* (1975, Jackson), *Dolemite* (1975, Martin), *Disco 9000* (1976, Martin), *The Human Tornado* (1976, Roquemore), *The Long Night* (1976, King). See chapters 4 and 5 for more on Williamson and Fanaka.

21. William Crain on *Blacula* and Michael Schultz on *Cooley High* (1975).

22. Exceptions to this are Ed Guerrero, who sees blaxploitation's start as 1969, and Novotny Lawrence, who marks the beginning as 1970 and the release of *Cotton Comes to Harlem*. See Ed Guerrero, *Framing Blackness: The African American Image in Film* (Philadelphia: Temple University Press, 1993); Novotny Lawrence, *Blaxploitation Films of the 1970s: Blackness and Genre* (New York: Routledge, 2008).

23. Guerrero, *Framing Blackness*, 69; Rhines, *Black Film / White Money*, 49–50; Mark A. Reid, *Redefining Black Film* (Berkeley: University of California Press, 1993), 90.

24. *Baadasssss Cinema*, Dir. Isaac Julien, DVD, IFC Films, 2002.

25. David Puttnam, *Movies and Money* (New York: Vintage, 2000), 213.

26. Mitch Tuchman, "Helter Shelter," *Film Comment* 13, no. 1, January/February 1977.

27. Ibid.

28. Van Peebles released a low-budget film of his stage play *Don't Play Us Cheap* (1973), a cinematically unambitious canned-theater project that only received minimal distribution.

29. Josef Gugler, "Wole Soyinka's Kongi's Harvest from Stage to Screen: Four Endings to Tyranny," *Canadian Journal of African Studies* 31, no. 1 (1997): 34.

30. "Countdown at Kusini," *Ebony*, April 1976, 90.

31. Delta Sigma Theta has tried to distance itself from *Countdown at Kusini*. The film has never been released on video or DVD, and no known prints exist, having either been destroyed, lost, or kept out of sight, possibly in a Delta member's basement or attic. At this point it is considered a lost film.

32. Gordon Parks, *Eagle in the Air*, screenplay dated December 10, 1969, Gordon Parks Papers, Box 22-6.

33. The third film in the series, *Shaft in Africa* (1973), was made by white director John Guillermin.

34. Gordon Parks, *An Endless Silence*, screenplay dated October 1972, Gordon Parks Papers, Box 22-7.

35. The total budget for the film was $2,235,699, of which $2,050,000 was provided by Paramount. Film budget, *Leadbelly*, Gordon Parks Papers, Box 23-1.

36. "Fiery Crash Claims Life of Gordon Parks Jr., 44," *Jet*, April 19, 1979, 60.

37. "Black Movie on Angel Dust Picked Up by ABC," *Jet*, May 31, 1979, 58. The film stars Philip Michael Thomas, and after his success on *Miami Vice* the film was released on home video under the new title *Death Drug*, intercut with footage shot in the 1980s of Thomas explaining the context of the story, as well as a music video for his 1985 pop song "Just the Way I Planned It."

38. Rhines, *Black Film / White Money*, 7.

39. Hoping to find a crossover audience with this black-cast adaptation of *The Wizard of Oz*, Universal and producer Berry Gordy of Motown created a film

that ostensibly had all of the earmarks of a blockbuster. Its star-studded cast featured Diana Ross, Michael Jackson, and Richard Pryor; it was an adaptation of William F. Brown's enormously successful Broadway play; and it seemingly guaranteed ancillary profits through its soundtrack album. While the soundtrack sold well, it didn't come close to making up for the disastrous showing of *The Wiz* at the box office. With a reported budget of $35 million, its domestic gross of $21 million gave studios pause when considering tackling black-cast films in the blockbuster era. Donald Bogle, *Toms, Coons, Mulattoes, Mammies & Bucks: An Interpretive History of Blacks in American Films*, 4th ed. (New York: Continuum, 2001), 264; Box Office Mojo, "The Wiz," www.boxofficemojo.com/movies/?id=wiz.htm.

40. E. Newton and U. Gupta, "Fighting Back in Hollywood," *Black Enterprise*, September 1982, 36.

41. Ed Guerrero points out the success of *The Godfather* (1972, Francis Ford Coppola) and *The Exorcist* (1973, William Friedkin) with black audiences as early markers of this industrial "logic." Guerrero, *Framing Blackness*, 105.

42. Newton and Gupta, "Fighting Back in Hollywood," 36.

CHAPTER 2: OUR MAN IN HOLLYWOOD

1. Personal interview, Jamaa Fanaka, March 18, 2010, Los Angeles.

2. Ibid.

3. Personal interview, Michael Schultz, October 10, 2006, Santa Monica, California.

4. HistoryMakers interview with Michael Schultz, archived at HistoryMakers office, Chicago.

5. Gloria Schultz appeared on stage as Lauren Jones.

6. Lithgow founded the Antioch Shakespeare Festival in 1952. Allardyce Nicoll, ed., *Shakespeare Survey 18* (Cambridge, UK: Cambridge University Press, 1965), 132.

7. Douglas Turner Ward, "American Theater: For Whites Only?" *New York Times*, August 14, 1966.

8. Schultz interview.

9. Weiss's play had yet to be translated into English. While directing *Amphitryon 38* at Antioch, Schultz and Ward set about finding a translator for the play, eventually employing a German couple who taught at the university. Within a few weeks they had a finished translation. Following the end of Antioch's summer season, Ward and Schultz were back in New York assembling the cast, costumes, and set designs for the NEC's inaugural production.

10. Schultz interview.

11. Lorraine Hansberry, "Review: A Medal for Willie," *Masses and Mainstreams*, December 1951, 59–60.

12. Telephone interview, William Branch, February 8, 2007.

13. Branch was a neighbor of both Ossie Davis and Ruby Dee in New Rochelle,

New York, at the time. He saw production vans parked outside, went out to investigate, and ran into Schultz, who was directing a scene at the Davis/Dee house.

14. *Variety*, December 6, 1972, 16.

15. Branch interview.

16. *Dream on Monkey Mountain* opened at the Mark Taper Forum and starred Roscoe Lee Browne and Ron O'Neal.

17. Branch interview.

18. Thomas Schatz, *Boom and Bust: American Cinema in the 1940s* (Berkeley: University of California Press, 1997), 65.

19. Branch interview; *Variety*, December 6, 1972, 16.

20. Branch interview.

21. Ibid.

22. Later in the decade the film showed up briefly in Europe under the new title *Black Cream*, but there are few details as to which countries carried the film or how it fared critically or commercially.

23. Schultz interview.

24. *Variety*, October 9, 1972, 19.

25. Christopher W. E. Bigsby, *The Cambridge Companion to Modern American Culture* (Cambridge, UK: Cambridge University Press, 2006), 385.

26. Much like *Ganja & Hess*, *Honeybaby* would be recut and repackaged by Kelly/Jordan in the upcoming years. The film was released on home video in the early 1980s under the new title *Three Days in Beirut*, an attempt by Kelly/Jordan to capitalize on news coverage of the civil war in Lebanon.

27. Schultz interview.

28. Sam Arkoff, with Richard Trubo, *Flying Through Hollywood by the Seat of My Pants: From the Man Who Brought You "I Was a Teenage Werewolf" and "Muscle Beach Party"* (New York: Birch Lane, 1992), 204.

29. The first was William Crain's *Blacula*.

30. Peter Lev, *American Films of the 70s: Conflicting Visions* (Austin: University of Texas Press, 2000), 95.

31. As in *American Graffiti*, period music plays a central role in *Cooley High*, replacing the rock and roll that Lucas wrote into the margins of his screenplay with Motown singles. The choice of immersing the film in Motown music was one of Schultz's earliest decisions. Contacting Suzanne de Passe, then an up-and-coming executive at Motown, Schultz was able to secure rights to the entire Motown catalog for what he remembers as "next to nothing." Schultz's use of music is central to the film, as the Motown songs inform the pacing and tone of the film and tap into the collective memory of the audience.

32. The Preach character (Glynn Turman) was reworked into the lead character "Raj" (Ernest Thomas), while 1964 Chicago was replaced with a contemporary Los Angeles.

33. Katia Dunn, "For Classic TV Producer, Good Times No Longer," *National Public Radio: Weekend Edition*, July 29, 2006.

34. Schultz interview.

35. Telephone interview, Gary Stromberg, April 10, 2010.

36. Ibid.

37. George Alexander, *Why We Make Movies: Black Filmmakers Talk About the Magic of Cinema* (New York: Harlem Moon, 2003), 81.

38. Stromberg interview.

39. Perhaps the most inspired subtext of the picture comes from its recognition of film history and casting of Clarence Muse as the elderly shoeshine man Snapper. Muse doesn't stray far from a film career in which he played countless butlers, porters, cooks, and stewards, and *Car Wash* used his films from the 1930s and 1940s as intertext to reinforce the continuum of labor inequality and subservience.

40. Richard Dyer, "Is *Car Wash* a Black Musical?" in Manthia Diawara, ed., *Black American Cinema* (New York: Routledge, 1993), 97.

41. Pryor's character Daddy Rich serves as a clear stand-in for 1970s evangelist Rev. Ike, who was more famous for having a mansion, sixteen Rolls-Royces, and a wide array of mink coats than for his grasp of theology. At the time when *Car Wash* was released, Rev. Ike's materialistic sermons were being broadcast on 1,770 radio stations nationwide, earning him legions of followers for his system of "divine economics." See Charles Sanders, "The Gospel According to Rev. Ike," *Ebony*, December 1976, 152.

42. Janet Maslin, "Washed Out," *Newsweek*, October 4, 1976, 89.

43. Whitfield's score received a Grammy, and his theme song was nominated for a Golden Globe. Golden Globes are voted on by the Hollywood Foreign Press Association.

44. *Car Wash* was featured the same year that the Moscow Film Festival awarded its grand prize to *A Soldier's Story* (1984).

45. Dyer, "Is *Car Wash* a Black Musical?" 100.

46. Thom Mount video interview, online at www.artistshousemusic.org/videos/film+producer+thom+mount+on+creating+soundtracks+for+car+wash+smokey+and+the+bandit+and+other+films.

47. Schultz interview.

48. Van Peebles's musical *Ain't Supposed to Die a Natural Death* had its Broadway premiere four months after *Sweetback* hit theaters, followed by *Don't Play Us Cheap* in 1972.

49. Schultz interview.

50. For a detailed history of the formation of NASCAR, see Neal Thompson, *Driving with the Devil: Southern Moonshine, Detroit Wheels, and the Birth of NASCAR* (New York: Crown, 2006). Like most biopics, *Greased Lightning* strays from the true-life experience of its subject in order to fit the narrative formula expected by Hollywood. The film ends with Scott winning the 1970 Grand National title in triumphant fashion, proving his worth as a driver and the collective power of the black community as they pitch in to help him build his race car. Of course, he did not actually win the title, that year or any other. Scott competed in NASCAR for two decades, spending twelve years in the Grand National Series, the highest level of stock-car racing. He won one race in 1963 on the dirt track at

Jacksonville, but the majority of his career was defined by his inability to remain competitive in a sport that is capital-intensive and dependent on corporate sponsorship. See Brian Donovan, *Hard Driving: The Wendell Scott Story* (Hanover, NH: Steerforth, 2008).

51. In Robinson's rookie year, 1947, he played his home games in Brooklyn while competing in the other seven National League ballparks: Manhattan, Boston, Philadelphia, Pittsburgh, Chicago, Cincinnati, and St. Louis. The South would not have a professional baseball team until 1962 with the addition of the Houston Colt 45's. The number doubled in 1966 when the Milwaukee Braves relocated to Atlanta.

52. Donovan, *Hard Driving*, 270–274.

53. David Montejano, *Chicano Politics and Society in the Late Twentieth Century* (Austin: University of Texas Press, 1999).

54. Although it provided a platform for the United Farm Workers and talented Chicano performers, *Which Way Is Up?* was not primarily a project for El Teatro Campesino. The following year, Luis Valdez debuted his play *Zoot Suit* at the Mark Taper Forum, and in 1979 he took the play to Broadway, becoming the first Chicano director to preside over a production on the Great White Way.

55. Rufus is a clear reworking of Pryor's famous character Mudbone.

56. "'Which Way Is Up?' Now Top Grossing Black Film," *Jet*, May 18, 1978, 54. As stated earlier, film rental figures roughly equal half of a film's box-office gross, giving *Which Way Is Up?* a global box-office take of approximately $46 million.

57. Frampton had been recording for nearly a decade as a member of the Herd and Humble Pie and then as a solo artist before the release of *Frampton Comes Alive*, making the widely held impression that he was an overnight success wholly inaccurate.

58. Frank Rose, "How Can You Mend a Broken Band? The Bee Gees Did It With Disco," *Rolling Stone*, July 14, 1977, 46. Two of Stigwood's early successes on the London stage were *Hair* and *Jesus Christ Superstar*.

59. Schultz was finishing postproduction on *Which Way Is Up?* The shooting schedule for *Grease* could not be pushed back because of Travolta's television contract with ABC—where he starred in the sitcom *Welcome Back, Kotter*—locking the production into a tight schedule that could not wait for Schultz.

60. Rose, "How Can You Mend a Broken Band?" 46. Stigwood had a recent history of firing directors, having replaced John G. Avildsen with John Badham in the middle of shooting *Saturday Night Fever*.

61. The only acting experience came when Barry and Maurice starred in a television comedy special that aired on BBC in 1971 to accompany their album *Cucumber Castle* (1970). Robin had left the band at the time and did not take part in the recording of the album or the TV special.

62. Schultz interview.

63. Ibid.

64. Viewing dailies near the end of shooting, the blunder of the pantomime approach became abundantly clear, so Schultz suggested they attempt to use a voice-

over narration by George Burns, who played Mr. Kite, the mayor of Heartland. Burns introduces characters and sets the stage, guiding the spectator through the countless shifts in mood and locale. Unfortunately, the voiceover only slightly alleviates the confusing narrative, and often underlines the ridiculous nature of the story.

65. "Oh! Darling" was the first single released from the soundtrack album and reached number fifteen on the Billboard singles chart, the only track off the album to crack the Top Forty. Although it was only a modest chart success, "Oh! Darling" is a rare late 1970s example of Robin's soulful vibrato being featured, as Barry's falsetto began to dominate the Bee Gees' output following "Jive Talkin'" in 1975.

66. This observation was made at the time of the film's release by Charles M. Young in "Pepper Is the Pits," *Rolling Stone*, August 8, 1978, 16.

67. Schultz interview.

68. Ian MacDonald, *Revolution in the Head: The Beatles' Records and the Sixties* (New York: Henry Holt, 1994).

69. Janet Maslin, "Son of 'Sgt. Pepper': Many Forms Involved," *New York Times*, July 21, 1978.

70. Melinda Bilyeu, Hector Cook, and Andrew Mon Hughes, *The Bee Gees: Tales of The Brothers Gibb* (London: Omnibus, 2001), 462. Reportedly, boxes upon boxes of unsold records were thrown in the trash after having been returned by record stores.

71. Schultz interview.

72. Ibid.

73. Ibid.

74. *Variety*, December 26, 1979, 12.

75. AVCO's biggest hits at the time were *Scanners* (1981, David Cronenberg), *Prom Night* (1980, Paul Lynch), *The Howling* (1981, Joe Dante), *Escape from New York* (1981, John Carpenter), *Time Bandits* (1981, Terry Gilliam), and *The Exterminator* (1980, Joe Glickenhaus). Coincidentally, Lear purchased AVCO Embassy in 1982 for $26 million. *New York Times*, January 5, 1982.

76. Douglas Brode, *Denzel Washington: His Career and Films* (New York: Birch Lane, 1997), 10.

77. John A. Williams and Dennis A. Williams, *If I Stop I'll Die: The Comedy and Tragedy of Richard Pryor* (New York: Thunder's Mouth, 1991).

78. David Handelman, "Richard Pryor: Sick, Alone and in Shambles," *Toronto Star*, January 26, 1982.

79. Schultz interview.

80. Ibid.

81. Pryor originally wanted Jane Fonda to play the role of Vivian Perry, but as a result of myriad circumstances Cicely Tyson was cast instead.

82. Box Office Mojo, "Bustin' Loose," www.boxofficemojo.com/movies/?id=bustinloose.htm.

83. Schultz, HistoryMakers interview.

84. Schultz interview.

85. Ibid.

86. Before working on *Car Wash*, Schultz contacted Gordy in hopes of directing *Bingo Long*.

87. In addition to the above-mentioned films, Motown also produced *Scott Joplin* (1977, Jeremy Kagan), *Big Time* (1977, Andrew Georgias), *Thank God It's Friday* (1978, Robert Klane), and *Almost Summer* (1978, Martin Davidson).

88. Schultz interview.

89. At times Gordy uses the film as a promotional tool for Motown. The film includes a number of musical interludes, featuring DeBarge's song "Rhythm of the Night," the lead single off of the soundtrack, which was meant to serve as a springboard for a family band that Gordy envisioned as a 1980s answer to the Jackson 5. Motown's most pronounced influence on the film comes with the casting of Vanity as Leroy's love interest. A protégé of Prince, who built the girl group Vanity 6 around her sexually suggestive persona, Vanity had left Prince and Warner Bros. to sign as a solo artist with Motown in 1984. Vanity's over-the-top sexuality is placed in stark contrast with Leroy's innocence, creating a natural tension that humanizes the hero, even if her song "7th Heaven" seems wildly inappropriate for a family-friendly movie.

90. Box Office Mojo, "The Last Dragon," www.boxofficemojo.com/movies/?id=lastdragon.htm.

91. Director's commentary, *The Last Dragon* (1985), DVD, Columbia TriStar Home Entertainment, 2001.

92. Schultz interview.

93. Ibid.

94. Spike Lee, *Spike Lee's Gotta Have It: Inside Guerilla Filmmaking* (New York: Fireside, 1987), 174.

95. Box Office Mojo, "Krush Groove," www.boxofficemojo.com/movies/?id=krushgroove.htm.

96. Rubin worked with artists as diverse as the Red Hot Chili Peppers, Johnny Cash, Slayer, Weezer, Tom Petty and the Heartbreakers, AC/DC, Danzig, Neil Diamond, System of a Down, Josh Groban, Lady Gaga, and the Dixie Chicks.

97. Lee, *Spike Lee's Gotta Have It*, 174.

98. Schultz interview.

99. Their first three albums on Sutra were *Fat Boys* (1984), *The Fat Boys Are Back* (1985), and *Big and Beautiful* (1986).

100. The soundtrack for *Disorderlies* featured only one track by the Fat Boys ("Baby, You're a Rich Man"), as the producers attempted to widen the appeal by including pop and rock acts like Bananarama and Bon Jovi, supplying an alternative for those who were not interested in hip-hop.

101. Curiously, the Beach Boys collaborated on the song despite the fact that "Wipe Out" was not one of their hits. Instead, the 1963 song was recorded and made famous by the Surfaris.

102. I take the term "ghetto action film cycle" from S. Craig Watkins, *Representing: Hip Hop Culture and the Production of Black Cinema* (Chicago: University of Chicago Press, 1998).

103. Dave Kehr, "A Troubled Past, but Promise for the Future," *New York Times*, October 1, 2004.

104. Kris Wilton, "Tracking Shots," *Village Voice*, September 28, 2004.

105. Rebecca Louie, "Prophet Margins," *Vibe*, April 2005, 136.

106. Schultz interview.

CHAPTER 3: WRITING HIS SECOND ACT

1. Dan Barry, "About New York: He Conned the Society Crowd but Died Alone," *New York Times*, July 19, 2003.

2. John Guare, *Six Degrees of Separation* (New York: Dramatist Play Service, 1990), 18.

3. Poitier's acting peers in the 1960s cannot be classified as stars in the strictest sense. Be it the failure to transition Sammy Davis Jr. into a successful leading man, or the commercially marginal roles of Ivan Dixon and Ossie Davis, the fact remains that no other black actor came close to Poitier's success. His closest peer, Harry Belafonte, did not appear in any feature films between *Odds Against Tomorrow* (1959, Robert Wise) and *The Angel Levine* (1970, Ján Kádar), while his so-called successor Jim Brown did not headline a film until 1969 with *Riot!* (Buzz Kulik) and *100 Rifles* (Tom Gries).

4. *Los Angeles Times*, September 20, 1983.

5. "Poitier Wants to 'Escape' the 'Black' Director Tag," *Jet*, January 31, 1980, 22.

6. Lester J. Keyser and André Ruszkowski, *The Cinema of Sidney Poitier: The Black Man's Changing Role on the American Screen* (New York: A. S. Barnes, 1980), 164.

7. Aram Goudsouzian, *Sidney Poitier: Man, Actor, Icon* (Chapel Hill: University of North Carolina Press, 2004), 215.

8. See Goudsouzian, *Sidney Poitier: Man, Actor, Icon*, 157–166, and Wil Haygood, *In Black and White: The Life of Sammy Davis, Jr.* (New York: Alfred A. Knopf, 2003), 281–295. Although Belafonte had his own production company (Harbel) and had some element of control in creating his own opportunities, his disappearance from feature films for eleven years following his refusal to star in *Porgy & Bess* suggests that Belafonte fell victim to the very fate that Poitier feared should he refuse the role.

9. Poitier willingly admits that he has regretted two of his films. During a teleconference interview with Ian Strachan (on February 26, 2010, during the Sidney Poitier International Conference and Film Festival in Nassau, Bahamas), Poitier admitted that one of the two films was indeed *Porgy & Bess*. He has not specified what the second one was, but biographer Aram Goudsouzian has speculated that it is *The Long Ships* (1964, Jack Cardiff), which was more of an artistic miscalcula-

tion than a racially problematic film like *Porgy & Bess*. Goudsouzian, *Sidney Poitier: Man, Actor, Icon*, 274–275.

10. He earned the Academy Award for Best Actor in *Lilies of the Field* (1963, Ralph Nelson), and his three consecutive hit films—*To Sir, with Love* (1967, James Clavell), *In the Heat of the Night* (1967, Norman Jewison), and *Guess Who's Coming to Dinner?* (1967, Stanley Kramer)—made Poitier the highest-paid film star in the country at the decade's end.

11. Clifford Mason, "Why Does White America Love Sidney Poitier So?" *New York Times*, September 10, 1967.

12. Donald Bogle, *Toms, Coons, Mulattoes, Mammies, & Bucks: An Interpretive History of Blacks in American Films*, 4th ed. (New York: Continuum, 2001), 220–223.

13. Goudsouzian, *Sidney Poitier: Man, Actor, Icon*, 215.

14. Ibid., 209, 270.

15. Ibid., 320.

16. Dustin Hoffman and Steve McQueen became partners in First Artists the following year. Goudsouzian, *Sidney Poitier: Man, Actor, Icon*, 354.

17. Ibid., 326, 347.

18. *Buck and the Preacher*, in some ways, is the realization of a long-planned Poitier-Belafonte western that was first discussed in 1959 under the title *The Exodusters*. Ibid., 196–197.

19. Keyser and Ruszkowski, *Cinema of Sidney Poitier*, 150.

20. Ibid., 342.

21. The concept of *Buck and the Preacher* as a revolutionary film comes from Mia Mask's paper "Black Masculinity on Horseback: From *Duel at Diablo* to *Buck and the Preacher* . . . and Beyond," delivered February 26, 2010, at the Sidney Poitier International Conference and Film Festival, Nassau, Bahamas.

22. For a thoughtful and detailed history of the disease, see Keith Wailoo's *Dying in the City of the Blues: Sickle Cell Anemia and the Politics of Race and Health* (Chapel Hill: University of North Carolina Press, 2001).

23. Ibid., 169.

24. Ibid., 3.

25. Ibid., 170.

26. Ibid., 182.

27. A year after *A Warm December* was released, the disease was given a more pronounced, albeit bizarre, cinematic treatment in the blaxploitation actioner *Three the Hard Way* (1974, Gordon Parks Jr.). The film stars Fred Williamson, Jim Brown, and Jim Kelly, and the black heroes rush to put an end to an elaborate plot by white supremacists to poison the water supply with a special strain of sickle cell anemia that will kill off the entire African American population. Needless to say, genocide is averted as the Hammer, Brown, and Kelly shoot, punch, and kick the neo-Nazis into submission.

28. Goudsouzian, *Sidney Poitier: Man, Actor, Icon*, 344.

29. Ibid., 345.

30. Personal interview, Richard Wesley, October 7, 2009, New York.

31. Wesley worked on rewrites on *Across 110th Street* (1972, Barry Shear), although he did not receive screen credit. He also worked on the unrealized *The Elmira Express*, a proposed biopic of Syracuse running back Ernie Davis. Wesley interview.

32. Ibid.

33. On Poitier's hesitancy to direct himself, see Keyser and Ruszkowski, *Cinema of Sidney Poitier*, 170. Information on the proposed casting of Foxx and Pryor comes from Wesley interview.

34. Keyser and Ruszkowski, *Cinema of Sidney Poitier*, 170.

35. Goudsouzian, *Sidney Poitier: Man, Actor, Icon*, 353.

36. Walker and Amos had been catapulted to fame via the sitcom *Good Times*, which was at the height of its success in 1975.

37. Goudsouzian, *Sidney Poitier: Man, Actor, Icon*, 353.

38. Ibid., 348–349.

39. Sidney Poitier, *This Life* (New York: Alfred A Knopf, 1980), 327.

40. For a discussion of the Poitier-Cosby films as a trilogy, see Mark Anthony Neal, *Soul Babies: Black Popular Culture and the Post-Soul Aesthetic* (New York: Routledge, 2002), 28.

41. Richard Majors, *Cool Pose: The Dilemmas of Black Manhood in America* (New York: Simon and Schuster, 1993).

42. Examples include *Claudine* (1974, John Berry), *Cornbread, Earl and Me* (1975, Joseph Manduke), *The Monkey Hu$tle* (1976, Arthur Marks), and *Together Brothers* (1974, William A. Graham), to name a few.

43. Cosby's work on educational television fare like *Fat Albert and the Cosby Kids* and *The Electric Company* coincided with his earning a doctorate in education from the University of Massachusetts-Amherst.

44. Goudsouzian, *Sidney Poitier: Man, Actor, Icon*, 358.

45. First Artists moved away from its initial concept and began producing pictures that did not feature its members as actors, beginning with *The Gumball Rally* (1976, Charles Bail) and including *Bobby Deerfield* (1977, Sydney Pollack), *The One and Only* (1978, Carl Reiner), *Zero to Sixty* (1978, Don Weis), and *Stevie* (1978, Robert Enders).

46. Pamela G. Hollie, "First Artists: Star-Crossed Child of the 1960's," *New York Times*, December 23, 1979.

47. Poitier, *This Life*, 343.

48. Gene Wilder, *Kiss Me Like a Stranger: My Search for Love and Art* (New York: St. Martin's, 2005), 184.

49. Box Office Mojo, "1980 Domestic Grosses," www.boxofficemojo.com/yearly/chart/?yr=1980&p=.htm.

50. Gary Arnold, "Slapstick in the Slammer," *Washington Post*, December 12, 1980.

51. Michael Schultz had already made *Sgt. Pepper's Lonely Hearts Club Band* (1978) and *Scavenger Hunt* (1979), while Bill Gunn's *Stop* (1970) and Gordon

Parks's *The Super Cops* (1974) provide earlier examples of black directors making films with largely white casts.

52. Shooting wrapped the last week of May 1980, and the Northridge fire incident happened June 11, 1980.

53. John A. Williams and Dennis A. Williams, *If I Stop I'll Die: The Comedy and Tragedy of Richard Pryor* (New York: Thunder's Mouth, 1991), 142.

54. Goudsouzian, *Sidney Poitier: Man, Actor, Icon*, 360.

55. *Los Angeles Times*, September 20, 1983.

56. Bob Thomas, Associated Press, March 3, 1985.

57. Poitier, *This Life*, 350.

58. Ibid.

59. Wesley interview.

60. Ibid.

61. Among the directors Jackson worked with are John Landis, Francis Ford Coppola, Martin Scorsese, Spike Lee, and John Singleton.

62. *Fast Forward* grossed $2.7 million, while *The Breakfast Club* grossed $45 million. Box Office Mojo, "Fast Forward," www.boxofficemojo.com/movies/?id=fastforward.htm, and "The Breakfast Club," www.boxofficemojo.com/movies/?id=breakfastclub.htm.

63. Mark Pendergrast, *For God, Country, and Coca-Cola: The Definitive History of the Great American Soft Drink and the Company That Makes It*, 2nd ed. (New York: Basic, 2000), 340–385.

64. Goudsouzian, *Sidney Poitier: Man, Actor, Icon*, 361.

65. Ibid., 369.

66. Cosby authored the autobiographical *Fatherhood* (Garden City, NY: Doubleday, 1986); *Time Flies* (New York: Doubleday, 1988); and *Love and Marriage* (New York: Doubleday, 1989).

67. *The Cosby Show* guest performers included Bill Gunn, Roscoe Lee Browne, Moses Gunn, Joe Williams, Nancy Wilson, Dizzy Gillespie, Lena Horne, Sammy Davis Jr., Norman Beaton, Pam Grier, Miriam Makeba, Howard Sims, Al Freeman Jr., Clarence Williams III, Joe Seneca, and Margaret Avery.

68. Box Office Mojo, "Ghost Dad," www.boxofficemojo.com/movies/?id=ghostdad.htm.

69. Gilles Whittel, "Sidney Poitier Is Made President of Walt Disney," *The Times* (London), November 25, 1994; Gerard Evans, "Sidney Poitier Lands the Top Job at Disney," *Evening Standard* (London), November 24, 1994.

70. Disney's string of successes following *The Little Mermaid* (1989, Ron Clements and John Musker) tapered off in Poitier's years on the board, with disappointing grosses on increasingly expensive films, including *Pocahontas* (1995, Mike Gabriel and Eric Goldberg), *The Hunchback of Notre Dame* (1996, Gary Trousdale and Kirk Wise), *Hercules* (1997, Ron Clements and John Musker), *Mulan* (1998, Tony Bancroft and Barry Cook), and *Tarzan* (1999, Chris Buck and Kevin Lima).

71. See James B. Stewart, *Disney War* (New York: Simon and Schuster, 2005).

72. Percival Everett, *I Am Not Sidney Poitier* (Minneapolis: Graywolf, 2009).
73. Dave McNary, "DGA Honors Poitier," *Variety*, February 26, 2001.

CHAPTER 4: THINK LOCALLY, ACT GLOBALLY

1. Williamson drew the comparison himself, stating, "I saw myself as Clark Gable, John Wayne, all these people, but Hollywood didn't see me that way. I figured the only way I could do that was to start making my own movies." George Alexander, *Why We Make Movies: Black Filmmakers Talk About the Magic of Cinema* (New York: Harlem Moon, 2003), 61.
2. Telephone interview, Fred Williamson, May 23, 2014.
3. Ibid.
4. Ibid.
5. Williamson was drafted by the National Football League's San Francisco 49ers and then traded to the Pittsburgh Steelers at the start of his rookie season. In 1961, he jumped to the upstart American Football League, signing with the Oakland Raiders. Williamson played four seasons with the Raiders before joining the Chiefs for his final three years in the AFL. His final game was against the Green Bay Packers in the inaugural Super Bowl.
6. Williamson interview.
7. "Bachelors for 1964: Leap Year Arouses Special Interest in Eligible Men," *Ebony*, June 1964, 212.
8. Mark Kriegel, "Now Playing . . . Hammer Time Fred Williamson Enjoys a Super Run in Movies," *New York Daily News*, January 14, 1996.
9. Following the 1967 season with the Kansas City Chiefs, Williamson played another year with the Montreal Alouettes of the Canadian Football League.
10. Williamson interview.
11. In addition to *Julia*, Williamson made a number of TV appearances in 1969, including episodes of *Star Trek*, *The Outsider*, and *The Bold Ones: The Protectors*. Williamson interview.
12. "Football Heroes Invade Hollywood," *Ebony*, October 1969, 202.
13. Williamson interview.
14. "Black-White Team to Make Film About Mixed Love," *Jet*, April 23, 1970, 57.
15. When I talked to Williamson, he said that he held a press conference in the early 1970s where he first presented his rules for representation on screen.
16. Alexander, *Why We Make Movies*, 61.
17. The opening credits of the film say that it is based on the historical research of C. Eric Lincoln, the renowned scholar of African American religious experiences.
18. Spangler had a brief history of working with football players in a mainstream entertainment context, producing the short-lived talk show *The Joe*

Namath Show in 1969 and Namath's feature-length western *The Last Rebel* (1971, Denys McCoy).

19. Louis Paul, *Tales from the Cult Film Trenches: Interviews with 36 Actors from Horror, Science Fiction, and Exploitation Cinema* (Jefferson, NC: McFarland, 2007), 281–286.

20. Universal came late to the game with blaxploitation, not distributing a single black-focused film in 1972. *Bolt*, along with *Trick Baby* and *Willie Dynamite*, came later, but actually lost money for the studio. See chapter 6 for more details.

21. *Three the Hard Way* had a production budget of $1.8 million, one of the largest for a black-focused film financed outside of the major studios. The film was cofinanced and distributed by Allied Artists. See "Fred Williamson to Star in Hubert Julian Film," *Jet*, July 5, 1973, 53.

22. Williamson's stay on *Monday Night Football* was brief. He was fired midway through his first season after the tension in the booth between him and Howard Cosell became palpable for viewers. ABC bought Williamson out of his contract, which also included a deal to make three television movies for the network. The TV movies never came to fruition. See Paul, *Tales from the Cult Film Trenches*, 281.

23. "Fred Williamson Signs to Co-produce New Film," *Jet*, September 26, 1974, 60.

24. Williamson interview.

25. Ibid.

26. "Dells to Score Fred Williamson Picture," *Jet*, March 11, 1976, 63. The budget has been alternately listed at $60,000 and $75,000.

27. Williamson interview.

28. This sense of cutting corners with the budget extends to the soundtrack. The Gamble and Huff composition "Do It Any Way You Wanna," a 1975 hit for the group People's Choice, was repurposed for the film, but with an instrumental version of the song. The opening credits give the false impression that the song was written for the film. Despite the involvement of a number of high-profile soul and R&B musicians in scoring and performing songs for black-focused films in the 1970s, including Curtis Mayfield, Isaac Hayes, Marvin Gaye, and James Brown, Gamble and Huff had no interest in participating in the blaxploitation cycle. They were offered the score for *Shaft in Africa*, but they turned it down because of reservations about the "negative" impact of black action features, drawing conclusions about representation that were aligned with the views of the Coalition Against Blaxploitation.

29. The original title for the film was *Peace Is Hell*, but it was changed before it was released in theaters. See "F. Williamson to Star *Mean Johnny Barrows*," *Jet*, December 11, 1975, 75.

30. Williamson interview.

31. Infernal Blues Machine's title song for *Adios Amigo* makes the connection to the modern-day ghetto explicit in its lyrics, with the groove disrupting any notion that the film is to be read as a literal reflection of the 1800s. Repeating the

line numerous times in the film, the chorus reads, "Adios amigo / might not be the ghetto."

32. "Williamson, Pryor to Co-Star in New Film," *Jet*, May 22, 1975, 64.

33. Williamson interview.

34. Martin Weston, "Richard Pryor: 'Every Nigger Is a Star,'" *Ebony*, September 1976, 57.

35. Williamson interview.

36. Ibid.

37. Ibid.

38. "Fred Williamson Finds Success as a Filmmaker," *Jet*, April 8, 1976, 58–61.

39. "Group Urges Boycott of Fred Williamson's Films," *Jet*, April 29, 1976, 61.

40. Williamson interview.

41. "People Are Talking About," *Jet*, June 17, 1976, 40. Williamson said he shot two to three days' worth of footage in Mexico, but decided to abandon *Greed* after corrupt border officials demanded bribes in order to allow him to bring the negatives into the United States. Realizing just how precarious making a film in Mexico could be, he decided to scrap the project altogether rather than navigate the channels of Mexican authority. Williamson interview.

42. Williamson interview.

43. "Williamson Buys Rest of Dirty Harry Films; To Work on His Own Character," *Jet*, April 7, 1977, 58. Eastwood had just finished filming his third Dirty Harry picture, *The Enforcer* (1976, James Fargo). He eventually returned to the character with *Sudden Impact* (1983, Clint Eastwood) and *The Dead Pool* (1988, Buddy Van Horn).

44. "Wilson, Robinson Signed for Fred Williamson Flick," *Jet*, September 28, 1978, 60; "Williamson Hints He'll 'Expose' How He Makes Love," *Jet*, May 10, 1979, 59.

45. Williamson interview.

46. "How to Survive in Hollywood Between Gigs," *Ebony*, October 1978, 34.

47. Ronald E. Kisner, "Is the Future Vanishing for Black Film Stars?" *Jet*, April 5, 1979, 14–16, 58–59.

48. "Disgusted with Hollywood, Fred Williamson Moves Film Works to Canada," *Jet*, May 22, 1980, 22.

49. Roger Ebert, "Fred Williamson: 'I Like the Life,'" *Chicago Sun-Times*, May 17, 1983.

50. In *Vigilante* he plays another black buddy character to Robert Forster, who appears in a Charles Bronson–*Death Wish* type role as a frustrated family man taking on street gangs. Williamson delivers an impassioned monologue about the dangers of urban youth and the need for swift and violent justice that problematizes his relationship with a black audience. The narrative fabric of *Vigilante* relies on the most audacious myths of black criminality put forth in Reagan's first term.

51. Audio commentary, *One Down, Two to Go*, DVD.

52. "One More for the Po' Boys," *Black Enterprise*, September 1982, 38.

53. *One Down, Two to Go* commentary.

54. Ibid.

55. "Celebrity Beat," *Jet*, October 4, 1982, 54.

56. "One More for the Po' Boys," *Black Enterprise*, September 1982.

57. Pat Borzi, "Williamson Succeeding, Just Like in Movies," *Miami Herald*, February 8, 1983.

58. Will Hermes, *Love Goes to Buildings on Fire: Five Years That Changed Music Forever* (New York: Faber and Faber, 2011), 33.

59. Ibid., 290.

60. Cruz was part of a much broader three-day concert series that was realized more than thirty years later as a documentary concert film with *Soul Power* (2008, Jeffrey Levy-Hinte).

61. Masucci also came up with the story concept, which Williamson fleshed out into a screenplay.

62. Blades and Colón had a long working relationship together, most successfully in recording the album *Siembra* (1978), the best-selling record in Fania's history. The film also features World Boxing Council featherweight champion Salvatore Sánchez, who died in a car crash shortly after shooting his scene for the film. The final credits of *The Last Fight* dedicate the film to his memory.

63. The *Dirty Harry* films are set in San Francisco.

64. The film features veteran actors John Saxon, Ed Lauter, Frank Pesce, Joe Spinell, Chelcie Ross, Bruce Glover, and James Spinks as well as Williamson's old friends D'Urville Martin and Richard Roundtree. Nancy Wilson also appears as Hooks's love interest, finally working together with Williamson years after they first discussed their long-rumored project *Blues for a Hundred Yards*. Wilson performs a song in the film, as does jazz pianist Ramsey Lewis.

65. "Actor D'Urville Martin Dies of Heart Attack," *Jet*, June 11, 1984, 14. Williamson was especially close to Martin, saying that "D'Urville was my right arm" when remembering his friend and colleague. Williamson interview.

66. "D'Urville Martin Slated for 3 Flicks This Year," *Jet*, February 27, 1984, 55.

67. Alessandro Portelli, "The Problem of the Color-Blind: Notes on the Discourse of Race in Italy," in Paul Spickard, ed., *Race and Nation: Ethnic Systems in the Modern World* (New York: Routledge, 2005).

68. Alexander, *Why We Make Movies*, 66.

69. Paul, *Tales from the Cult Film Trenches*, 289.

70. "Fred Williamson Denied British Work Visa, Won't Star in 'Dirty Dozen' Film," *Jet*, December 3, 1984, 30.

71. *Half Nelson* took the place of NBC's female detective agency show *Partners in Crime* in early 1985.

72. Williamson had appeared years earlier as part of the retired-athlete ensemble that populated the TV ads for Miller Lite.

73. The term "malt liquor" itself simply connotes a beer with alcohol content over the limit to legally be marketed as "beer" in the United States.

74. Philip Van Munching, *Beer Blast: The Inside Story of the Brewing Industry's Bizarre Battles for Your Money* (New York: Times Business, 1997), 236–241.

75. The advertising of malt liquor took a turn in 1991 when Anheuser-Busch and Miller dropped their price point, forcing other producers of malt liquor (Heileman's Colt 45, Stroh's Schlitz Malt Liquor, McKenzie River's St. Ides, and Pabst's Olde English "800") to actively convince consumers that their brands stood out from the crowd and were worth the extra cost. Some plastered inner cities with billboards and point-of-sale advertising in corner liquor stores, or flooded radio and television programs targeting young black men with commercials featuring hip-hop performers like Ice Cube, Scarface, King Tee, Notorious B.I.G., 2Pac, Snoop Dogg, and Dr. Dre, all professing their love for malt liquor.

76. Williamson had named the Jesse Crowder character after a childhood friend, only to later be sued by the real Jesse Crowder. Although Williamson had the case dismissed, he chose to abandon using the name in subsequent films to avoid any more legal entanglements.

77. Kriegel, "Now Playing . . . Hammer Time."

78. Williamson interview.

79. Massi directed the second and third *Black Cobra* films (1988 and 1990) under the American-sounding pseudonym "Dan Edwards."

80. Alexander, *Why We Make Movies*, 62.

81. Ibid., 59.

CHAPTER 5: OUTSIDE OF SOCIETY

1. Ed Guerrero, *Framing Blackness: The African American Image in Film* (Philadelphia: Temple University Press, 1993), 137.

2. Manthia Diawara, *African Cinema: Politics & Culture* (Bloomington: Indiana University Press, 1992), 133–135.

3. Clyde Taylor, "New U.S. Black Cinema," *Jump Cut*, no. 28, April 1983, 46.

4. I am using *Child of Resistance* as Gerima's first feature, although with a running time of 57 minutes, this designation is debatable.

5. Taylor, "New U.S. Black Cinema," 48.

6. Manohla Dargis, "Whereabouts in Watts? Where Poetry Meets Chaos," *New York Times*, March 30, 2007.

7. "Internship Participants Named by Film Institute," *Boxoffice*, August 22, 1977, 39. This connection may have played a role in Clark casting Clarence Muse in *Passing Through*, as Muse had worked with Schultz a few years prior on *Car Wash*.

8. Larry Clark, interview with Phyllis Klotman, April 24, 1984, Black Film Center / Archive at Indiana University, Bloomington.

9. Personal interview, Jamaa Fanaka, March 18, 2010, Los Angeles.

10. Ibid.

11. Ibid.

12. Mike Davis, *City of Quartz: Excavating the Future in Los Angeles* (New York: Vintage, 1992), 296.

13. Fanaka has alternated on the details of his incarceration, often denying that he was ever in prison altogether. He personally told me about his time in jail, but did not explain the specifics of his arrest or conviction.

14. Fanaka interview.

15. Ibid.

16. In addition to *Dolemite*, Dimension released the blaxploitation-era features *Tough* (1974, Horace Jackson), *Boss Nigger* (1975, Jack Arnold), *Deliver Us from Evil* (1975, Horace Jackson), *The Bad Bunch* (1976, Greydon Clark), *Black Shampoo* (1975, Greydon Clark), *Dr. Black, Mr. Hyde* (1976, William Crain), *Ebony, Ivory and Jade* (1976, Cirio H. Santiago), and *The Muthers* (1976, Cirio H. Santiago).

17. "Past, Present Stars Meet at Black Filmmakers Confab," *Jet*, March 23, 1978, 28–30.

18. Ibid.

19. Fanaka interview.

20. "'Penitentiary' Success Paves Way for Sequel," *Jet*, June 12, 1980, 60.

21. Robert E. Johnson, "Leon and Jayne Tell Why Their Good Marriage Turned Bad," *Jet*, November 26, 1981, 57.

22. Fanaka interview.

23. Ibid.

24. *Boxoffice*, October 1980, 10.

25. Boxing was always a popular genre, but *Rocky*'s success spawned a decided spike in boxing films, including *The Greatest* (1977, Tom Gries and Monte Hellman), *The Champ* (1979, Franco Zeffirelli), *The Main Event* (1979, Howard Zieff), *The Prize Fighter* (1979, Michael Preece), and *Raging Bull* (1980, Martin Scorsese), not to mention the sequels *Rocky II* (1979, Sylvester Stallone) and *Rocky III* (1982, Sylvester Stallone).

26. *Penitentiary II* was released on April 2, 1982, while *Rocky III* hit theaters May 28, 1982. Over the next few years Mr. T would star on *The A Team*, make his own Saturday morning cartoon, appear in the main event at the inaugural *Wrestlemania*, and have his likeness used on everything from action figures to his very own breakfast cereal.

27. See Julian Bond and Sondra Kathryn Wilson, *Lift Every Voice and Sing: A Celebration of the Negro National Anthem* (New York: Random House, 2000).

28. Box Office Mojo, "Penitentiary II," www.boxofficemojo.com/movies/?id=penitentiary2.htm.

29. "Hollywood Report," *Boxoffice*, February 1984, 8.

30. Ed Halter, "Secrets and Thighs," *Village Voice*, December 2, 2003.

31. *Knights of the City* was going to feature Sammy Davis Jr. in a supporting role, but his three days of shooting were cut out of the film after a new producer took over postproduction duties. Kennedy had befriended Davis in the 1970s and was looking to pay him back for the advice and encouragement he had received. Davis had gone so far as to mention *Penitentiary* during an appearance on *The Tonight Show* in 1980 to help gain exposure for the film. See Wil Haygood, *In Black and White: The Life of Sammy Davis, Jr.* (New York: Alfred A. Knopf, 2003), 461–462.

32. Cannon's involvement and his shared credit with Kennedy as producer have played a role in *Penitentiary III* being Fanaka's only film without a DVD release, as he owned all of his other films outright.

33. Kessler is credited as the Haiti Kid, his professional wrestling name. He had worked territories for over a decade before joining the World Wrestling Foundation (WWF) in the mid-1980s, where he appeared in *WrestleMania 2* and *WrestleMania III*.

34. Brown had appeared in a number of films, beginning with *Shaft*.

35. L. John Wertheim, "The New Main Event," *Sports Illustrated*, May 28, 2007.

36. Bureau of Justice Statistics, "Key Facts at a Glance," www.bjs.ojp.usdoj.gov/content/glance/tables/corr2tab.cfm; Manning Marable, "Racializing Justice, Disenfranchising Lives: Toward an Anti-Racist Criminal Justice," in Manning Marable, Ian Sternberg, and Keesha Middlemass, eds., *Racializing Justice, Disenfranchising Lives: The Racism, Criminal Justice, and Law Reader* (New York: Palgrave MacMillan, 2007), 4.

37. Box Office Mojo, "Penitentiary III," www.boxofficemojo.com/movies/?id=penitentiary3.htm.

38. Frederic Wasser, *Veni, Vidi, Video: The Hollywood Empire and the VCR* (Austin: University of Texas Press, 2002).

39. Fanaka interview.

40. Ibid.

41. Ibid.

42. The credits refer to the fictitious production company as Bob, Bea and Bee Honey Productions on *Street Wars*, with Fanaka's parents being joined by his aunt Winifred Ushery as a financier for the project. Ushery was credited with wardrobe on *Welcome Home Brother Charles*.

43. Ntongela Masilela, "The Los Angeles School of Black Filmmakers," in Manthia Diawara, ed., *Black American Cinema* (New York: Routledge, 1993), 109.

44. Taylor, "New U.S. Black Cinema."

45. Ibid.

46. Fanaka interview.

CHAPTER 6: DREAMS DEFERRED

1. Information on Moses's childhood and background comes from a telephone interview and personal correspondence with his sister, Carol Moses-Robinson, including a letter dated May 23, 2010.

2. An elementary teacher, Richard Eisenhaur, introduced Moses to Karamu House. Moses-Robinson correspondence.

3. "Karamu House: Negro Art Center in Cleveland Is a Milestone of Racial Amity," *Life*, June 18, 1951.

4. Arnold Rampersad, *The Life of Langston Hughes*, vol. 1, *1902–1941: I, Too, Sing America* (New York: Oxford University Press, 1986), 317.

5. Jack Warfel, "Karamu Play Captures Feelings of a Boy," *Cleveland Press*, February 23, 1955, 15.

6. Oberlin College had ties to Karamu House as the alma mater of the Jelliffes and a sponsor of its programs.

7. Moses attended before the Sorbonne, or the University of Paris, was reorganized and divided into thirteen separate universities in 1970.

8. Mel Gussow, "Gilbert Moses Dead at 52," *New York Times*, April 18, 1995.

9. Robert Penn Warren, *Who Speaks for the Negro?* (New York: Random House, 1965), 68–71.

10. Evers died June 12, 1963. Moses left Paris sometime in 1963, but the exact date of his departure, and the details of how he ended up in Mississippi, are unclear. Moses may have worked for the paper before Evers's assassination, or the publicity surrounding his death may have been what prompted Moses to set out for Jackson. But by the end of the year, he was certainly in Jackson working for the *Mississippi Free Press*.

11. Martha M. Jones, "An Interview with Gil Moses," *Black Creation*, Winter 1972, 20.

12. Prefiguring his work in decades to come, *Roots* incorporates filmed elements ("with funds willing," as the written play instructs), showing a cinematic train of thought that predates Moses's involvement in film production.

13. Thomas C. Dent, Richard Schechner, and Gilbert Moses, eds., *The Free Southern Theater by the Free Southern Theater: A Documentary of the South's Radical Black Theater, with Journals, Letters, Poetry, Essays and a Play Written by Those Who Built It* (Indianapolis: Bobbs-Merrill, 1969), 48.

14. "Friends of the FST" included Brock Peters (cochair circa 1968), while "those deserving special mention for their repeated response to emergency calls" were listed as follows: "Max Roach, Abby [*sic*] Lincoln, Ruby Dee, Leon Bibb, Harry Belafonte, Ossie Davis, Diana Sands, George Tabori, Viveca Lindfors, Madeline Sgerwood, Paul Newman, Sidney Poitier, Rod Steiger, Frederick O'Neal, and John O. Killens." This acknowledgment was signed Thomas C. Dent, Richard Schechner, John O'Neal, and Gilbert Moses, NYC 1968. Dent et al., *Free Southern Theater*, xiii.

15. John O'Neal, "Motion in the Ocean: Some Political Dimensions of the Free Southern Theatre (1968)," in Annemarie Bean, ed., *A Sourcebook of African-American Performance: Plays, People, Movements* (New York: Routledge, 1999), 115.

16. Dent et al., *Free Southern Theater*, 9; see also Roscoe Orman, *Sesame Street Dad: Evolution of an Actor* (Portland, OR: Inkwater, 2006), 41.

17. Orman, *Sesame Street Dad*, 42.

18. His enrollment at NYU was verified by Oberlin archivist Ken Grossi, correspondence dated August 2, 2010. His time in Chicago comes from Carol Moses-Robinson correspondence.

19. Jones, "Interview with Gil Moses," 19.

20. Ibid., 20.

21. Ibid.

22. Telephone conversation with Moses's second wife, Wilma Butler, March 3, 2010.

23. "Eli's Game" was first released in the United Kingdom on the 1994 compilation of Hi Records tracks *Name of the Game*, and has since appeared as a bonus track on *Let's Stay Together* and various Al Green box sets and rarities collections. Green was later attached to another unrealized Gilbert Moses film, 1974's *Mimi*.

24. If it can be assumed that Green's lyrics are structured along the lines of a number of contemporary soul soundtracks, namely Curtis Mayfield's *Super Fly*, Isaac Hayes's *Shaft*, and James Brown's *Black Caesar*, then we can look at the song for possible insight into the film's plot and focus.

25. Cutler wrote the story concept with Joe Keyes Jr.

26. Orman, *Sesame Street Dad*, 79.

27. The Eldorado was also the car of choice of both Priest in *Super Fly* and Goldie in *The Mack*, although Willie's customized additions are of comedic proportion.

28. Moses, quoted in press book for *Willie Dynamite*, Black Film Center / Archive at Indiana University, Bloomington.

29. Orman, *Sesame Street Dad*, 73–74.

30. Sands gives a standout performance; unfortunately, it would be her last, as she was diagnosed with cancer halfway through shooting, causing a break in production as she rested. Diana Sands seemed to be on the precipice of screen stardom in the early 1970s, one of the great stage talents who could benefit from Hollywood's sudden embrace of black themes. She made a supporting appearance in *The Landlord* (1970, Hal Ashby) and played the lead in Michael Schultz's low-budget *Honeybaby, Honeybaby* and the Maya Angelou–penned *Georgia, Georgia* (1972, Stig Björkman) before she was cast to play the title role in *Claudine* (1974, John Berry). Sands succumbed to cancer before she could play the part (it was eventually filled by Diahann Carroll), making *Willie Dynamite* the coda of her acting career.

31. Orman, *Sesame Street Dad*, 79.

32. Emory Lewis, "Gilbert Moses in Search of Black Theater," *Sunday Record* (New Jersey), May 25, 1975, B27.

33. "People Are Talking About," *Jet*, July 4, 1974, 61.

34. Other cast members attached to the project included Melba Moore, Al Green, and Lola Falana.

35. Lewis, "Gilbert Moses in Search of Black Theater," B27.

36. There are differing accounts as to why Moses was fired from *The Wiz* and how much control he had as director. In Geoffrey Holder's HistoryMakers interview, April 16, 2003, archived at HistoryMakers office, Chicago, he claims to have been initially slated to direct off-Broadway, but says that he turned down the job to focus on costuming and sets after the producers of the show insisted he take on an assistant director. Moses's firing, from Holder's perspective, was simply a case of the producers relenting to Holder's initial wish for full creative control.

This version of events, however, seems unlikely given Moses's talent and reputation at the time.

37. This was Moses's third and final marriage, as he had previously been married to Denise Nicholas and Wilma Butler. He and Bridgewater divorced in 1982.

38. The other directors, Marvin J. Chomsky, John Erman, and David Greene, were all white. Although the source material came from Haley, the screenwriting for the miniseries was credited exclusively to white writers. The 1979 follow-up, *Roots: The Next Generation*, was somewhat more inclusive than its predecessor, featuring black screenwriter Sydney Glass as well as black directors Georg Stanford Brown and Lloyd Richards. See Cecil Brown, "Blues for Blacks in Hollywood," *Mother Jones*, January 1981.

39. Tsia Moses interview.

40. Dashev managed the a cappella group the Persuasions, while Stromberg ran a public relations firm that had Earth, Wind & Fire, Elton John, the Doors, and the Rolling Stones as clients.

41. Telephone interview, Gary Stromberg, April 6, 2010.

42. Telephone interview, David Dashev, April 6, 2010.

43. Ibid.

44. Ibid.

45. Over twenty NBA players appeared in the film, most notably Kareem Abdul-Jabbar, Connie Hawkins, and Bob Lanier, while University of Nevada–Las Vegas head coach Jerry Tarkenian served as a technical consultant for the game sequences. The film also featured basketball announcers Chick Hearn and Marv Albert.

46. Pat Putnam and Jane Gross, "The NBA Said No Way," *Sports Illustrated*, October 28, 1974.

47. Pat Puttnam, "The Doctor Opens Up His Medicine Bag," *Sports Illustrated*, May 17, 1976.

48. Erving was traded by the financially struggling Nets for $3 million upon their arrival in the NBA.

49. See Terry Pluto, *Loose Balls* (New York: Simon and Schuster, 1991).

50. Todd Boyd, *Young, Black, Rich and Famous: The Rise of the NBA, the Hip Hop Invasion, and the Transformation of American Culture* (New York: Doubleday, 2003), 29–30.

51. Dashev and Stromberg interviews.

52. Ibid.

53. With a few strings pulled by Lorimar, Moses, Dashev, and Stromberg were given photographer's passes for the Lakers' 1977–1978 season. Moses developed personal relationships with a number of the players, and Lakers guard Norm Nixon eventually met his wife, Debbie Allen, through Moses.

54. Tsia Moses interview.

55. Dashev and Stromberg admittedly were battling drug addiction at the time, and Moses and Bridgewater were arrested by the Pittsburgh Police Department

and charged with possession of cocaine and stolen property. See "Actor Gilbert Moses, Wife Nabbed on Drug Charges," *Jet*, October 19, 1978, 60; "Free Dee Dee Bridgewater of Drug Charges, Husband Gilbert Moses Faces Rap," *Jet*, October 26, 1978, 59.

56. Dashev interview.

57. Stromberg interview.

58. The NBA-produced home video *Michael Jordan: Come Fly with Me* (1989) became a perennial best-seller, followed by *Michael Jordan's Playground* (1990) and *Michael Jordan: Air Time* (1993).

59. The most notable exception to the declining popularity was Teddy Pendergrass, whose solo career far outpaced his previous success as a member of Harold Melvin & the Blue Notes.

60. Frank Deford, "The 'Fish' Gets a Dismal Dunking," *Sports Illustrated*, November 25, 1979.

61. Tsia Moses interview.

62. Tsia Moses and Carol Moses-Robinson interviews. Moses had also spent time exploring Buddhism and Hinduism. His flirtation with conservative Christianity is an odd contrast to his earlier train of thought. As Robert Penn Warren sized Moses up when interviewing him in 1963, "he [Moses] is anti-religious, anti-theological, thinks that religion has been a 'great stumbling block,' for it prevents thought." Warren, *Who Speaks for the Negro?*, 69.

63. The project had received funding, likely from PBS, before Moses's passing. Correspondence with Carol Moses-Robinson, June 30, 2014.

64. Stan Lathan, HistoryMakers interviews, June 25, 2003, and April 23, 2004, archived at HistoryMakers office, Chicago.

65. Ibid.

66. Ibid.

67. Ibid.

68. NET would be replaced by the Public Broadcasting Service (PBS) in 1970.

69. Lathan, HistoryMakers interview.

70. Devorah Heitner, *Black Power TV* (Durham, NC: Duke University Press, 2013).

71. Robinson had been a close friend of Lathan's older brother Bill, who was eight years his senior.

72. "Save the Children: Documentary Film on 1972 PUSH EXPO Will Help Fund Fight for Black Rights," *Ebony*, October 1973, 48.

73. Lathan, HistoryMakers interview.

74. Wil Haygood, *In Black and White: The Life of Sammy Davis, Jr.* (New York: Alfred A. Knopf, 2003), 422–440.

75. Lathan, HistoryMakers interview. Neither version of the film has been made available in VHS or DVD, largely due to the complicated nature of securing the licensing for all of the music in the film.

76. Ibid.

77. "Matthew Robinson, Jr., 65; Original Cast Member of 'Sesame Street,'" *Los*

Angeles Times, August 8, 2002. Robinson played Gordon from the program's inception in 1969 until 1972. Hal Miller played Gordon in the interim before Orman took over the role in 1974.

78. For a detailed and thoughtful analysis, see Larry Tye, *Rising from the Rails: Pullman Porters and the Making of the Black Middle Class* (New York: Owl, 2004).

79. "Stan Lathan Named New Director of Sanford & Son," *Jet*, February 14, 1974, 63.

80. Champ Clark, *Shuffling to Ignominy: The Tragedy of Stepin Fetchit* (Lincoln, NE: iUniverse, 2005), 126–127.

81. Matt Robinson's biggest success after *Amazing Grace* was as a producer and staff writer for *The Cosby Show*. Unfortunately, Robinson battled Parkinson's disease for twenty years before his death in 2002, which limited his ability to complete more projects.

82. Lathan, HistoryMakers interview.

83. Elsie A. Williams, *The Humor of Jackie Moms Mabley* (New York: Garland, 1995), 53.

84. Mabley appears as herself in *Killer Diller* (1948, Josh Binney), a music and comedy revue produced by All-American News and released by Sack Amusements, and *Boarding House Blues* (1948, Josh Binney), a collection of vaudeville routines produced and distributed by All-American News.

85. Washington was appointed mayor of DC in 1967 by Lyndon B. Johnson. He became the first elected mayor of the city in 1974 when Congress granted the District of Columbia home rule.

86. David R. Goldfield, *Black, White and Southern: Race Relations and Southern Culture, 1940 to Present* (Baton Rouge: Louisiana State University Press, 1990), 177.

87. Baltimore would not get its first black mayor until 1986, when Clarence H. Du Burns was appointed mayor by the departing William Schaefer, who had been elected governor. Kurt Schmoke became the first black mayor elected in Baltimore the following year.

88. Lathan, HistoryMakers interview.

89. Thomas A. Mascaro, "Charged with a New Sense of Responsibility: Stan Lathan," *Journal of Popular Film and Television* 33, no. 2 (2005): 90–93.

90. "Black Family Breakthrough on Public Television," *Ebony*, February 1981, 74–80.

91. "People Are Talking About," *Jet*, June 22, 1978, 40. Richard Wesley was to write the screenplay. Hankerson's film ambitions never materialized after *Pipe Dreams*, and he and Knight would file for divorce in 1978.

92. "My Dinner with Luddy," *Mother Jones*, December 1984, 32.

93. Jeff Chang, *Can't Stop Won't Stop: A History of the Hip-Hop Generation* (New York: Picador, 2005), 193.

94. The credits of *Beat Street* contain a special note from the producers, who "gratefully acknowledge the research provided by Tony Silver and Harry Chalifant, Producers of 'Style Wars.'"

95. Kimberley Monteyne, *Hip Hop on Film: Performance Culture, Urban Space,*

and Genre Transformation in the 1980s (Jackson: University Press of Mississippi, 2013), 54–65.

96. Chang, *Can't Stop Won't Stop*, 193.

97. "Strangers in a Strange World" is performed by Jenny Burton and Patrick Jude. The song was written by pop-folk singer-songwriter Jake Holmes, a friend and collaborator of Belafonte's, whose credits range from cowriting Frank Sinatra's album *Watertown* (1970, Reprise) to composing advertising jingles for the US Army ("Be All That You Can Be") and Dr. Pepper ("Be a Pepper").

98. Chang, *Can't Stop Won't Stop*, 193.

99. See Lys Stevens, "Urban Youth Street Dances Go to the Movies and Become 'Breakdancing'," in *Dance/Diversity/Dialogue: Bridging Communities and Cultures*, World Dance Alliance Global Assembly, compiled by Karen Rose Cann, 2006, 364.

100. Ibid., 365.

101. Adolfo "Shabba-Doo" Quiñones from *Breakin'* was one of the hundreds of dancers accompanying Lionel Richie at the closing ceremonies.

102. Box Office Mojo, "Beat Street," www.boxofficemojo.com/movies/?id=beatstreet.htm; Box Office Mojo, "Breakin'," www.boxofficemojo.com/movies/?id=breakin.htm; Box Office Mojo, "Breakin' 2," www.boxofficemojo.com/movies/?id=breakin2.htm.

103. Christopher Vaughn, "Russell Simmons' Rush for Profits," *Black Enterprise*, December 1992.

104. The political subjects and dramatic tone of *Roc* brought the show into conflict with the network, which canceled the show after three seasons. *Martin* was made partially responsible through Martin Lawrence's popularity as the host for *Def Comedy Jam*.

105. Robin R. Means Coleman, *African American Viewers and the Black Situation Comedy: Situating Racial Humor* (New York: Routledge, 1998), 130; Lathan HistoryMakers interview.

CHAPTER 7: DIRTY MINDS REFORMED

1. Marjorie Garber, "Our Genius Problem," *The Atlantic*, December 2002.

2. Two years before his self-titled debut comedy album was released, Pryor made his film debut inauspiciously with a bit part in the Sid Caesar comedy *The Busy Body* (1967, William Castle). With the surge of black-focused films released in 1972, Pryor returned to the screen as Piano Man in *Lady Sings the Blues*. The next year he appeared in two more black-focused features, playing supporting roles in *The Mack* (1973, Michael Campus) and opposite Billy Dee Williams in *Hit!* (1973, Sidney J. Furie), while also appearing in a supporting role in *Some Call It Loving* (1973, James B. Harris) and as himself in the concert film *Wattstax* (1973, Mel Stuart).

3. Robert A. De Leon, "Richard Pryor Looks to '75," *Jet*, January 9, 1975, 56–61.

Also see John A. Williams and Dennis A. Williams, *If I Stop I'll Die: The Comedy and Tragedy of Richard Pryor* (New York: Thunder's Mouth, 1991), 69–70.

4. Personal interview, Michael Schultz, October 10, 2006, Santa Monica, California.

5. Ibid.

6. Williams and Williams, *If I Stop I'll Die*, 69–70. Pryor's inclusion in *Blazing Saddles* as a writer was tempered by Warner Bros. vetoing him as a star in the film, where he was set to play the role eventually filled by Cleavon Little. Pryor was deemed unsuitable for another major role that same year, but he took a cameo in *Uptown Saturday Night* as Sharp Eye Washington. It was a small role written specifically for Pryor after Warner Bros. rejected Poitier's pitch for the film to star Pryor and Redd Foxx.

7. Warner Bros. picked up Pryor's comedy album *That Nigger's Crazy* (1974) after his record label, Stax, defaulted on its contract. The album was certified gold and won the Grammy as Best Comedy Album. Over the next few years, Warner Bros. would release Pryor's albums . . . *Is It Something I Said?* (1975) and *Bicentennial Nigger* (1976), both of which were best-sellers and won Grammys. See Rob Bowman, *Soulsville, U.S.A.: The Story of Stax Records* (New York: Schirmer, 1997), 323.

8. "Pryor's Various TV, Movie Deals Make Him $20-Million-Dollar Man," *Jet*, May 19, 1977, 63.

9. Martin Weston, "Richard Pryor: 'Every Nigger Is a Star,'" *Ebony*, September 1976, 57.

10. "Pryor, Warner Bros. Sign Big Movie Deal Partnership," *Jet*, August 11, 1977, 55.

11. Williams and Williams, *If I Stop I'll Die*, 135.

12. "New York Beat," *Jet*, April 8, 1976, 57.

13. Ronald E. Kisner, "Richard Pryor's Richest Xmas," *Jet*, December 29, 1977, 56–58.

14. "Pryor Asks Saxman to Teach One Song for Film," *Jet*, December 7, 1978, 56.

15. "Pryor to Team with Mel Brooks in Comedy Movie," *Jet*, February 7, 1980, 61.

16. Gerald Nachman, *Seriously Funny: Rebel Comedians of the 1950s and 1960s* (New York: Random House, 2003), 583.

17. Williams and Williams, *If I Stop I'll Die*, 140, 150.

18. Richard Pryor, with Todd Gold, *Pryor Convictions* (New York: Pantheon, 1995).

19. "Richard Pryor, Comedy Legend, 1940–2005," *Jet*, January 9, 2006, 10.

20. Williams and Williams, *If I Stop I'll Die*, 174.

21. "Pryor Fires Brown as Head of His Company," *Jet*, January 2, 1984, 58–59.

22. Ibid.

23. Ibid.

24. Williams and Williams, *If I Stop I'll Die*.

25. Sidney Lumet, who was attached to the adaptation in the late 1970s, wanted Pryor to star as Malcolm. For a more complete discussion, see Keith Corson,

"Bringing Malcolm to the Masses: The Long Journey from Page to Screen," *Souls* 12, no. 1 (2010): 70–88.

26. "Pryor Fires Brown as Head of His Company," *Jet*, January 2, 1984, 58–59. One of the cofounders of the Negro Ensemble Company and a successful stage actor in the 1960s and 1970s, Hooks was thought to have been a clear candidate for creative control behind the camera during the blaxploitation cycle. He made his most prominent foray into feature films when he starred in *Trouble Man* (1972, Ivan Dixon), but by the 1980s he was largely working as a character actor on television.

27. "Charles Smiley Named Head of Pryor's Indigo Productions Company," *Jet*, March 12, 1984, 64; "Pryor Announces Revamp of Indigo; He'll Take a Lighter Load," *Jet*, November 26, 1984, 64.

28. Children's programming, particularly during the Reagan era, emphasized topical issues ranging from peer pressure to drug abuse and child abduction. See Hal Erickson, *Sid and Marty Krofft: A Critical Study of Saturday Morning Children's Television* (Jefferson, NC: MacFarland, 1998), 207–213.

29. "Richard Pryor Says, 'I Want to Dispel the Rumors That I Have AIDS,'" *Jet*, December 8, 1986, 54–55.

30. Pryor, with Gold, *Pryor Convictions*, 9–13.

31. Williams and Williams, *If I Stop I'll Die.*

32. Pryor, with Gold, *Pryor Convictions.*

33. See Martin Torgoff, *Can't Find My Way Home: America in the Great Stoned Age, 1945–2000* (New York: Simon and Schuster, 2004), 372–386.

34. Richard Zoglin, *Comedy at the Edge: How Stand-Up in the 1970s Changed America* (New York: Bloomsbury, 2008), 61.

35. Pryor appears with short-cropped hair and a clean-shaven face for scenes set in the 1960s. Rather than shooting these scenes last, cutting away layers of hair as he went along, Pryor had to use a wig and fake mustache to play the 1980s version of himself.

36. Erickson, *Sid and Marty Krofft*, 210.

37. Charles Whitaker, "Richard Pryor Changes Direction," *Ebony*, July 1986, 132–138.

38. Ibid.

39. Gabriella Oldham, *First Cut: Conversations with Film Editors* (Berkeley: University of California Press, 1992), 215.

40. Bambi Haggins, *Laughing Mad: The Black-Comic Persona in Post-Soul America* (New Brunswick, NJ: Rutgers University Press, 2007), 66–67; Box Office Mojo, "Jo Jo Dancer, Your Life Is Calling," www.boxofficemojo.com/movies/?id=jojo danceryourlifeiscalling.htm.

41. Pryor, with Gold, *Pryor Convictions*, 210.

42. *See No Evil, Hear No Evil* casts Pryor as a blind man who had a logical excuse to be clinging to someone else, while in *Harlem Nights* he appears almost exclusively in scenes where he is sitting down. By the time of Pryor's last major starring

role in *Another You* (1991, Maurice Phillips), yet another buddy comedy opposite Gene Wilder, his disease was impossible to hide.

43. Pryor, with Gold, *Pryor Convictions*, 113–116.

44. One of the most detailed accounts of working on one of these abandoned projects comes from Kevin Smith, who relates a story in *An Evening with Kevin Smith* (2002, JM Kenny) of being hired to direct a documentary for Prince at his Paisley Park studios. They shot a few days' worth of footage only to have the project later dropped.

45. Pryor, with Gold, *Pryor Convictions*, 144.

46. Prince worked with television writer William Blinn on an outline for the screenplay, with Blinn writing a first draft for the film based on their conversations. The screenplay received an extensive rewrite by Albert Magnoli when he signed on to direct. According to Magnoli, the final version of the screenplay is approximately 90 percent his, with only 10 percent remaining from Blinn's first draft. Both Magnoli and Blinn received screen credit. See DVD commentary on *Purple Rain*.

47. Lynn Norment, "Prince: What Is the Secret of His Amazing Success?," *Ebony*, June 1985, 162–170. The film cracked the top ten grossing films of the year, and it earned Prince an Academy Award for Best Original Song Score. Curiously, Prince was not nominated for Best Original Song, which went to Stevie Wonder's "I Just Called to Say I Love You," from *The Woman in Red* (1984, Gene Wilder).

48. What makes these inter-band conflicts compelling is how the fictitious world of *Purple Rain* relates to Prince's actual output and the mysteries surrounding his records. In effect, the Time and Apollonia 6 (a stand-in for the recently disbanded Vanity 6) were merely extensions of Prince, as he wrote the music, produced it, and conceptualized these bands under the pseudonym Jamie Starr. Vanity, the centerpiece of the girl group Vanity 6, was initially supposed to play the role filled by Apollonia Kotero, but she parted ways with Prince to pursue other film roles and signed a solo recording deal with Motown. Vanity was reportedly being considered by Martin Scorsese for a role in *The Last Temptation of Christ*. Her two biggest film roles came in Michael Schultz's *The Last Dragon* and *Action Jackson* (1988, Craig R. Baxley).

49. Per Nilsen, *Dance, Music, Sex, Romance: Prince: The First Decade* (London: Firefly, 1999), 176, 185.

50. Prince, notoriously shy, felt he would have been too out of place to contribute to the song. He also had artistic qualms with performing on a track penned by Michael Jackson and Lionel Richie. Instead, he wrote and recorded a track for the *We Are the World* album ("4 the Tears in Your Eyes"). This decision allowed him to contribute to the project without having to sacrifice his musical integrity.

51. Michael Shore, "The Prince Interview," *Rock & Soul*, April 1986. This interview is an unabridged version of the televised interview that aired on MTV in December 1985. Despite protests from Warner Bros., Prince insisted that the album be released without a single to help guide listeners to consider the album

as a cohesive whole. Prince would eventually release singles, starting a month after the album's release. "Paisley Park" was a British single and "Raspberry Beret" was the first American single off the record. Prince would ask for a similar release strategy for his album *Lovesexy* (1988). He started his own record label, Paisley Park, and began work on a new record before *Around the World in a Day* was even released, never touring to support the album.

When Prince finally relented to pressure from Warner Bros. to release singles and provide videos for MTV, he did so under the condition that he could direct the videos himself, which he did for "Raspberry Beret" and "America."

52. Nilsen, *Dance, Music, Sex, Romance*, 217.

53. Ibid., 222.

54. Shore, "Prince Interview." During the interview, which was conducted before shooting began, Prince was asked whether he would like to direct in the future, to which he enthusiastically replied, "Yes, yes, yes!"

55. Another possible reason for Lambert being hired may have been Prince's rumored interest in casting Madonna as his love interest, seeing that Lambert was the director for Madonna's videos "Borderline" and "Material Girl." Madonna reportedly passed on the film after meeting with Prince and the female lead was recast, with Kristin Scott Thomas making her feature film debut. Nilsen, *Dance, Music, Sex, Romance*, 223.

56. Ballhaus made over a dozen films with Rainer Werner Fassbinder. Following Fassbinder's death in 1982, he moved to the United States and served as cinematographer on *Baby, It's You* (1983, John Sayles) and *After Hours* (1985, Martin Scorsese).

57. Nilsen, *Dance, Music, Sex, Romance*, 225.

58. Ibid., 226.

59. Shore, "Prince Interview." Stamp was replaced by Steven Berkoff, who at the time was a go-to antagonist after his roles in *Beverly Hills Cop* (1984, Martin Brest) and *Rambo: First Blood, Part II* (1985, George P. Cosmatos).

60. Shore, "Prince Interview."

61. Ibid.

62. "Prince Completes 'Moon': June Release Scheduled," *Jet*, March 17, 1986, 60.

63. Nilsen, *Dance, Music, Sex, Romance*, 230.

64. For a broader history of African Americans in Paris, see Tyler Stovall, *Paris Noir: African Americans in the City of Light* (Boston: Houghton Mifflin, 1996). For an analysis of France's attraction to and curiosity about blackness, see Pretine Archer-Straw, *Negrophilia: Avant-Garde Paris and Black Culture in the 1920s* (New York: Thames and Hudson, 2000).

65. Cutler Durkee, "Prince Charming," *People*, July 21, 1986.

66. See Matthew Carcieri, *Prince: A Life in Music* (Lincoln, NE: iUniverse, 2004), 41–42.

67. Nilsen, *Dance, Music, Sex, Romance*, 239, 245.

68. See James F. English, *The Economy of Prestige: Prizes, Awards and the Circulation of Cultural Value* (Cambridge, MA: Harvard University Press, 2005), 100–106.

69. Nilsen, *Dance, Music, Sex, Romance*, 293–294.

70. Ibid., 262.

71. Ibid., 263.

72. With the album recorded, manufactured, and shipped out to stores, Prince ordered Warner Bros. to recall all of the copies of the album on the eve of its release. *The Black Album* was never officially released, although copies that failed to be returned to Warner Bros. were bought and sold among Prince fans illegally.

73. Alex Hahn, *Possessed: The Rise and Fall of Prince* (New York: Billboard, 2004), 157.

74. Ibid., 159.

75. The Time's original lineup reunited for the film, with Jimmy Jam, Terry Lewis, and Monte Moir, all of whom had left the group prior to *Purple Rain*, taking part in *Graffiti Bridge*.

CONCLUSION

1. David Puttnam, *Movies and Money* (New York: Vintage, 2000), 230–231. Before leaving the studio, Puttnam would play a role in Columbia's financing of Lee's first studio film, *School Daze* (1988).

2. Langston Hughes, *The Big Sea* (New York: Alfred A. Knopf, 1940), 223–233.

3. The double-dolly shot appeared even earlier in Melvin Van Peebles's *The Story of a Three-Day Pass* (1968).

4. Box Office Mojo, "Spike Lee," www.boxofficemojo.com/people/chart/?id=spikelee.htm.

5. "Spike Lee Come Home," *New Yorker*, June 30, 2014.

6. The eight highest-grossing stand-up concert films all feature black comedians. See Box Office Mojo, "Stand-Up Comedy Concert," www.boxofficemojo.com/genres/chart/?id=standup.htm.

Bibliography

BOOKS

Alexander, George. *Why We Make Movies: Black Filmmakers Talk About the Magic of Cinema*. New York: Harlem Moon, 2003.

Altman, Rick. *The American Film Musical*. Bloomington: Indiana University Press, 1987.

Archer-Straw, Pretine. *Negrophilia: Avant-Garde Paris and Black Culture in the 1920s*. New York: Thames and Hudson, 2000.

Arkoff, Sam, with Richard Trubo. *Flying Through Hollywood by the Seat of My Pants: From the Man Who Brought You "I Was a Teenage Werewolf" and "Muscle Beach Party."* New York: Birch Lane, 1992.

Bean, Annemarie, ed. *A Sourcebook of African-American Performance: Plays, People, Movements*. New York: Routledge, 1999.

Bigsby, Christopher W. E. *The Cambridge Companion to Modern American Culture*. Cambridge, UK: Cambridge University Press, 2006.

Bilyeu, Melinda, Hector Cook, and Andrew Mon Hughes. *The Bee Gees: Tales of The Brothers Gibb*. London: Omnibus, 2001.

Biskind, Peter. *Easy Riders, Raging Bulls: How the Sex-Drugs-and Rock 'n' Roll Generation Saved Hollywood*. New York: Touchstone, 1998.

Bogle, Donald. *Toms, Coons, Mulattoes, Mammies, & Bucks: An Interpretive History of Blacks in American Films*, 4th ed. New York: Continuum, 2001.

Bond, Julian, and Sondra Kathryn Wilson. *Lift Every Voice and Sing: A Celebration of the Negro National Anthem*. New York: Random House, 2000.

Bowman, Rob. *Soulsville, U.S.A.: The Story of Stax Records*. New York: Schirmer, 1997.

Boyd, Todd. *Young, Black, Rich and Famous: The Rise of the NBA, the Hip Hop Invasion, and the Transformation of American Culture*. New York: Doubleday, 2003.

Brode, Douglas. *Denzel Washington: His Career and Films*. New York: Birch Lane, 1997.

Brown, Jim, with Steve Delsohn. *Out of Bounds*. New York: Zebra, 1989.

Carcieri, Matthew. *Prince: A Life in Music*. Lincoln, NE: iUniverse, 2004.

Chang, Jeff. *Can't Stop Won't Stop: A History of the Hip-Hop Generation*. New York: Picador, 2005.

Clark, Champ. *Shuffling to Ignominy: The Tragedy of Stepin Fetchit*. Lincoln, NE: iUniverse, 2005.

Coleman, Robin R. Means. *African American Viewers and the Black Situation Comedy: Situating Racial Humor*. New York: Routledge, 1998.

Cook, David A. *Lost Illusions: American Cinema in the Shadow of Watergate and Vietnam, 1970–1979*. Berkeley: University of California Press, 2000.

Davis, Mike. *City of Quartz: Excavating the Future in Los Angeles*. New York: Vintage, 1992.

Dent, Thomas C., Richard Schechner, and Gilbert Moses, eds. *The Free Southern Theater by the Free Southern Theater: A Documentary of the South's Radical Black Theater, with Journals, Letters, Poetry, Essays and a Play Written by Those Who Built It*. Indianapolis: Bobbs-Merrill, 1969.

Diawara, Manthia. *African Cinema: Politics & Culture*. Bloomington: Indiana University Press, 1992.

Diawara, Manthia, ed. *Black American Cinema*. New York: Routledge, 1993.

Donahue, Suzanne Mary. *American Film Distribution*. Ann Arbor: UMI Research Press, 1987.

Donalson, Melvin. *Black Directors in Hollywood*. Austin: University of Texas Press, 2003.

Donovan, Brian. *Hard Driving: The Wendell Scott Story*. Hanover, NH: Steerforth, 2008.

English, James F. *The Economy of Prestige: Prizes, Awards and the Circulation of Cultural Value*. Cambridge, MA: Harvard University Press, 2005.

Erickson, Hal. *Sid and Marty Krofft: A Critical Study of Saturday Morning Children's Television*. Jefferson, NC: McFarland, 1998.

Everett, Percival. *I Am Not Sidney Poitier*. Minneapolis: Graywolf, 2009.

Flamming, Douglas. *Bound for Freedom: Black Los Angeles in Jim Crow America*. Berkeley: University of California Press, 2005.

Friedman, Thomas L. *From Beirut to Jerusalem*. New York: Farrar, Straus and Giroux, 1989.

George, Nelson. *Blackface: Reflections on African Americans and the Movies*. New York: HarperCollins, 1994.

Gerstner, David A., and Janet Staiger, eds. *Authorship and Film*. New York: Routledge, 2003.

Goldfield, David R. *Black, White and Southern: Race Relations and Southern Culture, 1940 to Present*. Baton Rouge: Louisiana State University Press, 1990.

Goudsouzian, Aram. *Sidney Poitier: Man, Actor, Icon*. Chapel Hill: University of North Carolina Press, 2004.

Grant, Barry Keith, ed. *Auteurs and Authorship: A Film Reader*. Malden, MA: Blackwell, 2008.

Guare, John. *Six Degrees of Separation*. New York: Dramatist Play Service, 1990.

Guerrero, Ed. *Framing Blackness: The African American Image in Film*. Philadelphia: Temple University Press, 1993.

Gunn, Bill. *Black Picture Show*. Berkeley, CA: Reed, Cannon and Johnson, 1975.

———. *Rhinestone Sharecropping*. Berkeley, CA: I. Reed, 1981.

Haggins, Bambi. *Laughing Mad: The Black-Comic Persona in Post-Soul America*. New Brunswick, NJ: Rutgers University Press, 2007.

Hahn, Alex. *Possessed: The Rise and Fall of Prince*. New York: Billboard, 2004.

Haygood, Wil. *In Black and White: The Life of Sammy Davis, Jr.* New York: Alfred A. Knopf, 2003.

Heitner, Devorah. *Black Power TV*. Durham, NC: Duke University Press, 2013.

Hermes, Will. *Love Goes to Buildings on Fire: Five Years That Changed Music Forever*. New York: Faber and Faber, 2011.

Hughes, Langston. *The Big Sea*. New York: Alfred A. Knopf, 1940.

Jakes, T. D. *Woman, Thou Art Loosed!* New York: Berkley, 2004.

Katz, Ephraim, Fred Klein, and Ronald Dean Nolan. *The Film Encyclopedia*, 3rd ed. New York: Harper Perennial, 1998.

Keyser, Lester J., and André Ruszkowski. *The Cinema of Sidney Poitier: The Black Man's Changing Role on the American Screen*. New York: A. S. Barnes, 1980.

Klotman, Phyllis Rauch. *Frame by Frame: A Black Filmography*. Bloomington: Indiana University Press, 1979.

Klotman, Phyllis Rauch, and Gloria J. Gibson. *Frame by Frame II: A Filmography of the African American Image, 1978–1994*. Bloomington: Indiana University Press, 1997.

Kofsky, Frank. *Black Nationalism and the Revolution in Music*. New York: Pathfinder, 1970.

Lawrence, Novotny. *Blaxploitation Films of the 1970s: Blackness and Genre*. New York: Routledge, 2008.

Lee, Shayne. *T. D. Jakes: America's New Preacher*. New York: New York University Press, 2005.

Lee, Spike. *Spike Lee's Gotta Have It: Inside Guerilla Filmmaking*. New York: Fireside, 1987.

Lev, Peter. *American Films of the 70s: Conflicting Visions*. Austin: University of Texas Press, 2000.

Lewis, Jon. *Hollywood v. Hardcore: How the Struggle Over Censorship Saved the Modern Film Industry*. New York: New York University Press, 2000.

MacDonald, Ian. *Revolution in the Head: The Beatles' Records and the Sixties*. New York: Henry Holt, 1994.

McCarthy, Todd. *Howard Hawks: The Grey Fox of Hollywood*. New York: Grove, 1997.

McGee, Mark Thomas. *Fast and Furious: The Story of American International Pictures*. Jefferson, NC: McFarland, 1984.

Majors, Richard. *Cool Pose: The Dilemmas of Black Manhood in America*. New York: Simon and Schuster, 1993.

Marable, Manning, Ian Sternberg, and Keesha Middlemass, eds. *Racializing Justice, Disenfranchising Lives: The Racism, Criminal Justice, and Law Reader*. New York: Palgrave MacMillan, 2007.

Mask, Mia. *Divas on Screen: Black Women in American Film*. Urbana: University of Illinois Press, 2009.

Massood, Paula. *Black City Cinema*. Philadelphia: Temple University Press, 2004.

Massood, Paula, ed. *The Spike Lee Reader*. Philadelphia: Temple University Press, 2010.

Montejano, David. *Chicano Politics and Society in the Late Twentieth Century*. Austin: University of Texas Press, 1999.

Monteyne, Kimberley. *Hip Hop on Film: Performance Culture, Urban Space, and Genre Transformation in the 1980s*. Jackson: University Press of Mississippi, 2013.

Nachman, Gerald. *Seriously Funny: Rebel Comedians of the 1950s and 1960s*. New York: Random House, 2003.

Neal, Mark Anthony. *Soul Babies: Black Popular Culture and the Post-Soul Aesthetic*. New York: Routledge, 2002.

Nicoll, Allardyce, ed. *Shakespeare Survey 18*. Cambridge, UK: Cambridge University Press, 1965.

Nilsen, Per. *Dance, Music, Sex, Romance: Prince: The First Decade*. London: Firefly, 1999.

Oldham, Gabriella. *First Cut: Conversations with Film Editors*. Berkeley: University of California Press, 1992.

Orman, Roscoe. *Sesame Street Dad: Evolution of an Actor*. Portland, OR: Inkwater, 2006.

Paul, Louis. *Tales from the Cult Film Trenches: Interviews with 36 Actors from Horror, Science Fiction, and Exploitation Cinema*. Jefferson, NC: McFarland, 2007.

Pendergrast, Mark. *For God, Country, and Coca-Cola: The Definitive History of the Great American Soft Drink and the Company That Makes It*, 2nd ed. New York: Basic, 2000.

Pierson, John. *Spike, Mike, Slackers & Dykes: A Guided Tour Across a Decade of American Independent Cinema*. New York: Hyperion, 1997.

Pluto, Terry. *Loose Balls*. New York: Simon and Schuster, 1991.

Poitier, Sidney. *The Measure of a Man: A Spiritual Autobiography*. San Francisco: HarperSanFrancisco, 2000.

———. *This Life*. New York: Alfred A. Knopf, 1980.

Pollock, Dale. *Skywalking: The Life and Films of George Lucas*. New York: Da Capo, 1999.

Prashad, Vijay. *Everybody Was Kung Fu Fighting: Afro-Asian Connections and the Myth of Cultural Purity*. Boston: Beacon, 2001.

Pryor, Richard, with Todd Gold. *Pryor Convictions*. New York: Pantheon, 1995.

Puttnam, David. *Movies and Money*. New York: Vintage, 2000.

Rampersad, Arnold. *The Life of Langston Hughes*. Vol. 1, *1902–1941: I, Too, Sing America*. New York: Oxford University Press, 1986.

Reed, Ishmael. *Airing Dirty Laundry*. Reading, MA: Addison-Wesley, 1993.

Reid, Mark A. *Redefining Black Film*. Berkeley: University of California Press, 1993.

Rhines, Jesse Algeron. *Black Films / White Money*. New Brunswick, NJ: Rutgers University Press, 1996.

Schatz, Thomas. *Boom and Bust: American Cinema in the 1940s*. Berkeley: University of California Press, 1997.

Schrader, Paul. *Schrader on Schrader*. New York: Faber and Faber, 2003.

Sieving, Christopher. *Soul Searching: Black-Themed Cinema from the March on Washington to the Rise of Blaxploitation*. Middletown, CT: Wesleyan University Press, 2011.

Simmons, Russell, with Nelson George. *Life and Def: Sex, Drugs, Money and God*. New York: Crown, 2001.

Spickard, Paul, ed. *Race and Nation: Ethnic Systems in the Modern World*. New York: Routledge, 2005.

Stewart, James B. *Disney War*. New York: Simon and Schuster, 2005.

Stigwood, Robert, and Dee Anthony. *The Official Sgt. Pepper's Lonely Hearts Club Band Scrapbook*. New York: Wallaby, 1978.

Stovall, Tyler. *Paris Noir: African Americans in the City of Light*. Boston: Houghton Mifflin, 1996.

Stromberg, Gary, and Jane Merrill. *Second Chances: Top Executives Share Their Stories of Addiction and Recovery*. New York: McGraw-Hill, 2009.

Thompson, Neal. *Driving with the Devil: Southern Moonshine, Detroit Wheels, and the Birth of NASCAR*. New York: Crown, 2006.

Torgoff, Martin. *Can't Find My Way Home: America in the Great Stoned Age, 1945–2000*. New York: Simon and Schuster, 2004.

Tye, Larry. *Rising from the Rails: Pullman Porters and the Making of the Black Middle Class*. New York: Owl, 2004.

Van Munching, Philip. *Beer Blast: The Inside Story of the Brewing Industry's Bizarre Battles for Your Money*. New York: Times Business, 1997.

Wailoo, Keith. *Dying in the City of the Blues: Sickle Cell Anemia and the Politics of Race and Health*. Chapel Hill: University of North Carolina Press, 2001.

Warren, Robert Penn. *Who Speaks for the Negro?* New York: Random House, 1965.

Wasser, Frederic. *Veni, Vidi, Video: The Hollywood Empire and the VCR*. Austin: University of Texas Press, 2002.

Watkins, S. Craig. *Hip Hop Matters: Politics, Popular Culture, and the Struggle for the Soul of a Movement*. Boston: Beacon, 2005.

———. *Representing: Hip Hop Culture and the Production of Black Cinema*. Chicago: University of Chicago Press, 1998.

Wilder, Gene. *Kiss Me Like a Stranger: My Search for Love and Art*. New York: St. Martin's, 2005.

Williams, Elsie A. *The Humor of Jackie Moms Mabley*. New York: Garland, 1995.

Williams, John A., and Dennis A. Williams. *If I Stop I'll Die: The Comedy and Tragedy of Richard Pryor*. New York: Thunder's Mouth, 1991.

Williams, Lucy Chase. *The Complete Films of Vincent Price*. Secaucus, NJ: Carol, 1995.

Zoglin, Richard. *Comedy at the Edge: How Stand-Up in the 1970s Changed America.* New York: Bloomsbury, 2008.

PERIODICALS

Atlantic
Black Creation
Black Enterprise
Boxoffice
Canadian Journal of African Studies
Chicago Sun-Times
Cleveland Press
Ebony
Evening Standard (London)
Film Comment
Jet
Journal of Popular Film and Television
Jump Cut
Life
Los Angeles Times
Masses and Mainstreams
Miami Herald
Mother Jones
New York Daily News
New York Times
New Yorker
Newsweek
People
Rock & Soul
Rolling Stone
Shakespeare Survey
Sports Illustrated
Sunday Record (New Jersey)
Time
Times (London)
Variety
Vibe
Village Voice
Washington Post

PERSONAL INTERVIEWS

Branch, William. Telephone interview. February 8, 2007.
Dashev, David. Telephone interview. April 10, 2010.
Fanaka, Jamaa. Personal interview. March 18, 2010. Los Angeles.
Moses, Tsia. Personal interview. March 3, 2010. New York.
Moses-Robinson, Carol. Telephone interview. May 19, 2010.
Schultz, Michael. Personal interview. October 10, 2006. Santa Monica, CA.
Stromberg, Gary. Telephone interview. April 10, 2010.
Wesley, Richard. Personal interview. October 7, 2009. New York.
Williamson, Fred. Telephone interview. May 23, 2014.

ARCHIVED INTERVIEWS

Michael Schultz (October 5, 2004), Stan Lathan (June 25, 2003, and April 23, 2004), and Geoffrey Holder (April 16, 2004). HistoryMakers, Chicago, www.thehistorymakers.com.

SPECIAL COLLECTIONS

Black Film Center / Archive at Indiana University. Bloomington.
Ossie Davis and Ruby Dee Papers. Schomburg Center for Research in Black Culture, New York Public Library, New York.
Gordon Parks Papers, 1946–1991. Manuscript Division, Library of Congress, Washington, DC.

Index